THE
LAST
HILL

THE
LAST
HILL

The Epic Story of a
Ranger Battalion and the
Battle That Defined WWII

BOB DRURY
AND TOM CLAVIN

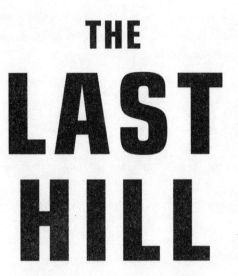

ST. MARTIN'S PRESS
NEW YORK

First published in the United States by St. Martin's Press,
an imprint of St. Martin's Publishing Group

www.stmartins.com

Endpaper credits: map © Michelle Bridges / Alamy; soldier © Vintage_Space/Alamy;
forest © Milosz Maslanka / Shutterstock; soldiers © George Peters / Getty Images;
US tanks © Topical Press Agency / Stringer / Getty Images

Frontispiece photograph courtesy of the National Archives.

Maps created by David Lindroth Inc.
Design by Michelle McMillian

Library of Congress Cataloging-in-Publication Data

Names: Clavin, Tom, 1954– author. | Drury, Bob, author.
Title: The last hill : the epic story of a ranger battalion and the battle
    that defined WWII / Tom Clavin, and Bob Drury.
Other titles: Epic story of a ranger battalion and the battle that
    defined WWII
Description: First edition. | New York : St. Martin's Press, 2022. |
    Includes bibliographical references and index.
Identifiers: LCCN 2022021367 | ISBN 9781250247162 (hardcover) |
    ISBN 9781250247179 (ebook)
Subjects: LCSH: United States. Army. Ranger Battalion, 2nd. | World War,
    1939–1945—Campaigns—France—Normandy. | World War,
    1939–1945—Regimental histories—United States.
Classification: LCC D769.31 2nd .C53 2022 | DDC 940.54/2142—
    dc23/eng/20220504
LC record available at https://lccn.loc.gov/2022021367

First Edition: 2022

10 9 8 7 6 5 4 3 2 1

For Nat Sobel, a Great Good Friend

Contents

Rain and snow had turned the roads into lakes of cold and slimy mud. The so-called paved roads, once adequate for peacetime traffic, were beginning to give way under the effect of freezes and thaws and the continuous pounding of tanks and trucks. The smaller lanes, which at best had only a little stone or gravel on them, were no more.

—MASTER SERGEANT FORREST POGUE,
U.S. ARMY, WORLD WAR II COMBAT HISTORIAN

THE
LAST
HILL

Prologue

A Vast Green Cave

Omaha Beach. Pointe du Hoc. Fortress Brest. Crucibles all. None had prepared the men of the United States Army's 2nd Ranger Battalion for the Hürtgen Forest. It was as if they were walking into the imaginations of the Brothers Grimm. With more bloodshed.

The roughly sixty-square-mile patch of densely timbered hills and gorges straddling the Belgian-German frontier screened the southern rim of the ancient fortress of Aachen, the first German city to fall to the Allies in the Second World War. It was at Aachen, more than a millennium earlier, that the emperor Charlemagne had established his seat of power, and his bones were interred there. Had the ghost of the king of the Franks miraculously arisen to greet the American Rangers on the morning of November 14, 1944, he would not have recognized the cheerless slagscape of bombed-out collieries, smashed smokestacks, and blackened railheads that now surrounded the capital city he had known as Aix-la-Chapelle. He would, however, have been quite at home among the pristine Hürtgen conifers whose one-hundred-foot canopy cast the forest floor in shimmering blue shadow, a perpetual twilight even at high noon.

The sodden ground beneath the towering trees was nearly devoid of underbrush, and as the Rangers slogged through ankle-deep mud along a man-made firebreak, they stooped to pass beneath low-hanging pine boughs that lent the woodland a claustrophobic ambience. One trooper, noting the loamy tang rising from the forest floor, likened it to walking into a vast green cave. The utter absence of wildlife, even birdsong, compounded the eeriness. "Everywhere the forest scowled," the generally sober U.S. Army's official history records in a jarring flight of anthropomorphism. "Wet, cold, and seemingly impenetrable."

The first snowstorm of the season had swept through the Hürtgen a day earlier, and the Rangers had only broached the forest's southwestern edge when a relentless mix of sleet and freezing rain again began to fall. According to army meteorologists, there was no end in sight to the grim overcast. The wretched weather blowing in from the west, in fact, portended the most dismal winter recorded in the region in almost a century.

The waning sunlight was near to being swallowed by the night when the Ranger battalion reached the base of their ridgeline bivouac, eleven miles into the wood. The heights loomed not so much to climb but, like Calvary, to suffer. "Frost and cold making life so miserable . . . wet snow dogging our every footstep . . . had us all bitching and cursing," the Able Company private first class Morris Prince jotted in his journal. "Slime and filth soaked our shoes, and great mud splotches blended into the wetness of our [wool] overcoats."

The raw conditions not only cut to the bone but, as the Rangers knew well, the low cloud cover would continue to prevent Allied aircraft from leaving their tarmacs in liberated Belgium. Over the past thirty days, the number of Army Air Forces and RAF sorties providing close air support to American infantry and armor advancing against the dug-in Germans had fallen by a third. In the coming weeks those prospects appeared even more bleak.

The autumn murk, however, could not obscure the bloody detritus of months of forest fighting—the scattered rucksacks and bullet-riddled helmets; the smashed hulks of burned-out Sherman tanks and jeeps; the blackened corpses of American boys fused together for eternity by direct artillery hits. Near the rotting remains of a German supply horse—one of hundreds of thousands killed that autumn—a Ranger rifleman absentmindedly kicked at a lone American combat boot by the side of the footpath. A foot fell out; the putrescent strips of flesh and muscle still clinging to the bone were thick with maggots. Farther on, dead GIs, bloated and turning gray, were stacked along the trail in haphazard rows, waiting to be tagged and bagged. To the Rangers they appeared to have been speared by medieval pikemen, their bodies punctured and shredded when razor-sharp wooden shards sheared from the treetops by airburst shells rained death on the forest floor. At first a light patter, then a heavy downpour.

The 2nd Ranger Battalion, one of only two American special operations units operating in the European Theater, was a collection of some five hundred recon men and night fighters; cliff climbers and bunker busters; athletes and aesthetes as adept with an M3 trench knife as a .30-caliber machine gun. Led by the rough-hewn former college football star Lieutenant Colonel James Earl Rudder, they thought they had seen the worst of what war had to offer. But as they spiraled deeper into the Hürtgen, even the most battle-scarred among them were staggered by the sight of the soldiers from the U.S Army's 28th Infantry Division they had come to relieve.

After twelve days of continuous combat, the Germans had nicknamed the storied 28th the *Blutiger Eimer*—the Bloody Bucket—a reference to the shape and color of the division's red keystone badge. It is unlikely that the Wehrmacht soldiers had any idea that the outfit's ancestry dated to units stood up by Benjamin Franklin during the Revolutionary War, or that its insignia paid tribute to those origins in Pennsylvania, the Keystone State. Not that it would have mattered. For here, in the Hürtgen, the Bloody Bucketeers—as the division's survivors had sardonically taken to calling themselves—had lived up to the sobriquet.

Less than eight weeks earlier the proud soldiers of the 28th Division—combat boots polished, sunlight reflecting off the metallic blue barrels of their M1 rifles—had strutted down the Champs-Élysées to the raucous cheers of Parisians crowding the sidewalk. Now, as the Rangers approached, these same GIs emerged from rime-crusted foxholes and tumbledown bunkers like wraiths, their drawn faces tinged ashen, as if dipped in soot. Their eyes were hollow, without expression. Some looked as if daylight would hurt them, others resembled pallbearers in search of a funeral. The foul stench of gas gangrene from infected wounds was omnipresent, permeating the woodland like a crepuscular mist.

There is an ancient battlefield bromide: rarely believe a casualty and never believe a straggler. In this case, the soldiers of the 28th did not have to speak for the Rangers to piece together what had occurred. When the Ranger battalion's chief medical officer, Captain Walter E. "Doc" Block, stumbled into a former German troop shelter that had been converted into an American aid station, he was appalled to find wounded GIs left unattended, their rasping voices pleading for water or, in some cases, to be put out of their misery. Block managed to salvage one of the few working jeeps from the 28th's ravaged motor pool and, after jury-rigging a litter to the vehicle, he and his aid men stuffed their musette bags with bandages, plasma, and temporary splints and began combing the forest in search of more wounded. Picking their way through random artillery and small-arms fire, avoiding impassable roads and keenly aware that German sappers had rigged the trailside trees with mines, they managed to gather nineteen more survivors before Lt. Col. Rudder called a halt to their efforts.

"You might get hit," was Rudder's terse explanation. Rudder could ill afford to lose his battalion surgeon.

Not far from Doc Block's makeshift aid station, Able Company platoon leader Lieutenant Bob Edlin spotted a bomb-battered chapel, veiled in mist and rising from the floor of a moss-green dell like a ghostly clipper ship impaled on a reef.

What an odd place for a church, Edlin thought as he moved closer to inspect the wreckage. When he neared the crumbling structure he blanched at the plethora of American rifles scattered about. He could only conclude that soldiers seeking sanctuary in the little shrine had tossed their weapons in flight. It had not done them any good. Twenty-one days earlier the 28th Division and its various attachments had entered the forest with approximately twenty-five thousand effectives. Over six thousand of those men were now dead, wounded, or missing.

More than a few Rangers were startled by the ferocity with which the Germans, on the run for months since D-Day, fought in the Hürtgen. Lt. Edlin in particular felt the pangs of the carnage more sharply than most. Before volunteering for the Rangers, he had been a member of the 28th Infantry Division's 112th Regiment and had known many of the GIs who would now never return home. Not long after his inspection of the chapel, Edlin crossed paths with one of his best friends from his old outfit, a captain named Preston Jackson. Jackson begged Edlin to turn around and get out while he could.

Edlin was shocked. He remembered Jackson as a solid soldier, eager for action. Yet now Jackson stared at Edlin with vacant eyes, as if something had cankered his soul.

"I wish you wouldn't go," Jackson repeated in a numb voice. "I wish you'd just flat tell them you're not going any further." Jackson cocked his chin toward the enemy front. "It's the most miserable thing that you've ever seen in your life."

Edlin was not sure how to react. For a moment a baleful silence hung between the two. Finally, Edlin blurted, "Well, we'll calm things down." The pained look on his old companion's face made Edlin doubt his own words.

Similar misgivings were racing through the mind of Dog Company's 2nd Lieutenant Leonard "Bud" Lomell. The Ranger battalion's former sergeant major had only recently received a battlefield commission—one of thirty thousand U.S. enlisted men promoted into the officer ranks during the war—and still retained a noncom's connection to his men. As Lomell watched the anxious troopers absorb the ravages about them, he began to compile a mental list of ways to prevent them from meeting a similar fate. He vowed that wherever this mission led, the men of Dog Company would never be without hot coffee and clean socks. Quotidian goals, perhaps, but in the lethal heat of battle more important than any quests for glory or valor. How Lomell would accomplish this, he had yet to figure out.

Just as the Rangers were taken aback by the savagery of the fighting in the Hürtgen, the members of the general staff at Supreme Headquarters Allied Expeditionary Force (SHAEF), were equally baffled by the stiff German resistance. General Dwight D. Eisenhower and his war planners, only recently relocated from London to the Trianon Hotel in Versailles, were inexplicably slow to recognize that as precious as the capture of Paris or Brussels or Amsterdam may have once been to the Third Reich, its soldiers were now defending the Fatherland. "Stand or die" was Adolf Hitler's mantra. The Rangers were willing to oblige the Führer on the second count. Although as they trod further into the forest, more than a few recognized an irony as dark as the vast green cave.

In September and October, it had been the 9th American Infantry Division, accompanied by a smattering of tanks from the 3rd Armored Division, that had been tasked with driving the Germans from the Hürtgen. The combined units had suffered forty-five hundred casualties while moving forward less than two miles beneath sheets of artillery fire—one man down, the War Department's history of the campaign notes, for every three feet gained. Now it was the 28th Division that had failed to clear the forest. All told, upward of fifty thousand American soldiers had been thrown into the three attempts, suffering over fifteen thousand casualties.

Now it was the Rangers' turn, although a few of the outfit's veterans wondered what 27 officers and 485 enlisted men could accomplish where so many before them had faltered. If there was a sliver of saving grace to their unenviable task, at least the men of the 2nd Ranger Battalion understood what awaited them. It was the key to the woodland assault. The Germans called it *Burg-berg,* or Castle Mound, an homage to the ruins of the medieval schloss that had once dominated its precipice. American army historians, perhaps in deference, also referred to it as Castle Hill. On Allied topography maps it was known as Hill 400, for its height in meters. To the Rangers, it would become, simply, the Hill. The Last Hill.

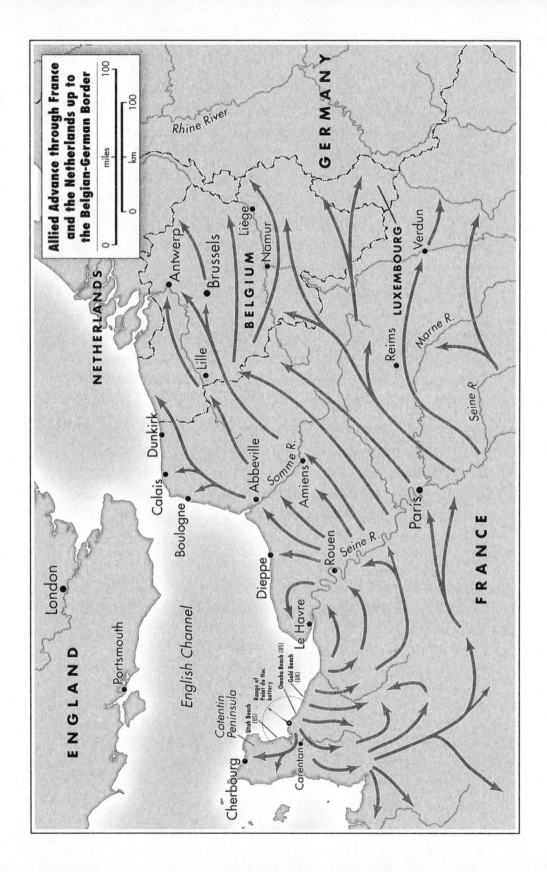

100

miles

100

km

0

0

Rhine River

GERMANY

NETHERLANDS

Antwerp

Brussels

Liège

Namur

BELGIUM

Verdun

LUXEMBOURG

Lille

Reims

Marne R.

Dunkirk

Seine R.

Calais

Abbeville

Somme R.

Boulogne

Amiens

Paris

FRANCE

London

Rouen

Seine R.

Portsmouth

Dieppe

ENGLAND

Le Havre

English Channel

Cotentin
Peninsula

Range of
Point du Hoc
battery

Omaha Beach (US)

Utah Beach
(US)

Gold Beach
(UK)

Cherbourg

Carentan

PART I

The Rangers

In general, when pushed upon by the enemy, reserve your fire till they approach very near.

—ROBERT ROGERS'S 13TH RULE OF RANGING, 1757

1

Commandos

I t only stood to reason that Winston Churchill and the British army's general staff would be more open to special operators than their American counterparts.

Even before the United Kingdom's inception as a unified country, much less a global empire, generations of Britishers had shared the prime minister's reverence for the sceptered isle's martial heritage. Most did not distinguish these traditions from the UK's sense of nationhood. Men and women, boys and girls, had reveled in the quests of Welsh Arthurian knights, forest-dwelling Merry Men, kilt-clad freedom fighters, and undercover spies chronicled by scribes from Malory to Kipling to Maugham. It was, after all, the eighteenth-century British general Thomas Gage who, during what came to be known as Pontiac's Rebellion in North America, had established and trained the country's first forest-fighting corps of irregulars to crush the Native American uprising.

Moreover, as a twenty-five-year-old war correspondent, Churchill had personally witnessed the havoc that Afrikaner "Kommando" companies had wreaked across the Transvaal during the Second Boer War. Now, four decades later as a second World War raged, these memories played into his famous 1940 instructions to his newly created Special Operations Executive to "set Europe ablaze." The SOE, an all-volunteer unit, was charged with igniting that fire via sabotage and subversion behind the lines of Hitler's "Fortress Europe."

The American officer corps, on the other hand, was far less keen regarding clandestine warfare. Their thinking was reflected in the United States Secretary of War Henry Stimson's famous quip, "Gentleman do not read each other's mail." This chauvinism toward commando forces even led some Stateside generals to dub Churchill's Special Operations Executive the "Ministry of Ungentlemanly Warfare."

As it was, the architects of the American military machine, intuiting Adolf Hitler's monomaniacal lust for his neighbors' lands— and foreshadowing Steinbeck's insight that "All war is a symptom of man's failure as a thinking animal"—had been quietly placed on a war footing by President Franklin D. Roosevelt long before Pearl Harbor. They now argued that despite the fact that both the British and the Germans had been conducting successful special operations since the outbreak of hostilities across the Atlantic, cloak-and-dagger combat had no upside. In their view, the concept not only failed to contribute to the big-picture war effort, but actually hampered military operations by siphoning manpower and funds from the regular army. In a classic case of fighting the last war, even the War Department's official history of Special Operations in World War II notes that on the eve of combat in Europe, "American officers . . . envisioned a future conflict along the lines of the Great War." That is, a continuation of the huge, blunt-force battles that had originated in America's War Between the States.

So it was that in the interwar years between the 1918 armistice and the 1941 Japanese strike on Hawaii, superannuated American military theory and subsequent mobilization plans emphasized straightforward conventional tactics. Much of this attitude stemmed from America's maturity into an industrial behemoth. As the United States flexed its manufacturing might in the twentieth century, the country's military planners similarly gravitated toward a vision of "big-unit" warfare conducted by large conscript armies slugging it out across the European plains. To American generals preparing to face the German Wehrmacht, that remained the template. The names Ulysses S. Grant and John "Black Jack" Pershing might as well have been verbs, with Grant's battering-ram campaign against Robert E. Lee's Army of Northern Virginia standing out as *the* valued lesson. The successes of harassing tactics practiced during the Revolutionary War by the likes of Daniel Boone, Francis "Swamp Fox" Marion, George Rogers Clark, and Ethan Allen and his Green Mountain Boys had been reduced to fanciful fables.

This mindset was not altered by the fact that by the time America formally entered World War II, both the Germans and the British had successfully employed special operators to great advantage. It was the elite German *Fallschirmjäger* paratroopers and glider men who had captured the "impregnable" Belgian fortress of Eben-Emael in May 1940, opening the pathway into France. Conversely, even as Luftwaffe bombs devastated London during the Battle of Britain, the British SOE was arranging for supplies to be air-dropped to partisans in occupied Europe while simultaneously conducting coastal commando raids. One SOE operative dropped behind enemy lines managed to sabotage six Wehrmacht railway engines in eastern France, while another, working with the French resistance known as the Maquis, orchestrated the destruction of a massive Peugeot factory complex now churning out German tanks and planes. Though but military pinpricks, the British found these forays effective at keeping the Germans off balance. The American generals, however, were not impressed.

Given the clashing martial viewpoints between the United States and Great Britain, America's general staff was mildly annoyed when, in June 1942, the decorated World War I veteran Colonel William Donovan filled the country's special-operations vacuum by convincing his old Columbia Law School classmate Franklin Roosevelt to let fly an "arrow of penetration" behind enemy lines. Donovan's enthusiasm for sabotage, subversion, propaganda, and small-unit guerrilla warfare was as palpable as the collection of ribbons and decorations, including the Medal of Honor, he sported upon his return from the Western Front twenty-four years earlier. The scars, and Purple Heart commendations, he carried from his three war wounds only served to solidify his reputation. The result was the establishment of the covert Office of Strategic Services (OSS). Despite the War Department's pique at what it considered the now-civilian Donovan's intrusion onto its military turf, the generals and admirals grudgingly recognized that the man nicknamed "Wild Bill" had the president's ear. To that end, the uniformed brass concluded that if the foreign agents and Ivy League toffs flocking to Donovan's new OSS planned to swan about Europe playing at cowboys-and-indians, so be it—as long as they stayed out of the way of the true war fighters.* If that meant the army or navy occasionally lending an officer or two to Donovan's enterprise, such was the small price to pay.

Fortunately for America's war effort, there was one significant exception to this anti-commando wave of indifference and disdain; one soldier who perceived the value in both Churchill's and Dono-

---

* Recent military historians note the irony of regular-army brass looking down its collective nose at what they mockingly referred to as Donovan's "Oh So Social" outfit, particularly after the OSS commandeered the Congressional Country Club in suburban Maryland as a training site. In fact, during the interwar years, its own peacetime army officer class had developed quite the "gentlemanly" affinity for bridge foursomes and polo chukkers.

van's ardor for special operators. He happened to be the United States Army's chief of staff, General George C. Marshall.

It was the British vice admiral Lord Louis Mountbatten's penchant for bold strikes that caught Gen. Marshall's eye. In October 1941, Mountbatten—King George VI's nephew and Winston Churchill's trusted friend—had been appointed to lead Britain's Combined Operations Services in planning and executing the hit-and-run sorties on the continent that the prime minister so valued. Striking from Norway to Crete, these predominantly nighttime stealth assaults culminated in a commando-led amphibious attack on the strategic German-occupied dry dock of St. Nazaire, on France's Normandy coast. The success of the raid not only rendered a crucial *Kriegsmarine* repair station unusable for the remainder of the war but went far to plant the seed in Marshall's mind for standing up an American quick-strike force with similar capabilities.

As it happened, Gen. Marshall had arrived in Great Britain in early April 1942—one week after the successful St. Nazaire operation—to present Churchill with the American plan for a cross-Channel invasion, code-named Operation Sledgehammer, the following year. While in London Marshall went out of his way to meet with Mountbatten and work out an arrangement for select American soldiers to train at Great Britain's Commando Headquarters at Fort William in the western Scottish Highlands. That the training depot was tucked away behind a series of rugged hills dominated by the seventeenth-century Achnacarry Castle in the heart of the ancient Clan Cameron country only added to the romance and allure.

Marshall had been planning for an assault on the European continent since 1939, when President Roosevelt had appointed him the U.S. Army's chief of staff. The former cavalryman had watched closely when, as part of Roosevelt's New Deal legislation six years earlier, the president had placed the Civilian Conservation Corps under the aegis of the U.S. Department of War. Known informally as Roosevelt's Tree Army, the CCC's recruits were supervised by army officers as they cleared forests, fought fires, built roads, and maintained the country's infrastructure. Though they were not issued weapons, their camps were run with a military efficiency that not only exposed the recruits to the physical challenges of deployments under arduous conditions, but also taught them the more mundane details of military life, ranging from standing at attention to marching in sync. When, at Marshall's urging, the United States instituted the country's first peacetime draft in September 1940, many of the three million graduates of the CCC—about 5 percent of the country's male population—became noncommissioned officers in the regular army.

Across the ensuing months Marshall oversaw a series of military maneuvers in the American South involving hundreds of thousands of these inductees. Their aim was to allow America's expanding military to test new equipment ranging from rifles to artillery to tanks. By the time the United States entered World War II, Marshall was convinced that the exercises had elevated the U.S. Army into a serious professional fighting force. But Churchill, having already spent several desperate war winters in what Henry David Thoreau called the "harvest of thought," considered the American cross-Channel invasion plan a potential debacle.

In his meetings with Marshall, it took the prime minister's most silver-tongued eloquence to convince the American general that his misguided "iron-mongering" would result in disaster. At this point, Churchill argued, Allied forces in general and the Americans in particular remained too ill-prepared and untested to engage in a direct confrontation with the Third Reich's Wehrmacht.

The hubris of the American high command, Churchill admitted

to confidants, was matched only by his own nation's depleted armories. With Great Britain's army grievously underequipped, with British factories barely able to turn out planes for the Royal Air Force, and with the Royal Navy shedding capital ships daily to Nazi U-boats, Churchill knew from hard experience what Marshall had yet to comprehend—a landing on the well-defended French seacoast would prove an Allied catastrophe on a scale to make Dunkirk appear inconsequential.

Instead, Churchill proffered an alternative. Why not, he suggested, allow the Soviet Union to weaken Hitler's armies on the war's eastern front while Marshall's raw American troops, with British Tommies by their side, tasted first blood in Axis-controlled North Africa? Victories across the Sahara would not only give U.S. soldiers much-needed combat experience, but also act as a springboard for Allied forces to jump the Mediterranean and invade the Reich's "soft underbelly" of Fascist Italy.

Marshall was indeed intrigued by the idea of throwing his new divisions against the enervated Vichy forces garrisoning Morocco and Algeria. Once battle-tested against such irresolute opponents, his thinking went, the Americans would be toughened enough to stand toe-to-toe with Field Marshal Erwin Rommel's Afrika Korps farther east in Tunisia. It could not hurt, Marshall told confidants, if salted among those armies rolling into North Africa was a cadre of special operators whose British tutors had whetted them to a bayonet's sharp edge as leaders, teachers, and killers.

[2]

Darby's Recruits

Given his personality and experience, General George Marshall's concept of America's new special forces was naturally more buttoned-up than "Wild Bill" Donovan's notion of a secret strike force composed, as the saying went, of Ivy Leaguers who could win a bar fight. Marshall was well aware that working side by side with Donovan's college grads were Czarist officers who had fled Russia after the revolution, combat-addled veterans of the Spanish Civil War, would-be adventurers too unmanageable for regular-army strictures, and, in one OSS instructor's words, "tough little boys from New York and Chicago [anxious] to get over to the old country and start throwing knives." Marshall, on the other hand, envisioned a more disciplined version of Donovan's charges—soldiers first, scout-saboteurs second. To that end he tapped the newly promoted Brigadier General Lucian K. Truscott to stand up America's initial special-operations battalion.

In the forty-seven-year-old Truscott, Marshall had chosen the ideal officer to mold America's latest iteration of irregulars. The son of a Texas rancher who had once cowpoked along the Chisholm Trail, Truscott possessed what one subordinate described as a "predatory" face whose gap-toothed snarl was complemented by a voice gravelly enough to walk on. A career soldier, Truscott was no stranger to explosive expletives, strong liquor, and tobacco, and in his two and a half decades in uniform he had honed a martial ethos that stressed "speed, vigor, and violence"—the consummate qualities he envisioned in his new charges.

Truscott initiated a series of meetings with Vice Admiral Mountbatten, and during their initial strategy sessions—around the same time that *Newsweek* magazine informed its readers that the War Department was seeking a name for newly established American units whose duties would correspond to those of British commandos— Truscott received a message from Dwight D. Eisenhower. Eisenhower, then still a major general leading the Planning Division at the War Department, advised Truscott that the term "commando" was already too associated with the British, and suggested he find another name for his special operators. For his part, Truscott was an admirer of the key role the colonial New England frontiersman Robert Rogers had played in what was known in the western hemisphere as the French and Indian War. Truscott settled on Rogers's coinage for his motley group of backwoods fighters—"Rangers."*

Truscott's next task was culling volunteers from the 34th Infantry Division and the 1st Armored Division, then training in Northern Ireland—some thirty-five thousand American soldiers in all, and the first U.S. combat troops to arrive in Europe since the Great War. Once his Ranger team was assembled, he proposed that they not only train with their British counterparts, but even accompany Mountbatten's commandos on their surreptitious raids into enemy

---

* Truscott had undoubtedly also seen the movie *Northwest Passage*, released two years earlier, in which Spencer Tracy portrayed Rogers. To this day, Rogers's "28 Rules of Ranging," compiled in 1757 and only slightly modified in 1942, are considered the standing orders for all modern Ranger activities.

territory. At the very least, he thought, this would provide the American operatives with a modicum of combat experience. After this temporary deployment attached to British raiders, the Rangers could then return to their former units to impart their experiential knowledge. The concept was remarkably similar to George Washington's command to the Prussian mercenary Baron Friedrich von Steuben at Valley Forge in 1778—to forge a nucleus of sub-trainers who would then fan out among the regiments of the Continental Army to convey their newfound professionalism. As it happened, the *temporary* aspect of Truscott's vision would not quite come to pass.

On June 19, 1942, Truscott officially issued orders activating the 1st Ranger Battalion. Its roster listed zero members. Truscott delegated the job of mustering the outfit's personnel to the thirty-one-year-old West Point graduate Captain William O. Darby, whom he plucked from the staff of General Russell Hartle, commander of all American forces stationed in Northern Ireland. Darby was charged with building his team from scratch. The enthusiastic, likable, and, most important, indefatigable Capt. Darby proved more than up to the assignment.

Darby established his initial base in the seventh-century Gaelic fortress town of Carrickfergus, on the north end of Lake Belfast, and began circulating flyers among Hartle's troops calling for volunteers. More than two thousand enlisted men stepped forward while Darby personally interviewed prospective junior officers. Once selected, this new officer corps was tasked with culling and molding a battalion from among the disparate riflemen, tank drivers, and antiaircraft-artillery operators flocking to Carrickfergus. Darby stressed to his staff that he was looking for venturous athletes willing to push beyond their assumed physical limits. He also wanted intelligent soldiers capable of thinking for themselves in an emergency. A few regular-army unit commanders attempted to use the opportunity to rid their outfits of slackers and misfits—"eight balls," in the vernacular. But Darby's filtering process proved rigorous, and they were rapidly bounced.

At the onset of World War II, a conventional United States infantry battalion generally consisted of some 860 enlisted men and 40-odd officers. Darby pictured his stand-alone Ranger unit as a smaller force, perhaps half that size. Within a month he and his subordinates had selected 570 candidates, wisely factoring into his thinking losses from injuries and last-minute defections. By the time their training was complete, 447 enlisted men and 26 officers would form the initial nucleus of the 1st Ranger Battalion. Darby then divided the outfit into a headquarters company and six line companies of 67 men each.

The recruits were, as Darby had hoped, an eclectic cross section of America, hailing from all forty-eight states and ranging in age from eighteen to thirty-five. Though the composition of the unit came nowhere close to the Donovan-esque type of eccentrics drawn to the OSS, the army's official Ranger history nonetheless reports that the initial roster of the 1st Ranger Battalion ran the gamut from oil rig roustabouts to electrical engineers to bartenders to medical school students and included more than a few former high school and college football stars, a full-blooded Sioux Indian scout, and even a circus lion tamer.

The battalion's next stop was the British commando school at Fort William. Upon debarking from their troopship, the unit received its first taste of "Rangering" by marching seven miles in full gear to its new garrison in the shadow of the ancient Achnacarry Castle. The grueling trek kicked off three months of day-and-night exercises supervised by British commando instructors. They included what the Americans took to calling "Limey Humps"— quick-step marches through freezing rivers and up and over the region's mountainous terrain. These footslogs bookended training in hand-to-hand combat and tank-ambush tactics, booby-trap and demolition courses, and navigation of small lake boats. During one early war game an American enlisted man saluted a major in the Royal Marines. His reward was a swagger stick to the solar plexus and a verbal dressing-down. On a real battlefield, he was told, he would have just made the officer a prime sniper's target.

Following British commando custom, the exercises stressed realism. This meant crawling through obstacle courses beneath spitting machine gun slugs and disposing of live hand grenades casually tossed by British subalterns into the midst of the Yank apprentices. Every evening, at the shrill blast of an instructor's whistle, the Rangers would dash to the nearest "felled forest" for the dreaded log-lifting drills. The exercise consisted of six men hefting a heavy tree trunk between ten and fourteen feet long to one shoulder and, on command, shifting the burden to their other shoulder in unison. As time went on the orders to shift shoulders became more rapid, resulting in the heads of the weary soldiers being rapped incessantly. Even less appreciated were the unnerving "death slides," in which a Ranger would climb a forty-foot tree and, as live fire rent the air about him, slide down a single rope suspended over a raging river. Every Ranger was required to participate.

From time immemorial, professional-army boot camps had been intentionally structured not only to instill in trainees the practicalities of war fighting, but to be as difficult and draining as possible in order that the shared suffering and stresses would forge a strong esprit de corps. Because men washed out of Darby's battalion daily, the captain made frequent trips back to Northern Ireland in search of replacements. As Darby hoped, the recruits who did manage to survive soon fell into a training groove that so stiffened morale that, in their rare down times, the Rangers practiced applying green and black camouflage paint to each other's faces and teaching new arrivals how to break down and operate enemy small arms.

In early August the 1st Ranger Battalion packed its gear and bade farewell to Achnacarry Castle. Its next assignment was a forty-five-mile, full-gear march south through the crofted landscape to the Royal Navy training center at Argyll. There the Americans—having picked up the sobriquet "Darby's Rangers"—were drilled in amphibious landings before crossing the Highlands to Dundee, on Scotland's east coast, to rehearse the techniques and tactics of attacking pillboxes. It was at Dundee that, at the insistence of President Roosevelt, fifty of Darby's troopers—six officers and forty-four enlisted men—were selected to accompany British and Canadian commando battalions spearheading the 2nd Canadian Division's amphibious assault on the German-held port city of Dieppe in northern France. This was the American Rangers' baptism of fire, and it proved a disaster for the Allies.

Unlike the raid on St. Nazaire, the August 19 attack on Dieppe was conducted in daylight. Lacking sufficient air cover as well as the element of surprise, thirty-three of the Royal Navy's landing craft as well as a destroyer were sunk by German torpedo boats while Wehrmacht machine gunners and mortarmen positioned on the chalk cliffs to either side of Dieppe's harbor decimated the Canadians who made it to shore. The rout was so thorough that Marshal Philippe Pétain, leader of the Vichy French government, forwarded congratulations to the German High Command.

Churchill and Mountbatten attempted to put the best face they could on the fiasco, citing lessons learned that would be applied to a grander cross-Channel invasion—primarily the need for coordinated naval gunfire and bomber support, better obstacle-removal and beach-control assignments, and even the utility of adapting tanks for amphibious landings. Similarly, in his own after-action report, Capt. Darby—who had been rebuffed when he volunteered to lead the Ranger contingent on the cross-Channel mission—emphasized that his troopers had fought with valor.

To an extent the whitewash worked. American newspapers trumpeted the deeds of the first U.S. soldiers into European combat, with *The New York Times* leading the boosterism. The paper of record rejoiced that "for the first time United States troops took part in a raid on the continent." Disingenuously if hilariously ignoring the tiny role the Rangers had played, the newspaper added that "the raiding force also included Canadians, British, and fighting French." Despite the gloss, however, of the more than six thousand Allied troops who had taken part in the landings on Dieppe's flint-stone beaches, over half had been killed, wounded, or taken prisoner—including three Rangers killed in action, eleven wounded in action, and four missing and presumed captured.

No one was more aware of the truth of the operation's appalling failings than Gen. Truscott, who had observed the action from an offshore ship. As War Department publicists basked in the positive news coverage, Truscott was left with a counterintuitive takeaway from the mission. In an effort to follow the template of returning the Rangers to their original units after a taste of combat, Darby's troopers had been dispersed haphazardly among the British and Canadian commando teams—four here, twelve there; in a few cases even in ones and twos. Tagalongs, at best. Now it dawned on Truscott that perhaps the special operators might work and fight better as a single, cohesive unit.

Truscott did not know it, but his thinking was mirrored by Gen. Marshall. Post-Dieppe, Marshall began to reconsider his original idea for the deployments of America's Ranger force. For as it happened, the U.S. Army's highest-ranking officer now needed Darby's small and mobile outfit elsewhere.

[3]

Torch

The horror felt by the American public over the massive territorial gains being made by the Imperial Japanese war machine rolling across the Pacific Theater was a secondary concern to Franklin Roosevelt and his war counselors. Despite the nationwide thirst to avenge Pearl Harbor, U.S. strategists had long since decided upon a "Germany First" campaign that would initially allocate some 85 percent of all United States military resources to the destruction of Adolf Hitler's Third Reich. Eclipsing the Rising Sun would have to wait.

As such—and as evidenced by Roosevelt's personal insistence that members of the 1st Ranger Battalion be included in the Dieppe raid—by the late summer of 1942 the U.S. Joint Chiefs of Staff were under enormous pressure from the president to open a combat front somewhere—anywhere—against Germany and its European allies. Thus was the hard decision made to forgo an immediate cross-Channel invasion "to sever the Nazi jugular" and instead follow Churchill's recommendation to land troops in French North Africa. The compromise was a rather spot-on example of the British prime minister's possibly apocryphal maxim that Americans can usually be counted on to do the right thing after they have tried everything else.

The three-pronged North African assault—code-named Operation Torch—involved eighty-three thousand American troops and more than fifteen thousand British soldiers coming ashore from Casablanca to Algiers, and was scheduled for early November 1942. During planning sessions, American commanders recognized the need for a small, clandestine unit that could secure the beachheads in preparation for the main landings. At the port town of Arzew, hard by Oran on Algeria's Cap Carbon, this task fell to now-Major Darby and his 1st Ranger Battalion.

In the predawn hours of November 8, while close to twenty thousand GIs of the U.S. Army's 1st Infantry Division—the Big Red One—floated off the Algerian coast, two of Darby's companies slipped into Higgins boats, broke through the boom guarding the entrance to Arzew Harbor, scrambled over a concrete seawall, and fell on the French-occupied Fort de la Pointe. The outpost's startled garrison, some sixty naval gunners of the Vichy regime's so-called Armistice Force, surrendered within fifteen minutes. Simultaneously, a few miles to the north, Darby personally led his four remaining line companies on a stealth attack of another French battery, whose guns were trained on the landing zones. As the Rangers' 81 mm mortar shells exploded in their midst, another sixty Vichy cannoneers threw down their weapons and surrendered.

Two Rangers were wounded during the operation—one of whom later died—and for its successful and near-bloodless execution of the landings, the battalion was feted by a host of senior officers. But Darby's elation at his battalion's performance was soon muted when, following the Allied landings, two of his Ranger companies were folded into the force assigned to guard the beachhead. The grunt-work assignment did not sit well with the newly minted major, who became even more disturbed when his entire Ranger battalion was left behind as the Big Red One moved east toward Tunisia to confront Rommel's Afrika Korps. It was evident that army doctrine had yet to determine to what use it could put Darby's elite unit other than to secure landing zones.

As the months passed and Ranger morale ebbed, Darby attempted to keep his troops mentally sharp and in physical fighting trim with the kind of day-and-night training and amphibious operations the outfit had undertaken at Fort William. But arid North Africa was not the placid Scottish Highlands. There was a real war being fought in the east, and Darby and his men ached to be part of it. Worse for the special operators, word from the front trickling back to Oran indicated that it was the British who were taking the lead in covert raids on Rommel's scattered outposts. Particularly galling was the news that raiders from Britain's Special Air Service were serving as scouts behind enemy lines, led by a Belgian-born mathematician and engineer named Vladimir Peniakoff.

Needless to say, despite Peniakoff's accomplishments—he was awarded the British Military Cross and appointed a Companion of the Distinguished Service Order for his feats in the desert—America's military brass took a dim view of a partisan character with the vaguely sinister code name of "Popski" freelancing across the Sahara. There was something devious, even foreign, about the entire enterprise. It was this lingering skepticism toward unconventional warfare that Darby and his Rangers continued to face when, in early February 1943, Gen. Eisenhower sent word from Tunisia that he was in need of special operators to gather intelligence and harass the flanks of Rommel's desert army.

Over the next three months, Darby's Rangers initiated a series of lightning raids behind German lines, including a successful nighttime bayonet assault on the Italo-German outpost at Sened, in central Tunisia. When Rommel launched a counteroffensive through the Kasserine Pass, in west-central Tunisia's Atlas Mountains, and temporarily halted the American advance, it was the 1st Ranger Battalion's six companies who served as a rear guard protecting an area previously held by an Allied regiment.

Though Gen. Marshall continued to ponder his initial notion of eventually returning individual Rangers to their parent units as instructors, by the time of the Axis surrender in North Africa in May 1943, officers ranging from Eisenhower to General George Patton had convinced him of the efficacy of Darby's unit as shock troops for the planned invasion of Sicily. Two years earlier, in July 1941, Patton had rocketed to celebrity when he'd appeared on the cover of *Life* magazine as the personification of Marshall's new, professional army. Now the irascible tank leader lavished such encomiums on the Rangers—even letting it be known that if Darby's battalion were ever to be elevated to a regiment, he would want it to become part of his Seventh Army—that Marshall not only acquiesced to keeping the 1st Ranger Battalion together as a stand-alone unit but agreed to form up two more battalions of special operators. In the meantime, Darby split his time in North Africa not only planning the Sicilian landings but hopscotching among American troop-replacement depots on recruiting drives to staff his new units.

By the time Darby's Rangers landed on the southern Sicilian beachhead in July, picked their way across the mined sands, and captured the seaside town of Gela, they had been joined by the newly inaugurated 3rd and 4th Ranger Battalions. As Patton's Seventh Army convoyed inexorably toward its ultimate target of Palermo, on the island's north coast, the three Ranger battalions were fanned out and, with Darby somehow organizing a mule train over the rugged terrain, charged with serving as flanking scouts to seek out and eliminate any pockets of German resistance.

One of these was the imposing mountain fortress of Butera, an aerie four thousand feet high from which German artillery spotters directed pinpoint strikes on Patton's rumbling procession. It had previously been adjudged nearly impregnable, but a single Ranger company scaled Butera's razor's-edge ridgelines by night and captured it within hours. On another occasion, several platoons of Rangers secreted among a jumble of boulders overlooking an inland highway ambushed a dozen enemy vehicles attempting to flank the main American force. They obliterated the column, littering the road with corpses and taking forty German prisoners.

So it continued for the Rangers: an Italian artillery emplacement wiped out near Montaperto; twenty officers of the Italian command group controlling the Agrigento area taken without a fight; a stealth night assault securing the harbor at Porto Empedocle; a patrol of fifteen light tanks wiped out on the road from Lido Azzurro. As Patton reached Palermo and the Rangers prepared to lead the landings on the Italian peninsula proper, many felt that war could not be this easy. They were correct.

As Darby's Rangers were feted for their string of successes across North Africa and Sicily, another force of American special operators was being mobilized on a dusty army installation nearly five thousand miles to the west. Located in the shadow of Tennessee's southeastern highland rim, Camp Forrest had sprung into existence seventeen years earlier as a sleepy National Guard training facility. Following America's entry into the war, however, it evolved into an eighty-five-thousand-acre complex where infantry, artillery, engineering, and armored units—including Gen. Patton's famed 2nd Armored Division—rehearsed maneuvers before shipping overseas. It would now also serve as the mustering station of the 2nd Ranger Battalion.

The idea for the Ranger school was the brainchild of the sixty-three-year-old General Ben Lear, a career soldier who in 1940 had been appointed commander of the Second U.S. Army. Lear, a former Olympic equestrian, felt that in order for his troops to compete on a level playing field against their brutal Nazi counterparts, American servicemen must abandon whatever traditional ideas of sportsmanship they harbored and develop a lethal zeal "that will top the instinctive and naturally dirty fight that the blond, square-head, self-appointed supermen" of the Third Reich were waging. To that end he instituted a Ranger-like program at Camp Forrest that shuffled troopers from across the Second Army in and out of the installation for rigorous two-week courses with an emphasis on infiltration and close combat. Lear appointed the forty-one-year-old rifle battalion commander Lieutenant Colonel William Saffarans to run the exercises.

Much as they had with Gen. Marshall, however, events soon overtook Gen. Lear's notion of soldiers merely temporarily deployed to the Camp Forrest program. By early 1943, with plans for the invasion of France gaining traction, Gen. Lear decided that the Ranger school would now become home to a permanent unit of special operators recruited to spearhead that assault. Thus it was that on the first day of April 1943, 27 officers and 484 enlisted men, all volunteers, snapped to stiff-backed attention as Lt. Col. Saffarans formally introduced himself as the new commander of the 2nd Ranger Battalion.

[4]

Heat and Dust

Like Bill Darby's original troop of soldiers, the stateside
volunteers drawn to the nascent 2nd Ranger Battalion reflected the quilted fabric of the United States. There were
farm boys and city slickers, former high school athletes and
members of the choir; some had acted in class plays and others
had been members of the chemistry club. Except for the handful
who had grown up along America's rims and larked into Canada
or Mexico in search of beer, girls, or both, few had ever been out
of their home states before shipping off to basic training. There
were rich kids and poor kids; Lutherans, Roman Catholics, Bap-
tists, and Jews. Not to be outdone by the 1st Ranger Battalion's
lion tamer, there was a nightclub operator from Cleveland and even
a diminutive professional tap dancer from Plymouth, Massachusetts, named Antonio Ruggiero. There were no African Americans
or Asian Americans.*

---

* Despite the efforts of civil rights leaders, the African American press, and Black soldiers
themselves, the long-embedded history of the U.S. Army's Jim Crow ethos held fast, not least
in the designation "Camp Forrest," after the former Confederate general Nathan Bedford
Forrest, who went on to become the first Grand Wizard of the Ku Klux Klan. In 1941, for

On their first day in camp, Lt. Col. Saffarans called his recruits to attention under a baking Tennessee sun that seemed to wilt the ubiquitous scrub oaks. He brusquely informed them that for the duration of their training they would eat, shower, and sleep together in their isolated corner of the camp before sailing off to fight and die together in Europe. He motioned to a row of moth-eaten, conical tents a mile distant from the site's barracks area. Six enlisted men would be billeted in each of those tents, while individual officers would be allocated smaller canvas tepees. He then cited the feisty Gen. Lear, who had personally composed the school's motto: "Rangerism is the doctrine of a personal fight."

The outfit, Saffarans said, would have no rear-echelon staff—no noncombatant cooks or drivers or clerks. Most important, the iron rule would replace the golden rule—the 2nd Ranger Battalion would be tougher, meaner, and more lethal than any unit the Germans could throw into the fray. To emphasize the point, he distributed sets of brass knuckles to each man. Saffarans concluded with a warning—the United States Rangers were not equal opportunity employers. Not all of the men standing before him would make the cut. In fact, more than 50 percent of those present on that April morning would eventually be shipped back to their original infantry, armor, cavalry, and engineering outfits. These included several dozen who later that day would fail the required physical or could not complete the three full-gear shakedown marches of three miles, five miles, and nine miles in the allotted times.*

What most of the Ranger recruits would remember and come to

---

instance—even as Franklin Roosevelt was pressuring Winston Churchill to sign the Atlantic Charter guaranteeing the right of self-determination to Britain's postwar colonists—a division of Black soldiers was disinvited from one of George Marshall's vaunted American South maneuvers on the grounds that white enlisted personnel and junior officers would be uncomfortable saluting a Black superior.

* In thirty-seven minutes, one hour, and two hours, respectively.

despise about the Tennessee training facility was the heat and especially the sand. The ubiquitous granules "rode the wind," said one
Ranger, describing the tiny tornado-like funnels whipping through
the patchy scrub oak and brush, settling permanently "into clothing, bedding, weapons, food, and water." Even spring rain showers
brought little relief, transforming the red soil beneath the camp's
gritty crust into a morass of cold, oozing mud that swallowed combat boots and vehicle tires alike. These were precisely the conditions that Gen. Lear and Lt. Col. Saffarans had counted on.

Even as the 2nd Ranger Battalion began its training, there remained
an innate regular-army reluctance toward the creation of yet another
unit of atypical war fighters. Lieutenant General Lesley McNair, the
head of U.S. Army Ground Forces and the officer most responsible for building and training George Marshall's "new" American
army, was a particular critic. McNair had no influence over Bill
Darby's battalions already fighting overseas, but the United States
was his turf, and he argued that the outlaw romance surrounding
the Rangers would dilute an already undermanned American military force by luring away too many of his best junior officers. He
also feared that the mere formation of more commando-type outfits
would eventually lead to their officers pushing for expensive and
unproductive missions as a way to justify their existence.

But Gen. Marshall, already a year into planning the cross-Channel
landings in France, was unpersuaded—reports of Ranger triumphs
in North Africa and Sicily were too hard to overlook. Marshall was
convinced of the need for some type of unconventional operators
serving as the tip of the spear for the first wave of the 160,000
American, British, and Canadian troops to be tasked with attempting the largest amphibious invasion in history. Little forethought
was given as to how, exactly, to use the special operators subsequent to the Normandy landings.

The beaches of France, however, were still far from Lt. Col. Saffarans's mind as he set about constructing his battalion. After delineating a headquarters staff and a fifteen-man medical section, he and his staff officers formed the remainder of the outfit into six assault companies, each consisting of sixty-five enlisted men and three officers, a mix of pugnacious veterans and young 2nd lieutenants fresh from Officer Candidate School, the so-called ninety-day wonders. The companies were further divided into two platoons containing a 60 mm mortar section and two rifle sections led by a 1st sergeant.

Within these teams, specialty positions—runner, sniper, communications specialist—were assigned to the fleet, to the lynx-eyed, to those with an engineering aptitude. The latter skill proved a temporary obstacle to overcome, for in its early stages of formation the battalion had not been issued any radios, only field telephones—with no wire. To remedy this, one moonless night several enterprising Rangers scrounged climbing belts and wire cutters and raided a line of telephone poles connecting Camp Forrest's military police to the main barracks area. Although an investigation was opened, the perpetrators were never caught, and even Lt. Col. Saffarans was left in the dark as to who committed the infraction.

Although all Rangers were given perfunctory lessons on how to sight, load, and fire the mortar tubes as well as operate the several .30-caliber light machine guns allocated to the battalion, no doubt was left that each man's rifle was his new best friend. The .30-caliber M1 Garand semiautomatic rifle was by this point the U.S. Army's primary infantry weapon, having replaced the bolt-action Springfield in 1936. Accurate to three hundred yards, with its bullets traveling nearly three thousand feet per second, the Garand was, according to Gen. Patton, "the greatest battle implement ever devised." The battalion's small-arms arsenal also included a modicum of surplus World War I weaponry, including Thompson submachine guns and Browning automatic rifles (BARs). When rapidly reloaded, the latter—twenty-pound behemoths, twice as heavy as the M1—were capable of spitting a stream of "walking fire" at 550 rounds per minute from their detachable twenty-round magazines.

Finally, and of particular menace, were the fragmentation hand grenades issued to each trooper. As opposed to the wooden-handled German *Stielhandgranate* "potato masher"—which packed more explosives and had been designed during World War I primarily for open field warfare—the American "pineapples" were manufactured with the fundamental intent of clearing bunkers, pillboxes, and other enclosed spaces. About the size of a baseball and weighing a touch over a pound, the grenade's surface consisted of fifty-eight pieces of cast iron serrated vertically and horizontally to ensure a consistent burst of the metal shards in a 360-degree ambit. Once the pin was removed and the safety lever released, the fuse would detonate the weapon in four to five seconds. Its "kill radius" averaged about thirty yards, although some fragments often flew farther.

At the Ranger base at Camp Forrest, all of this gear as well as sixty-pound combat packs and three-pound "steel pot" helmets were toted on speed marches ranging from twenty-five to seventy miles. The hikes were often routed through purposely flooded fields studded with barbed-wire barriers. To simulate the reality of advancement under bombardment, local crop dusters were hired to drop sacks of flour from their prop planes as the Rangers scampered for the cover of trenches and gullies on the near-treeless plains. The men were instructed to slough forward at a bent-knee dogtrot dubbed the "flexion step" that averaged six miles per hour, and the daily grind of these marathon marches further attenuated the outfit. Dozens of soldiers, prohibited from carrying canteens, either quit or dropped. The latter were scooped up by trailing vehicles, returned to their tents to gather their personal effects, and "ghosted" out of the battalion before their former teammates even returned.

If the constant calisthenics and forced marches did not convince certain recruits that they were not physically cut from the Ranger mold, the pit-fighting competitions often provided the coup de grâce. These exercises were held in a forty-foot-square hole dug three feet deep, bordered with stacked logs, and covered with several inches of sawdust soon infested with wood ticks. Sometimes separate squads or even individuals descended into the excavation to square off, although more often entire platoons jumped in to attack each other like ancient Spear-Danes, screaming lusty war cries that echoed throughout the camp. All that was missing was iron and oak. The object was to heave all opponents up and over the log rims until only men from a single platoon were left standing.

Once victory was achieved, the winning team was granted three minutes to prepare itself for the next combatants. Rules were few and seldom enforced; by the ordeal's conclusion the sawdust looked as if it had been coated with red paint and the pit itself smelled like the inside of a leper. Afterward, the battalion's medical team—whose members were not spared the crucible—found themselves treating gashes, sprains, dislocations, and a not-inconsiderable number of broken bones, sometimes their own.

At the end of these long days the Rangers returned to their tent city too exhausted to make the two-mile, round-trip walk to the barracks showers. Instead they squatted over open-air slit-trench latrines and washed and shaved as best they could from helmets filled with fetid water from a communal trough. Just as iron sharpens iron, the Rangers honed each other to a combat edge. Yet despite the camaraderie developed among all who to this point had survived the trials of Camp Forrest, there remained a hole in the soul of the 2nd Ranger Battalion. And the men knew it.

From early in his stewardship as chief of staff, George Marshall had made it clear that his army would be a meritocracy. His blind spot toward the institution's Jim Crow policies notwithstanding, he'd intuited that during the interwar years the military had become too reliant on an unofficial old-boys' network of West Point graduates who greased too many a promotional skid. It was to rectify this that he had initiated the series of prewar maneuvers across the Southern states intended not only to professionalize his fighting force, but to winnow the chaff from its officer corps. The result was a rolling overhaul, with over a thousand officers involved in just one Louisiana war game cashiered or reassigned, including thirty-one of forty-two corps and division commanders. Given Marshall's fastidious attention to detail, it was not long before the inadequacies of Lt. Col. Saffarans's Ranger training regimen came to his office's attention.

Some of the grievances revolved around issues as mundane as the battalion's clothing allocation. Upon arrival at Camp Forrest, each Ranger recruit had been issued boots, socks, underwear, and two sets of stained and tattered fatigue field uniforms previously worn by other soldiers. Much like the absence of radios and telephone wire, the Rangers took these recycled uniforms as just another sign that the regular army considered them second-class citizens. Similarly, whether through indifference or inefficiency, Lt. Col. Saffarans had failed to square away the battalion's supply section. The result was a dilapidated motor pool of broken-down trucks and jeeps, weary men standing on line for hours at the abandoned barn that served as a stock shed to secure a pair of socks or bootlaces to replace those destroyed on the marches, and even a dearth of printed forms that served as passes to the camp's post exchange, or PX.

Graver still were the mess hall failings. If, as Napoleon observed, an army travels on its stomach, the 2nd Ranger Battalion was in danger of moving in reverse. Given its isolation from the camp's professional kitchens, the unit was forced to make do for itself—basically a rotating cast of inexperienced "cookies" self-taught on the fly. Their primary culinary skills consisted of setting up gasoline-fired field ranges and boiling provisions to a watery slop in oversized pots whose greasy sheen matched that of the men's trays, plates, and utensils. Dysentery galloped through the camp during the first few weeks of training to the point where the makeshift outhouses were so overwhelmed that they had to be burned. Suspicions among the recruits that they were but an afterthought in the greater war effort were heightened when an enlisted man peeling potatoes in the cook shack spread word that the "lamb" on one dinner menu had been ladled from giant tins labeled as goat meat.

None of this helped morale, and for Lt. Col. Saffarans's superiors the final indignity may have been the fistfights in the nearby Tennessee town of Tullahoma. On the rare occasions when the Rangers were issued off-base passes, there were two options for men seeking libation stronger than the 3.2 percent alcoholic beer sold at the PX. Those with cars, predominantly officers, could drive to Chattanooga, two hours away, where the city's urban delights were enhanced by the secondary allure of a nearby WAC base. Most of the enlisted men, however, were content to hike the two miles into Tullahoma, whose sleepy, prewar population of five thousand had exploded with the wartime expansion of Camp Forrest. Saloons, dance halls, cheap gin joints, pawnshops, tattoo parlors, curio shops, and nickel automats sprouted like mushrooms.

The heady mix of boisterous, pent-up young men and cheap liquor made the military police a pervasive presence in the town. But even the ubiquity of the baton-swinging MPs could not prevent the inevitable Saturday-night hooleys. Local police reports—and bills for damages—presented to Camp Forrest commanders by irate city fathers always seemed to place the Rangers at the center of these brawls. It was as if Saffarans's men had relocated the fighting pit to Tullahoma's town square. More concerning were reports that the brawls were not confined to the battalion's enlisted men. Several back-channel communiqués placed the 2nd Ranger Battalion's heavy-drinking executive officer, Captain Cleveland Lytle, at the center of the donnybrooks. This left Lt. Col. Saffarans conflicted.

Saffarans considered the twenty-nine-year-old Lytle a good man and a good soldier. An honors graduate of Clemson University, while on duty he was as squared away as any soldier in the outfit; as tough as a drill bit on the training fields as well as a masterful tactician. "We're heading for pay dirt" was Lytle's oft-repeated gung ho cry as the Rangers neared the finish line of their exhausting marches. He even looked the part; with his ruddy face resembling a clenched fist and a tendentious attitude telegraphed by his shaved bullet head, Lytle bore more than a passing resemblance to Gen. Patton. But when granted leave, it was obvious to all that the captain transformed into a canker of a man whose wheel of fortune was oiled by whiskey. Yet such was Lytle's standing among the Rangers that one platoon leader, Lieutenant Stan White, volunteered his services as a driver who remained sober while Lytle tore up Tullahoma's taverns.

The final match was struck to this powder keg one night when a gunner from a tank outfit and a Ranger squared off over a dime-a-dance bar girl. What began as a simple tussle rapidly escalated into a city-wide brawl that jumped from saloon to saloon, tumbled into a local hotel lobby, and continued on the town's sidewalks. A Ranger chronicler of the skirmish gleefully described one member of the battalion involved as having "the look of a mad gorilla" and another possessing "the disposition of a constipated bull dog." It was strongly intimated that one of these gleeful descriptions applied to Capt. Lytle.

Such admiration for the battalion's street-fighting abilities may have pleased the writer's subjects. But not long after, reports of the melee spread up channels, all the way to Washington. It was not officially reported whether Lytle was involved, but sketchy witness sightings placed him at the scene. It appeared obvious that Lt. Col.

Saffarans had lost control of his unit, and the brass in the War Department decided that the army's remote jungle training school in Hawaii, far from any civilian population center, was in desperate need of his leadership abilities.

With Saffarans shipped out, a succession of officers briefly assumed command of the 2nd Ranger Battalion. Perhaps the oddest cameo was achieved by the former West Point football star Major Charles Meyer. A whirlwind of an athlete packed into a five-foot-nine, 143-pound frame, Meyer's combination of speed, strength, and agility had earned him the nickname "Monkey" during his playing days in the late 1930s. As he rose through the ranks, however, the sobriquet was judiciously and charitably shortened to "Monk." Meyer likely found that more palatable than an alternative tag—"Mighty Mite."

The Rangers were initially buoyed by the prospect of serving under the quarterback who in 1935 had finished second in the inaugural Heisman Trophy voting to the University of Chicago's legendary Jay Berwanger and whose Army team once held mighty Notre Dame to a tie score. Their excitement turned to dismay when, after several weeks in camp, Meyer stepped into his jeep one morning, rolled slowly to the end of the "company street" while receiving crisp salutes from the men standing before their tents, and continued driving, never to be seen again.* Various excuses for Meyer's disappearance were offered. The most plausible was that the ambitious career officer viewed commanding a ragtag Ranger battalion as a dead-end assignment. This, however, does not explain why Meyer had bothered to show up in the first place. At least the Rangers had been inspired, albeit temporarily, by Meyer's

---

* Meyer, who would retire as a brigadier general, went on to a stellar career leading troops in the Pacific Theater and again in Korea; wounded twice, he was awarded the Distinguished Service Cross—the United States' second-highest service commendation, next to the Medal of Honor—as well as two Silver Stars for "extraordinary heroism."

gridiron reputation. Their next commander earned the enmity of the battalion during his very first day on site.

Within hours of arriving at Camp Forrest, Major Lionel McDonald ordered a three-day, seventy-mile overland trek to take the measure of his new command. A fusty, elderly officer unencumbered with charisma, McDonald had arrived in Tennessee with his tunic bedizened with medals said to have been earned not on the battlefield, but in the peacetime Indiana National Guard. That alone raised eyebrows. Then, during the course of that initial march, he and his driver puttered alongside the struggling recruits in a shiny jeep ostentatiously gulping water while the Rangers, forbidden to drink, sweated beneath a searing sun. That night, battalion medics toted gallons of water to the dehydrated troops while treating bloody and blistered feet. As the Rangers spread their sleeping bags over the ground, Maj. McDonald and his adjutant drove off to their rented quarters in Tullahoma to dine with their wives.

There is an old soldier's adage that when the army spends time and money on you it isn't trying to save your life, but rather attempting to find a more efficient way for you to lose it. The aspiring Rangers at Camp Forrest did not fail to notice that they were not even receiving the equipment and leadership necessary to die competently. The combination of no radios, no showers, no new fatigues, no decent food, and vanishing or languorous commanding officers only enhanced the battalion's sense of isolation and inferiority. Change, however—like the swirling Tennessee sand—was in the wind. It arrived at Camp Forrest on the last day of June 1943.

5

"Big Jim" Rudder

I t was as if Major James Earl Rudder had been preparing for this role his entire life. It did not hurt that he looked the part.

At six feet tall and 220 pounds, the thirty-three-year-old Rudder still resembled the pile of muscle who had anchored the Texas A&M football team's offensive line nine years earlier. The only things missing from his chest were barrel staves. Yet despite the pounding he had taken playing center for the Aggies during the leather-helmet era of cauliflower ears and pulverized nose cartilage, Rudder's countenance had escaped the gridiron largely intact. In fact, with his wavy flaxen hair set atop a broad forehead, his pug nose, close-set blue eyes, and thin lips sloping to a protruding jaw, he resembled nothing so much as a sphinx without a riddle.

The second youngest of six children, Rudder was the progeny of three generations of Texans. His grandfather had fought for the Confederacy in the Civil War and his father, Dee, was a failed rancher turned real estate broker. Rudder rarely spoke about his dad—Concho County court records suggest that it was the fast-talking Dee who put the confidence in "confidence man"—but was effusive in his praise for his nurturing, aspirational mother, Annie.

It was Annie Rudder who imbued her children with an ecumenical ethos long before the term and concept were widely accepted.

Young Curly Jim, as he was known, grew up in the tiny prairie town of Eden, Texas, attending a Sunday school open to all Christian denominations and, following Annie Rudder's example, absorbing the fiery exhortations of itinerant preachers of every stripe who passed through the clapboard community. He received his primary education at Eden's one-room schoolhouse and struggled to finish his homework by the light of a kerosene lantern. By high school he had matured into an outstanding athlete known for his engaging personality. And though his grades were decidedly mediocre, his captaincy of Eden High's first-ever football team led to scholarship offers, first to John Tarleton Agricultural College, a junior college, and eventually to Texas A&M.

World War I had long concluded by the time Rudder arrived at A&M's College Station campus in the fall of 1930, yet a revered military ethos still pervaded the all-male institution's classrooms, dormitories, and athletic fields. The legacy was in large part due to the memories of the roles that the school's former students had played in the Great War. Nearly half of all A&M graduates had volunteered for military service at the height of the fighting—the highest percentage of any institute of higher learning in the United States—and in 1918 the university's entire senior graduating class had enlisted en masse.

The martial atmosphere seemed to flip some kind of a switch in Rudder's personality. He enrolled in the school's advanced ROTC program—spending each summer fulfilling his army-training obligations—and immersed himself in his studies in hopes of becoming a teacher. His previous indifference toward academics, he realized, would only hold him back. And though this new sense of motivation did not result in a complete turnaround—he graduated in 1932 with a solid-C grade point average—the self-direction he

had discovered would go far in shaping his career. Just not immediately.

For after his graduation, Rudder found that neither his bache-
lor of science degree nor his lieutenant's commission in the United
States Army Reserve opened many employment doors at the height
of the Great Depression. He supported himself hiring out for piecemeal manual labor jobs before landing a position at a local high
school that required him to wear multiple hats—teaching history,
mathematics, and chemistry as well as coaching the school's football
and basketball teams. The successes of both athletic squads took
him nearly full circle when, in 1938, he was offered the head football coaching job at the John Tarleton institution, where his annual
twenty-six-hundred-dollar salary provided the financial cushion he
needed to marry his longtime girlfriend, Margaret Williamson.

The athletic Williamson, known as Chick, was the socially connected daughter of one of central Texas's most prosperous ranchers
and horse breeders. Her father—the delightfully named Willie Walter Williamson—liked to joke that the songwriter Johnny Mercer
had his daughter in mind, albeit with reversed genders, when he
wrote the line "And I learned to ride 'fore I learned to stand" for his
hit song "I'm an Old Cowhand." But it was a more romantic tune
that cemented the relationship between the burly former football
star and the quintessential tomboy.

Rudder, venturing from Texas A&M's College Station campus,
had met Chick at a dance hall when she was a sorority girl at the
University of Texas. He was fond of telling friends that he knew
she was the one for him from the moment they embraced to the
tune of the trombonist and fellow Texan Jack Teagarden's hit song
"Chances Are." Moreover, though he feigned chagrin, Rudder secretly delighted in the fact that, even after their marriage when
Chick gave birth to a boy and a girl, he could never best her on the
tennis court.

Two years into Rudder's coaching tenure at John Tarleton and with war drums beating, all army reservists were summoned to active duty. Rudder, upon reporting to the 2nd Infantry Division at San Antonio's Fort Sam Houston, was promoted to captain. Following three months of field training at Fort Benning, he was next placed in charge of a unit guarding a chemical plant on the state's gulf coast. Eventually, in the aftermath of Pearl Harbor, he was selected to attend the army's Command and General Staff College at Fort Leavenworth in Kansas, the stepping-stone to his next posting as a training officer assigned to the Second Army's 83rd Division, based in Indiana.

It was there—after yet another whirlwind promotion, to major—where the combination of the personal empathy that Rudder had honed tutoring high schoolers and the bull-run tactics he had acquired on the football field caught the attention of the Second Army's new commanding officer, General Lloyd Fredendall, who had replaced the retired Gen. Ben Lear.

Fredendall had commanded a corps in North Africa during the battle of the Kasserine Pass, and had personally witnessed Bill Darby's 1st Ranger Battalion in action. There was something about Rudder's carriage and command that reminded Fredenhall of Darby. After a brief personal interview, the general acted on a hunch, and spontaneously reassigned Jim Rudder to take command of the 2nd Ranger Battalion at Camp Forrest.

It was immediately apparent to the Rangers at Camp Forrest that their new battalion commander preferred the view from the ranks, as opposed to the saddle. On Rudder's first morning in camp, he eschewed the offer of a jeep and matched his troopers, flexion step for flexion step, on a twelve-mile, full-gear speed march. That night one of the battalion's lieutenants saw the major decline a medic's offer to treat his feet. Instead, Rudder unsheathed his M3 trench knife, cut off his bloody socks, and bathed and bandaged his own swollen dogs. Word spread.

The next morning following a 6 A.M. reveille roll call and a hurried breakfast, Rudder gathered the battalion in a circle and laid out his philosophy. He was not a man renowned for the length of his fuse, he admitted, and he was not here to make friends. He told his troops that he had been assigned command of the outfit to "restore order" to what his superiors viewed as an increasingly ill-disciplined unit. Nonetheless, he added, he was not an animal trainer; thus the brute-strength pit fights were a thing of the past. In a bellowing drawl he barked that the speed marches and obstacle courses would still be emphasized—he considered endurance and agility the cornerstones of the Ranger ethos—but he also planned to introduce courses in prisoner-abduction techniques, knife-fighting, and a newfangled jujitsu regime. Rudder lumped these under the rubric "close-combat engagements." Most of his would-be special operators recognized this as a fancy term for hand-to-hand fighting.

Moreover, he said, from here on out riflemen would be graded daily on the firing range not only by targets hit, but by the percentage of bullets it took to attain kill shots. Those falling below his prescribed score two days in a row would be shipped out. He also planned to institute informal after-hours courses in field-leadership tactics on those rare evenings when the battalion was not rehearsing night raids. He informed his officers that they would be tutoring sergeants and corporals on their own time. If they objected to the extra work, well, they had volunteered in and they were free to "volunteer out." He also laid down another of what were rapidly becoming known as "Rudder's Rules"—all officers and sergeants were from this moment forward required to learn the names of every enlisted man in their outfits by the end of their first day with a new unit. Given the battalion's constant turnover, this was not as simple as it sounded.

Rudder emphasized that he had studied the progress of the conflict in Europe down to the minutiae that could save a man's life. Every German rifleman, he said for example, had been taught to distinguish the discarded cigarette butt of a French Gauloise from a British Woodbine from an American Lucky Strike. No man in his battalion was going to give away their position by carelessly flicking his spent smoke to the ground. To that end, the discipline of habit would begin immediately. He warned that if by the end of the day he saw so much as a single cigarette butt or, for that matter, any stray scrap of paper on the grounds of the battalion's lodgment, the entire outfit—smokers and nonsmokers—would be held responsible. First and foremost, he added, he was determined to shape the 2nd Ranger Battalion into the most physically and psychologically fit unit in the United States Army. Lethality would naturally ensue.

Rudder's promise to ride his recruits harder than any of their previous commanders came with a caveat. He would share equally in their every physical and mental hardship. His credo was simplicity itself: combat was a clash of opposing wills, an extreme trial of moral and physical strength. He envisioned the Ranger military doctrine as a sort of secular religion—Jesuits with guns. Rudder then challenged his charges—any man who felt that he was ready to take what the new commander planned to dish out should immediately gear up. For in ten minutes Rudder would personally be leading another full-gear speed march, this time with a twist. Overnight he had arranged to have a hiking course constructed that included ropes dangling from tall sawhorses over trenches filled with muddy water and barbed wire. The men would need to swing over these obstacles "Tarzan-style" while instructors lobbed lit charges of dynamite into the muck below them. This would be only the beginning of live-fire exercises.

Rudder concluded his speech with a rhetorical flourish. "Dig in fast and deep," he said. "Because first I'm going to make men of you, then I'm going to make soldiers of you, and then I'm going to make Rangers of you."

By the time the major was finished speaking his new nickname was already circulating behind his back: "Big Jim." There was a general feeling among the Rangers that if Rudder had been the *Titanic,* the iceberg would have sunk.

6

A New Beginning

Trrue to his word, James Earl Rudder proved nothing if not thorough. In the brief period between his command appointment and his arrival at Camp Forrest, he had managed to obtain from Gen. Fredendall's staff the personnel files of several of the 2nd Battalion's officers and pored over them on his flight to Tennessee. One of the first men to catch his attention was Lieutenant James Eikner, the outfit's chief communications officer.

"Ike" Eikner's résumé checked several of Rudder's boxes—he was athletic, he had received several commendations for leadership, and he was persistent, as evidenced by his multiple attempts to enlist after initially being turned away for having bad teeth. Equally as important, Eikner had been a Boy Scout, a trait that Rudder had come to particularly value as he'd bounced from one army assignment to another. He felt the Scouts instilled a certain esprit in a future soldier that usually set the tone for a stellar military career.

If Rudder was taken aback during his initial face-to-face encounter with Eikner, he did not say. For the lithe and compact lieutenant, with his stylish Clark Gable mustache, pomaded hair, and jauntily cocked garrison cap, might have been mistaken for a dashing RAF fighter pilot. Beneath the outward guise, however, Eikner was pure country stock, and during their introductory meeting Rudder was impressed by Eikner's backstory. The Mississippi-born Eikner was a twenty-nine-year-old son of the South who traced his forebears to the early seventeenth-century Jamestown settlement. His family tree included a sailor who had fought in the War for Independence aboard the *Bonhomme Richard* under John Paul Jones, and Eikner liked to tell the tale of his ancestor's post-Revolutionary adventures, wherein he had turned privateer and kidnapped and married a beautiful Malay princess. Though a tad self-conscious about the whole "kidnapping" aspect of the story, Eikner nonetheless boasted that he was descended from that union.

Eikner had graduated from Blackburn Junior College in Illinois, and afterward moved to Texas to work for Southwestern Bell as a telephone lineman, at the time a dangerous profession that involved constructing substations, setting and climbing wooden poles and metal towers, and stringing high-voltage wires—a "journeyman," in the trade's parlance. He was celebrating his twenty-eighth birthday when radios across the country erupted with news bulletins that the Japanese had bombed Pearl Harbor. Any restrictions regarding enlistees with bad teeth were papered over following the attack, and Eikner had sailed through both basic training and the ninety-day Officer Candidate School courses at Georgia's Fort Benning. After receiving his commission, he was assigned to the communications section of the Second Army's 80th Infantry Division. But he knew what he wanted. Within twenty-four hours he had volunteered for the Rangers.

Toward the end of their conversation, in the interest of full disclosure to his new skipper, Eikner offered a confession. It was he who had led the midnight raid on the base's telephone poles to secure the wire for the battalion's field phones. In fact, he still had several small spools hidden in reserve for emergencies. He was also responsible for the "borrowed" generator that had allowed the Rangers to string streetlights through the camp. Rudder was delighted. This was precisely the kind of enterprising self-sufficiency the new battalion commander was looking for in his officer corps. He then promised Eikner that he would soon have new radios to complement the pilfered wire.

Over the next several days between field exercises, the line of officers trooping into the tar-paper-roofed shack that Maj. Rudder used for his command post resembled a queue of Vatican supplicants. The major suspected that perhaps half of the men he was interviewing would wash out by the time the battalion deployed. He did, however, see potential in more than a few. One of these was the tall and lanky Fox Company commander, Captain Otto Masny, nicknamed "Big Stoop" by the troops after a gigantic character in the popular comic strip *Terry and the Pirates*. At six foot five, the twenty-six-year-old Masny towered over his fellow Rangers and possessed a cantilevered frame that lent him the appearance of a praying mantis walking on its hind legs. But it was his zeal for combat that drew Rudder's attention.

The Chicago-born Masny was the son of eastern European immigrants and had grown up listening to his Slovakian father and Moravian mother curse what Hitler and his Nazi regime had done to their homelands. With vengeance on his mind, he had enlisted in the Illinois National Guard straight out of high school, and his gung ho potential was evident to his first drill instructor, who successfully lobbied to have him promoted to sergeant at the conclusion of basic training. Recommended for Officer Candidate School not long after Pearl Harbor, he'd graduated a 2nd lieutenant and bided his time in an infantry division at Fort Dix, New Jersey, while accruing two more rapid promotions.

He told Maj. Rudder that he'd followed the exploits of Darby's Rangers as best he could from his stateside billet, and when he heard about a new Ranger battalion being stood up in Tennessee, he figured that this was his fastest track to an overseas deployment. His overwhelming desire, he said, was to right the Third Reich's wrongs. Rudder liked the ring of that and sensed that he had a keeper.

Rudder was also open-minded enough to disallow first impressions from taking root. This was good news for the twenty-three-year-old Lieutenant Ralph Goranson. On Rudder's first morning at the Ranger bivouac, he had screeched his jeep to a halt at the sight of a bareheaded trooper loping down the company main street. The young man—a handsome, fresh-faced blond whose gleaming white teeth appeared too big for his mouth—was clad in boots, fatigue trousers, and a dirty undershirt. Rudder bellowed, "Who the hell are you?"

The startled trooper threw out his chest and snapped off a salute.

"First Lieutenant Ralph Goranson, sir."

Affecting his best snarl, Rudder tried to bore holes through Goranson with a hard-ass stare. "How the hell am I supposed to know who you are? Get your ass back to your quarters and put on your rank insignia."

Goranson did just that, and later during morning formation stepped forward to apologize in front of the entire outfit. Rudder liked the fact that Goranson had not wilted under his harsh gaze. He also appreciated that the young officer had, unbidden, taken immediate responsibility for his sloppiness.

Day later, as Goranson stood before Rudder in the headquarters tent—cap in hand, his tattered khakis crisp and creased, his boots shined—the major had another opportunity to take the measure of the man. Goranson's story was fairly typical: tough Swedish American kid from Chicago—first Masny and now Goranson, what was in the Windy City's water?—attracted to the new special operations outfit as a means of seeing action sooner, particularly if it involved fighting behind enemy lines.

When possible, Rudder tried to assign enlisted men who had been buddies in their old parent outfit to the same Ranger companies, but he had also arrived at Camp Forrest planning to play a game of what one observer referred to as "musical chairs" with his officers and noncoms, mixing and matching them to squads, platoons, and companies until he felt he had the right combination. For the moment, Lt. Goranson was a platoon commander in Easy Company. But after a few days of observing Goranson train with his troops, Rudder felt he had the potential to lead a larger unit. He promoted him to captain, and placed him in charge of Charlie Company.

One of the last men to meet with Maj. Rudder was Captain Harold Slater. In Slater's case, first impressions did not do justice to the man's outsize presence. Tall, strapping, and nearly bursting out of his formal pink-and-greens—Slater made sure to look sharp in his first meeting with his new commandant—the twenty-four-year-old was one of the youngest captains in the United States Army.* Slater was the kind of soldier for whom crowds naturally parted. Even his nickname—"The Duke"—swaggered. In addition, he was inordinately handsome. If Slater's rippling forearms called to mind a circus strongman, he also bore an uncanny facial resemblance to the Broadway hoofer Gene Kelly, only just then making the transition to Hollywood stardom. The comparison was apt, for not only was Slater renowned for his endurance during speed marches and his "victories" in the fighting pit, his catlike agility on the obstacle course would have given the famously graceful Kelly a run for his money.

---

* The dress uniforms acquired the nickname because of the pinkish hue of one of the sets of pants.

Slater was the commanding officer of Dog Company, the only company that had been folded into the Ranger battalion as an intact unit. Slater had organized this development at Maryland's Fort Meade, where he'd been languishing when rumors reached him that the army was establishing a commando-like outfit in Tennessee. He'd immediately put in for a transfer from his post in Fort Meade's training cadre, and then looked for fellow volunteers among NCOs and enlisted men. A few of the recruits who turned up had never heard of the Rangers—one even thought he was joining some version of a horse cavalry based in Texas—but for the most part the unit Slater assembled consisted of men who had already survived Gen. Lear's two-week training school.

Maj. Rudder sensed, correctly, that Capt. Slater was not a soldier to mince words, and used most of the time during their first meeting to probe for his thoughts about his fellow Ranger officers. It is not recorded whether Rudder inquired, or Slater commented on, the battalion XO Cleveland Lytle's off-duty proclivities. What was reported was Slater's praise of Dog Company's 1st sergeant, Len Lomell. Slater went so far as to advise Rudder that if he was looking for possible "Mustang" candidates—that is, in the army vernacular, enlisted men field-promoted to the officer corps—he could do worse than to keep an eye on Lomell. Somewhat sheepishly, Slater added that Lomell was the only man to ever knock him out in a boxing match.

At first glance it was hard to picture Len Lomell as a Ranger, much less as a prizefighter who had coldcocked the seemingly indestructible Duke Slater. Soft-spoken to the point of shyness, the lanky, sandy-haired Lomell himself often wondered how he had ended up a special operator. In fact, the twenty-three-year-old New Jerseyan's reasons for volunteering were somewhat esoteric.

Lomell was ready to do his duty for God and country when war broke out, but unlike Otto Masny he did not burn for personal revenge on the Nazis. Nor was he particularly seeking medals, awards, or accolades. A curious sort, he viewed trying his hand at Rangering not only as an out-of-the-box military adventure, but also as a means to financially aid his elderly parents. He had been helping to support George and Pauline Lomell since high school, heading straight from the classroom to a succession of construction jobs and, during the summer, working double shifts as a brakeman on the Pennsylvania Railroad by day and sorting mail at his local post office at night.

Two years earlier, in June 1941, he had graduated with honors from Tennessee Wesleyan College and returned to his parents' home on the Jersey Shore. He had hoped to continue his postgraduate education at one of the service academies. But when both West Point and Annapolis requested his birth certificate, his parents shocked him by telling him that he had been adopted as an infant. Lomell recovered quickly from the surprise and had already engaged an attorney to help him locate his birth certificate when Admiral Isoroku Yamamoto's Japanese fleet interrupted his plans. Drafted in January 1942, Lomell completed boot camp and was assigned to the 76th Infantry Division at Fort Meade.

His natural intellectual and athletic prowess—a high school football star, Lomell had also boxed as an amateur in college—led his superiors to pluck him from the obscurity of "gruntland," as he called it, and appoint him to the elite Intelligence and Reconnaissance Platoon of the division's 417th Regiment. Lomell rose rapidly to the rank of platoon sergeant, and he was reassigned to the regiment's headquarters company, where he met Duke Slater.

Soon thereafter Lomell and some two hundred fellow enlisted men and draftees, most strangers to each other, were diverted from their various assignments and sent to Gen. Lear's nascent Ranger school at Camp Forrest. Much like George Marshall's original plan for Darby's Rangers, the 76th Division's commanding officer took to the idea of salting his outfit with soldiers schooled in Ranger tactics who, upon their return to Fort Meade, would pass along their newfound knowledge as combat instructors. For two weeks Lomell and his cohort—dressed in coveralls that displayed no rank—were run through the same grueling exercises that Darby had initiated in Northern Ireland. Men dropped out daily, and by the end of the course Lomell was one of only sixty soldiers to graduate.

Lomell returned to the Maryland camp and was only just gearing up for his new role as a combat instructor when, in March 1943, he received a call from Lt. Col. Saffarans asking if he would be interested in transferring into the new, permanent Ranger battalion. Lomell was reluctant. He explained that if he remained in his current position, there was a good chance that he would soon be promoted to 1st sergeant. The promotion, he said, came with a not inconsequential pay raise. He told Saffarans that he personally did not care about the money, but that he was the sole financial support for his septuagenarian parents. Saffarans's reply took him aback. "All right, Lomell," he said, "I'll promote you on the spot to first sergeant of the battalion's Dog Company."

The core of the company, Saffarans added, would consist of the fifty-nine soldiers from the 76th Division with whom Lomell had graduated Ranger school. Capt. Slater would be their company commander. By April 1, Lomell was back in Tennessee and, with the arrival of Maj. Rudder three months later, sensed that the peculiar outfit he was now a part of was about to undergo a sea change.

But for the moment there was a more immediate hurdle for Lomell to vault. Somehow Duke Slater had found out about his amateur boxing career and was pestering him for a fight. Lomell wanted no part of stepping into the ring with his company commander in front of an audience of his enlisted-man peers. It was, he felt, a lose-lose proposition. He would not mind a diverting exhibition bout, two guys dancing around each other and throwing half-hearted jabs. But by this time he knew Slater too well. The captain would fight the way he did everything else—lunging for a knockout blow with every swing. And with that, Lomell would have to take him out.

Slater's persistent taunts finally broke Lomell's resistance. To Slater's everlasting embarrassment, Lomell dropped him in the first round. Afterward, despite much cajoling, Lomell insisted that his boxing career was over. Whatever fight he had left in him, he'd save for the Germans.

7

Sea Change

I t did not take long for the sea change that Len Lomell anticipated to begin lapping over the 2nd Ranger Battalion. True to his word, Maj. Rudder soon had working radios issued to Ike Eikner's communications shop; crates of crisp new field uniforms were distributed the same day. The hand-me-down fatigues the men had worn for over three months were burned in a ceremonial bonfire.

Rudder may have been the catalyst for the sudden influx of new stores, but it was the battalion's chief logistics officer, Captain George Williams, who navigated the maze of the U.S. military's supply-line bureaucracy. In the lengthy annals of this planet's lethal conflicts, every successful military commander has recognized the need for a competent logistical unit to bridge the gap between forces deployed in combat operations and the means to keep them in the field—to sustain the channels and methods upon which they depended for weapons, food, clothing, and transportation. Someone had to forge the armor worn by Alexander the Great's Macedonian shock troops, to feed and care for Hannibal's war elephants, and to deliver longbows to Henry V at Agincourt. George Williams would have filled any of those roles. He was, in army parlance, a "scrounger" extraordinaire.

The 2nd Battalion's previous commanding officers, so intent on building a cutting-edge fighting unit, had perforce fairly ignored Williams's complaints that his requisition orders invariably went unanswered. But under Rudder, Williams and his small staff blossomed, not only procuring the hard-to-come-by radios and uniforms that had been likely destined for other regular army units, but also helping Rudder to devise a procedure wherein Ranger enlisted men were selected by lot and rotated in and out of Camp Forrest's Cooks and Bakers School in order to provide the outfit with edible meals. The break with past practices seemed complete when, within a week of his arrival, Rudder ordered the dusty tent city struck and his troopers relocated to barracks with beds, toilets, and showers.

Many if not all of these changes came as a response to the series of regular "gripe sessions" that Rudder instituted to allow his men to let off steam. It is a foxhole truism that when dealing with a bureaucracy like the United States Army, major decisions are made by a committee that never meets and the man you are talking to is never the man you need to see. Rudder proved the exception to this adage, personally hosting the forums to hear out every man's grievances. Though he likely did not recognize it at the time, his makeover of the Rangers cast him as a protean figure who by all accounts possessed not only a martial spirit, but also what Socrates described as the classic qualities of a judge—to hear courteously, to answer wisely, to consider soberly, and to decide impartially. Which is not to say that he lacked blind spots. One of them was his tendency to judge a man too harshly by outward appearances.

The underdressed Ralph Goranson's narrow escape notwithstanding, the major was known to order an unlucky volunteer sent back to his former outfit simply because he did not like "the cut of his jib." This was exemplified by Rudder's concern over the shambolic countenance of the Georgia farm boy William Elrod Petty, whose missing front teeth, both top and bottom, were an affront to the battalion commander's sense of order. Rudder had noticed the twenty-one-year-old Petty, a technical sergeant attached to Otto Masny's Fox Company, sitting silently in the back of the room during a few of his gripe sessions. Though Petty never spoke, he seemed to constantly seethe over some slight. Aside from the empty sockets in his mouth, the slight, pale-skinned sergeant nicknamed L-Rod also walked with a pronounced limp; one Ranger compared his gait to a duck's waddle.

Rudder had no idea that Petty, one of thirteen children, had clawed his way out of a boyhood of red-dirt poverty and paternal beatings to earn a football scholarship to the University of Georgia. Though Petty had ended his father's physical abuse at the age of fourteen with a timely swing of a pick mattock, the maltreatment had left him with an enigmatic spleen banked to an ember carefully tended. He could nurture a grudge like a dog worrying a bone, as evidenced, years later, when he spit on the casket at his father's funeral. Despite being a bright and eager student, Petty didn't mind being known as a place where trouble started. This accounted for the upper and lower incisors he had lost not only on the gridiron, but in a series of fights with other members of the team. It is not recorded how his fellow student-athletes reacted when Petty dropped out of college during his junior year to enlist.

Like veins in marble, the strains of Petty's rough upbringing were writ large on his face. With his sunken cheeks, heavy-lidded eyes, thin lips, and swirly eyebrows, he could have been cast as a lurking gunsel in a Hollywood gangster film. The effect was only enhanced when he broke both legs on his first parachute jump with his previous unit, the 13th Infantry Division, resulting in the lifelong limp. Yet when he doffed his service cap his appearance changed dramatically, with all eyes drawn to the snowy bloom of white-blond hair that might have been lifted from an arctic fox.

When Rudder pulled Otto Masny aside to inquire about Petty, the company commander assured him that despite the sergeant's bowed legs and flintlike temperament—hard and easily sparked— Petty's squad and platoon leaders had nothing but praise for his work ethic and physical dedication. Moreover, Masny said, Petty was a crack shot with an M1 and probably the company's best man with the BAR. As for the missing teeth, the army had issued him dentures, but Petty found them too uncomfortable to wear, particularly during training sessions. Rudder, however, remained conflicted; Petty's mien just did not reflect his notion of a "squared-away" Ranger, and his presence in the battalion sat like a burr under the major's saddle.

One day he summoned Petty to his office to personally break the bad news—he was about to sign the sergeant's transfer papers. Petty challenged the decision. He loved being a special operator, he told Rudder, and he was damned good at it. He had finally found the home he had never had. When Rudder mentioned Petty's broken-fence smile, the sergeant shot back that he did not plan on biting the Nazis to death.

For once, Rudder was pulled up short. Perhaps scanning the room for the owl of Minerva, he not only appreciated Petty's perspicacity and pluck, but agreed with the sergeant's reasonable take. It was a prescient decision. For despite his physical anomalies, those who served with Sgt. Petty would come to appreciate him as a comrade of boundless courage and compassion. In fact, Petty seemed destined to become, in the words of one Ranger, "the soul of Fox Company." If, that is, he made it out of Camp Forrest alive.

"Big Jim" Rudder knew well, and regularly reminded his officers, that the sins of the training field blossomed on the battlefield. To keep his troops sharp he lifted a page from the British commando instructors at Scotland's Fort William and implemented a series of live-fire exercises, studding the obstacle courses with hidden "enemy" positions spraying real rifle and machine gun bullets over the heads of troopers slithering under barbed-wire obstructions. Further, to try to simulate the terror of an armored attack, he made arrangements with one of the tank battalion commanders stationed at Camp Forrest to burst his M4 Shermans from a copse of trees and ambush Ranger platoons as they made their way across a clearing pocked with shallow foxholes. The dreaded "Easy Eights," as they were known, would roll over the troops as they dived into the holes.* Rudder expected casualties; he was not wrong.

One Charlie Company lieutenant was killed when an overcharged dynamite satchel detonated beneath him as he "Tarzan-ed" over a muddy trench; a sergeant from Dog Company lost his hand to a mistimed demolition charge, and an Easy Company enlisted man had a block of TNT detonate between his legs as he practiced inserting a timer. He survived; his private parts did not. It was not unusual for the ever-present battalion ambulance to return from rushing an injured soldier to the camp's infirmary only to immediately have to run the same route with another casualty. As one Ranger chronicler recorded laconically, "The dead were buried with honor, the wounded were sent to hospitals, and the men of the battalion got the training they needed."

One of these latter was the twenty-three-year-old Fox Company sergeant Herman Elias Stein. The red-headed Stein's lissome physical frame was offset by piercing dark eyes as well as a nimbleness on the obstacle course second only to Duke Slater's. The youngest

---

* Technically classified the M4A3E8 Sherman Tank, the vehicle received the "Easy Eight" nickname from its "E8" designation. Once deployed overseas, the M4s acquired a more ominous tag, "Ronson," a bleak reference to the Ronson cigarette lighter's advertising slogan, "Lights Every Time"—as did the Shermans too often after taking artillery fire.

child of a wealthy New York City family who had lost everything in the Great Depression, it was, paradoxically, the Steins' reduced financial circumstances that had occasioned the 2nd Ranger Battalion's good fortune when Stein arrived in Tennessee. For when Stein's father was forced to close his watchmaking business and sell the family's comfortable manse on Staten Island, the young Stein found himself living in the outer reaches of then-rural Westchester County, north of New York City. The relocation to "the boondocks" was a godsend for the boy known as "Bubby." With neighbors sparse, Stein spent hours alone tromping the thousands of acres of vast forests and climbing the sheer hills of his new environs, transforming himself from a chubby city kid into an agile pathfinder whose athleticism earned him a college baseball scholarship to New York University.

Drafted into the Army during the summer after his freshman year, Stein sailed through basic training and was assigned to the 76th Infantry Division, then staged at Maryland's Fort Meade. When the outfit shipped overseas just months after Stein's arrival, however, his natural affinity for handling weapons proved counterproductive to his strong desire for combat, and he was left behind to serve as a machine gun instructor. Chagrined and chafing at what he called the "training and waiting" of stateside life, Stein attempted to transfer into an Army Airborne unit to become a paratrooper, but his request was denied because of his poor eyesight. When he came across a bulletin-board notice seeking volunteers for the nascent 2nd Ranger Battalion, he eagerly signed on.

One dreary August day the entire battalion was trucked ten miles from Camp Forrest and deposited on the precipice of a ninety-foot crag rising from an abandoned quarry. The men were handed climbing ropes two inches thick and given rudimentary instructions in the art of rappelling. The first Ranger over the side lost his footing almost immediately and plunged to the bottom, landing with what one witness described as the thudding sound of an ax striking hickory. As the injured soldier twitched and moaned, it became apparent that no forethought had been given to an extraction in such circumstances. At this, Herm Stein slithered feetfirst over the cliff's edge and picked his way down the rock face. Someone tossed down a medical kit, and by the time several noncoms including Sgt. Petty had swung down, Stein had treated the recruit's open wounds with sulfa powder and was in the process of setting his several broken bones with makeshift splints. In the hour it took for an ambulance to reach the scene, the stopgap team of corpsmen kept the man alive, although he never returned to the battalion.

It was not, however, Stein's medical acumen that stuck with his fellow troopers afterward. It was the manner in which he had scampered down the cliff face. It led some Rangers to wonder if the New Yorker hadn't actually been a second-story man in his prewar years, and prompted L-Rod Petty to begin referring to his new-found climbing buddy as "My Pet Ape." Stein took the moniker in stride and, sensing a kindred spirit in Petty, from that day on stuck to him like a limpet. However incongruous, the strong bond that developed between the brooding and toothless good old boy from Georgia and the little New Yorker called Bubby made for one of the outfit's oddest friendships.

Not every volunteer, however, was as sanguine as Herm Stein and L-Rod Petty at the wearying precariousness of Ranger training. A narrative diary compiled by three headquarters Rangers tells the tale succinctly in several short paragraphs.

"Thirty-mile hikes at forced march," it begins. "For every mile a man fell out. Every day-light hour was full, and half the night.

"Classes in mortars, M-1s, pistols, LMGs [light machine guns], signals, wirelaying [sic], mines and booby-traps. Laying demolitions, fighting tanks, scouting and patrolling, sabotage. For hours on end the roar of charges filled the air as Engineer officers taught us to blow a bridge, pillbox, tanks or train. Hours in the water making boats from shelter halfs [*sic*] and the construction of toggle-rope bridges.

"Lay on hours on grinding gravel in the hot sun firing guns 'til your shoulder burst. Fire some weapon all day and clean it half the night.

"Night problems, of creeping and crawling through dew-wet grass freezing in cold, white light of flares. The crashing *whump* of satchel charges with the attendant sick, sweet, stinging smell of TNT and clods of flying dirt. Tracer bullets at night, infiltration and the rounds snicking at the wire. You crawled through dust, through more showers of exploded dirt 'til you are gagged at the smell of it.

"Not for every soldier."

Indeed. Through July and August, 16 officers and 227 enlisted men were either dismissed from the outfit or requested transfers. They were replaced by a revolving-door cast of recruits whom Rudder and his top subordinates personally interviewed during visits to various infantry bases. There was an added urgency to these trips, as Rudder had been informed by Gen. Fredendall that another Ranger battalion, designated the Fifth, was scheduled to be activated on September 1, 1943. As the date neared, soldiers from across the country poured into the Ranger camp in Tennessee, including sixty-eight enlisted men and five officers from the recently constituted 100th Infantry Division. Among them was 1st Lieutenant Sidney Salomon.

Beneath his short-cropped mop of wavy brown hair as thick as an otter's pelt and dark, penetrating eyes, Sid Salomon possessed a jaw that appeared carved rather than molded. The twenty-nine-year-old native of Newark, New Jersey, also possessed a baritone voice that could scour a stove, an attribute honed during his days bellowing commands from the coxswain's seat of his championship rowing team. Nine years earlier, having graduated from high school, Salomon had on a lark joined a local rowing club, a somewhat out-of-the-box decision for a city kid from Newark. However, so naturally adept was he at this most nonurban of sports that he and his team took first place in every competition they entered.

By the time Salomon enrolled in New York University to study commercial science, he was competing in two-, four-, and eight-man shells and regularly winning gold medals in regional competitions. This led to his selection as an alternate to the U.S. Olympic rowing team. The Games were scheduled to take place in the summer of 1940 in Helsinki, before being canceled when war in Europe broke out.

Almost three months to the day after Pearl Harbor, Salomon enlisted in the army. Following basic training, he was rapidly promoted from private to private first class to corporal, which allowed him to apply to Officer Candidate School at Fort Benning. He graduated with honors, was commissioned a 2nd lieutenant, and, following the usual odyssey of enlistees and draftees in the war's first year, bounced from base to base before winding up with the new 100th Division.

During his initial interview with Maj. Rudder, Salomon relayed how his friends joked that he was so angry with Hitler for causing the cancellation of the Helsinki Games that he ached to become a Ranger in revenge. He added that they were not far wrong. Rudder was also impressed by the fact that Salomon, like Ike Eikner, had been an avid Boy Scout troop leader. Finally, in the back of his mind the major must have felt that, given the turn that the Ranger training regimen was about to take, it could not hurt to have someone on the team who knew his way around water. Salomon was in.

8

Swim and Swat

On the morning of September 4, 1943, the five-hundred-odd officers and enlisted men of the 2nd Ranger Battalion staggered through a driving rainstorm under the weight of their weapons, field packs, and barracks bags. Their destination was a troop train leaving Knoxville, Tennessee, for the town of Fort Pierce in southeast Florida. It was a grim departure. Days earlier the battalion had taken part in a pass-in-review ceremony that Gen. Fredendall had arranged for a coterie of visiting officers. The Rangers had performed so sloppily that Fredendall dressed down Rudder. In turn, the furious major read the riot act to his troops, ending his harangue by challenging any man who didn't like the way he ran things to step forward to fight. No one, of course, accepted his offer, but the incident hung over the journey to Florida like a sullen vapor.

There was one Ranger officer conspicuous by his absence that day. Rudder had left the company commander Captain Otto Masny behind to oversee the formation of the 5th Ranger Battalion. He did not intend the transfer to be permanent. Asking Big Stoop to take over the training of a larger outfit, Rudder felt, would provide a solid test of the officer's administrative skills. The 5th Battalion had already attracted 34 officers and 563 enlisted men, but Rudder had privately advised Masny to keep recruiting volunteers, not only to replace the inevitable dropouts from this new unit but also with an eye toward filling holes in the 2nd Battalion. After the fiasco of the pass-in-review ceremony, Rudder was even keener to cull what he considered the "undesirables" unable to keep pace with the demanding physical regimen he had established. He suspected that ten days of beach recon and water exercises on a mosquito-infested island would go far toward attaining that goal.

From the railroad siding in Fort Pierce the Rangers were trucked to a scrubby spit of sand off the Atlantic coast named Hutchinson Island. The barrier island, part of the sprawling Fort Pierce military base, was home to the U.S. Navy's Amphibious Scouts and Raiders School. This was where Rudder's Rangers would hone their invasion landing skills. Hutchinson Island was as dreary as promised, its grasses and sand dunes alternately baked by the tropical sun or lashed by the pelting rains of Florida's hurricane season.

After the Rangers had erected their pyramid tents, hung mosquito netting, dug latrines, and established a rudimentary mess hall, the men were marched to a rickety classroom building near the ocean's edge. There, an army veteran of Lt. Col. Darby's North African landings and several navy swimming instructors issued life belts and led the newcomers to the water. As the sailors graded each soldier's ability to handle the frothing surf, no Ranger thought to ask why the waves were tinged with an odd, pinkish cast. That night, after eight hours of swimming exercises followed by a "short" beach hike of seven miles, medics scrambled from tent to tent treating a plethora of jellyfish stings.

What followed was a succession of seventeen-hour days that included the customary speed marches, calisthenics, and hand-to-hand combat drills supplemented by one particularly insidious discipline incongruously named the "swim and swat." Each morning after roll call, the men stripped to their skivvies and were told to dive into the sea before reassembling on the beach. They were then required to stand motionless while the island's ubiquitous sand flies, attracted by the ocean salt on their bodies, burrowed under their skin and, in one Ranger's words, "drew nearly all the blood and sanity from you." The men rapidly came to understand that the nickname "swim and swat" made no sense, as the first trooper to break formation to swat a fly or scratch an itch subjected his entire platoon to even more grueling physical training, if not the dreaded kitchen patrol duty.

Insect attacks aside, the primary purpose of the Hutchinson Island ordeal was to habituate the Rangers to water exercises and day-and-night boat training. The drills included climbing down cargo nets strung from a makeshift troop transport into bobbing landing craft, guiding rubber dinghies onto breakwaters through storm swells, and—to the horror of the outfit's landlubbers—learning to handle deep-water emergencies. In the latter exercises the Rangers were broken into seven-man squads that were loaded aboard the rubber "over-stuffed waffles" and towed several miles out to sea. There, beyond sight of land, each squad was ordered to intentionally capsize their craft, right the boat without losing their paddles, packs, or weapons, and find their way back to shore using only their compasses. After a few initial rehearsals, the Rangers boarding the towed vessels were told that hereafter the operations would be performed without life belts. No one drowned, although a few came close.

On September 14, three days before their planned departure from Florida, Rudder devised a final exam consisting of a war-game raid on the mainland. That night the battalion's assault teams executed blackout landings at various predetermined checkpoints and surreptitiously "captured" a series of "enemy" installations in and around Fort Pierce. That the objectives were guarded by U.S. Navy sentries who had been given advance warning of the Rangers' sneak attack only added to Maj. Rudder's satisfaction.

Amid the palpable sense of achievement permeating the outfit after the success of the war game, Rudder rewarded his men with graduation presents—two-day passes into town. Within twenty-four hours, however, loud complaints from Fort Pierce's naval commandant as well as the town's civil authorities over the brawling special operators forced him to recall the outfit and confine them to quarters. Even a stickler like Rudder could not tamp what one Ranger euphemistically called the men's "general exhilaration of spirit." There remains some doubt as to whether he really wanted to.

Whether it was this "general exhilaration of spirit" exhibited by the Rangers in the course of their training sessions, or perhaps during their abbreviated nights on the town, several of the naval swimming instructors petitioned their commanding officers to be allowed to volunteer for the battalion. Citing the prohibition on interservice transfers, their requests were denied. As word of Rudder's oddball outfit spread, however, his troopers became accustomed to welcoming an assortment of ambitious potential operators to the team. The battalion drew volunteers from Army Airborne units, engineering and armored regiments, and even a few men who had previously served in the U.S. Navy and reenlisted in the army with the outbreak of war. One of these, Charlie Company's 1st Sergeant Henry Golas, had once been the Pacific Fleet's middleweight boxing champion. Golas's pullet-sized fists could hospitalize a brick, and Rudder's men joked that any other swabbie who wanted onto their team would first have to put on the gloves and dance with him.

While the men of the 2nd Ranger Battalion were battling and sometimes floundering in the Florida surf during training exercises, half a world away their counterparts under Lt. Col. Darby were enduring the real thing. On September 9, 1943, Darby's three Ranger battalions spearheaded the U.S. Fifth Army's invasion of Salerno, on Italy's west coast. Maj. Rudder, in an effort to make certain that his fighters were as savvy as they were battle-ready, encouraged his men to stay abreast of the news trickling in from the European fronts. Despite the requisite wartime censorship, the stateside Rangers managed to follow the exploits of Darby's units as they attempted to claw their way up the spine of the Italian peninsula. They understood well what their brethren were facing—an additional sixteen Wehrmacht divisions pulled from France and the Russian front had been rushed into Italy to backstop the existing German presence, including the twenty-nine thousand enemy troops who had managed to escape the Allied advance through Sicily. Together these defenders formed what Field Marshal Albert Kesselring called his Gothic Line along the heights of the Apennine Mountains.

Though most of Rudder's Rangers could not have found an Apennine summit on a map, it took neither an advanced degree in European cartography nor a strategic military-planning background to recognize that the crack German units pouring into Italy served a single purpose. Hitler and the Nazi high command recognized that every acre of terrain lost as the Allies pushed north through Italy represented a potential airfield from which U.S. bombers could reach southern German cities as well as the Reich's primary oil depots in Romania. Though the Kingdom of Italy, as it was then still known, may have formally surrendered to the Allies in early September, the Germans occupying the country's northern tracts had no choice but to fight on.*

Meanwhile, back at the Fort Pierce rail yard, the creeping anxiety felt from time immemorial by every soldier facing combat pervaded the 2nd Battalion as it filed onto the rickety troop-transport cars attached to an ancient steam engine. Rolling north, word spread that

---

* They obeyed their orders all too well, at the eventual cost of over 150,000 dead German soldiers. Wehrmacht forces in Italy continued to battle Allied troops until late April 1945, when—one day before Hitler's suicide in Berlin—they finally laid down their arms in unconditional surrender.

Fort Dix, the army camp in south-central New Jersey, would be their final stop before heading overseas. During the thirty-six-hour journey the men sat stiffly on hard wooden seats contemplating the bleak news from the Italian front. Most concerning were the whispers that Darby and his troops had been trapped in a defensive pocket along the rocky heights of the Sorrentino peninsula while General Mark Clark's main landing force remained bottled up near the beaches of Salerno.

Rangers, alone and outnumbered. It would set a pattern.

There was no way that Lt. Col. Rudder and his men chugging toward New Jersey on that mid-September day could have known the extent to which Darby's outfits had been decimated during the Italian campaign's frigid mountain fighting, with his 1st Battalion alone taking 350 casualties. Yet the sparse news they did manage to glean was enough to lend an extra urgency to their advance drills at Fort Dix. This was particularly true of the artillery exercises, where a platoon of Rangers only just familiarizing themselves with a battery of heavier 81 mm mortars outgunned a veteran howitzer outfit in one precision-shelling competition. It was also at Fort Dix where the battalion's medical section finally cohered under the direction of an unlikely addition—a forty-year-old physician whose lifelong desire had been to enlist in the Army Airborne's paratroop corps.

With his genial smile, close-cropped dirty-blond hair, and sparkling blue eyes, Dr. Walter Block possessed the ecclesiastical mien of a village parson. His grit, however—and perhaps the hint of a pugilist's saddle nose—would belie the initial impression. A graduate of Northwestern University and Chicago Medical School, Block had once punched a blue-nosed professor for derogatorily referring to him by the surname Niedzwiecki, which his grandfather had legally changed after emigrating to the United States from Poland. On another occasion, after a movie date with his future wife, Alice, he startled the poor girl by letting the air out of the tires of a car he thought had parked too close to his vehicle.

Once married, Walter and Alice Block wasted no time starting a family, with son John and daughter Joan arriving close enough together to be considered "Irish twins." And despite beginning his medical practice in the depths of the Great Depression, the Blocks lived comfortably enough to afford to add a small addition to their Chicago home upon the birth of their third child, Jeffrey.

His patients, though, were often in financial straits. His urban practice notwithstanding, Doc Block—as the Rangers universally came to refer to him—often had more affinity for the barter payments of an old-time country circuit doctor than the professional billing system of a big-city physician. It was not uncommon for him to accept recompense in the form of crates of eggs, homemade cakes or pies, or shanks of beef conveniently gone missing from Chicago's plentiful slaughterhouses. And though not technically a pediatrician, Block gravitated toward tending to children. Once, after treating a bookmaker's daughter, his payment was rendered in a series of insider tips on horses running at nearby Arlington Park racetrack.

Given his age and parental responsibilities, Block was exempt from the draft when war broke out. But some combination of patriotism, his combative nature, and the well-known shortage of U.S. Army doctors caused his civilian status to gnaw at his conscience. Heretofore he had reluctantly bowed to Alice Block's wishes that he abandon his dream of joining the Army Airborne to jump out of perfectly good airplanes. But after hearing about the Rangers—possibly from his neighbors the Goransons, Lieutenant Ralph Goranson's parents—he traveled to New Jersey and offered his services to Maj. Rudder. In what is likely an exaggerated bit of family mythology, it was said that Alice was somehow under the impression that becoming a Ranger had something to do with tending to the nation's forests. Her husband did not disabuse her of the notion.

Although nearly twice the age of most of his battalion mates, Block, commissioned a captain, kept pace on the calisthenic fields, often jumping to—and keeping—the lead during the speed marches. Further, after a day's exercises were concluded, he was known to challenge the younger troopers to push-up contests. He also took seriously his role as the outfit's chief health officer, once turning away hungry men from a field kitchen after determining that the water used to wash the mess kits was not hot enough to kill germs. On another occasion, he ordered the battalion's rare movie night canceled upon discovering exhaust from a nearby generator seeping into the makeshift tent theater.

All of Block's assistants had been instructed in the rudiments of battlefield medicine during basic training—bandaging and suturing wounds, setting broken bones, applying the pre-penicillin silver sulfadiazine powder, known as sulfa, to fight infections. But Block took their practical education a step further, holding classes on how to differentiate a belly wound from a lung injury, how to read X-rays, and which drug therapies applied to which battlefield injuries. He was also not afraid of broaching taboo subjects and held regular discussions on how to recognize various combat mental disorders.

Naturally, Block's priorities also extended to the operating room—or, as he suspected, whatever field tent or farmer's hut would serve as a surgical center once the battalion entered combat. He foresaw the need for heightened concentration under such fraught circumstances and stressed to his charges to "always anticipate what the man who is doing the actual surgery will require next." He so professionalized the battalion's medical section that Maj. Rudder rearranged his command structure to make Block's fifteen-man unit a stand-alone, front-line squad. Rudder gave Block free rein to run the aid station as he saw fit, and Block in turn devised a schedule wherein one medic was always attached to a line company while the remaining nine aid men rotated in and out of various squads and platoons as needed.

Block, who spoke fluent French and played several musical instruments, was also appreciated for his droll sense of humor. Once, when a newly married Ranger asked him if he could devise a steel jockstrap to wear into combat, the doctor played a few mournful chords on his accordion before sardonically suggesting that if the man could somehow secure an extra helmet, a circular saw, a handful of bolts and T nuts, and perhaps a leather strap, he might be able to rig a contraption that could cover his precious family jewels. The trooper walked away from the conversation not certain whether the Doc was serious or not.

Moreover, Block possessed a dual distinction uniquely his own— deft surgical hands that were not averse to a good fight. As one Ranger was to observe, "Doc Block could cut a throat almost as well as he could sew one." Thus did the former family practitioner with the skittish wife enter the slipstream of 2nd Ranger Battalion lore.

On September 29, 1943, Maj. Rudder gathered his men on the Fort Dix parade ground for official battalion photographs, a sure sign that the push-off to Europe was imminent. Big Stoop Masny had returned to the outfit by this time, having handed over the reins of the 5th Ranger Battalion to yet another temporary commander, an officer promoted from within the unit. Masny was surprised to see so many new faces, including officers like Doc Block and a lanky, hawk-nosed lieutenant whose name tag read "Cook." Masny soon learned that prior to one "final readiness" exercise at Maryland's nearby Camp Ritchie, Rudder had been impressed with a glib knife-fighting instructor who seemed to understand more about Nazi strategy and tactics than any twenty-five-year-old junior officer had a right to know.

After the drill, the lieutenant introduced himself to Rudder as Harvey Cook, out of Philadelphia by way of Michigan State. Cook admitted that he was more or less bluffing his way through the knife-fighting class; he guessed that his commanding officer had only slotted him into the instructor's role because of the fast hands he'd developed playing high school and college baseball. His real goal, he said, was to work in army intelligence. Rudder replied that he could offer the next best thing. The 2nd Ranger Battalion was without an intelligence officer, he said. Would the erstwhile knife fighter be interested in the position? Thus did Lieutenant Harvey Cook become the battalion's S-2.

Back at Fort Dix, Rudder used the photo ceremony to unveil the outfit's new shoulder insignia—a patch with the capitalized word RANGERS shaded a yellow-gold and superimposed on a horizontal blue diamond edged with the same yellow-gold embroidery. Heretofore the men had merely worn the red-and-white "2" signifying their membership in the Second U.S. Army. Now, as Rudder distributed five of the patches to each man, he could feel the pride in their new separate and distinct identity.

Seven weeks later, on November 23, the 25 officers and 448 enlisted men of the 2nd Battalion trundled up the steep gangway of the converted luxury liner *Queen Elizabeth* at the terminus of New York City's West Forty-ninth Street. The ship, like its sister *Queen Mary*, had been painted a wartime gray and retrofitted to carry an entire infantry division. Before boarding, Rangers queued at the banks of telephone booths lining the docks to say final farewells to parents and wives. Among them was Bubby Stein, who had married his longtime girlfriend, Lena Toirac, only days earlier. Big Jim Rudder, now sporting the silver oak leaf of a lieutenant colonel, had also managed to get through to his wife. Their conversation, the contents of which are lost in the churn of history, was surely emotional. For Rudder began his next letter to Chick, "You will have to pardon my weakness, but somehow I couldn't help it."

In accordance with their special-operator status, the Rangers had been ordered to keep their new patches hidden aboard the *Queen Elizabeth* as they took up their first official duties as military police. Most, including Rudder, did not miss the cosmic irony—his rough-and-tumble bar brawlers had been charged with maintaining shipboard order among the fifteen thousand American GIs steaming off to war.

As it happened, the mere presence of men sporting MP top pots but no identifying insignia sparked frequent conversations as to the identities of the mysterious soldiers who appeared to belong to no unit. It would not be the last time that a group of Rangers left their fellow GIs in wonderment.

9

The Cliffs

At first, they sniggered at the destination. Baggy Point. The Brits with their silly place names. Then the Rangers saw the lichen-crusted cliffs. South-facing slabs of sheer sandstone rising nearly three hundred feet from the pounding surf on the North Devon coast. The smiles vanished.

In the tall gorse atop the promontory, British commandos had deployed .30-caliber machine guns. Short velvet bursts of live fire hissed over the Americans' heads as they pulled themselves up rope lines slippery with sea spray. The ropes, thinner by an inch than those they had trained on in the States, had been launched from small craft by specially equipped mortars reconfigured to fire grappling hooks instead of artillery rounds. The whoosh of the grapnels hurtling through the air combined with what the locals call "the sing of the shore"—waves breaking against rock—to produce a cacophonic melody so unfamiliar to the Rangers as to be alien.

Next came rehearsals on the Needles, three perpendicular stacks of white chalk rising like icebergs out of Alum Bay, on the west coast of the Isle of Wight. This time, along with the free rope lines, there were toggle ropes and portable steel ladders to wrangle. The latter came in four-foot tubular sections weighing four pounds apiece and designed to be fitted together as the men climbed. Once the Rangers topped the crags—again beneath live machine gun fire—they were instructed to rappel back down as rapidly as possible, before the incoming tide drowned the thin strip of scree that passed for a beach.

Climbing and rappelling; rappelling and climbing, until the flesh on their palms and fingers blistered and bled. The screeching caws of the cormorants and razorbills soaring overhead seemed to mock their efforts as the men slipped and fell at an alarming pace. Some were picked up by makeshift ambulances cruising the small beach when the tide allowed or by the small flotilla of British skiffs sluicing through the breaking sea-foam. The lucky ones, bruised and scratched, were returned to their platoons to repeat the process, the injuries mainly to their pride. Others were dragged unconscious from the rocky fill or fished from the water and rushed to emergency medical stations, never to return to the battalion. Once, a replacement recruit was spotted rifling through the pockets of an unconscious Ranger who had tumbled from the heights. The newcomer was dismissed and evacuated immediately, before he was beaten to a pulp.

After several weeks, the four "duck boats" arrived—two-and-a-half-ton DUKW amphibious trucks mounted with one-hundred-foot hydraulic ladders on loan from the London Fire Department. The ducks skimmed the ocean's surface and plowed onto the shingle spit, where their six wheels were deflated and chucked with jacks. The ladder ascent was perilous, with the pressure-propelled wooden steps swaying and swerving under the weight of the two water-cooled Vickers machine guns bolted to the top rungs. Exercises included the Rangers climbing one ladder in full gear, and then swinging over to descend another.

Incessant training honed experience and experience led to lessons learned. Early on, for instance, light machine guns were exchanged for Browning automatic rifles; the BARs may have been heavier but were less cumbersome for a single soldier to lug up a cliff face and lock and load for combat. Rope ladders may have at first glance appeared propitious, but the Rangers found that they were prone to tangling when fired from the mortar tubes. The first wave of climbers learned to drape them over their shoulders and, after scrambling to the top, unspooling them and tossing them down. The old telephone lineman Ike Eikner—again proving his value as the battalion's communications officer—devised a hands-free radio attached tight to the neck, like a hangman's noose, freeing up the Vickers gunners to fire both their weapons while simultaneously giving and taking instructions. Eikner's ingenuity earned him a promotion to captain. And some clever soul managed to affix spare ammo boxes to the ladders' side rails that fed directly into the Vickers' firing chambers.

It was rough work, long work, wet work, cold work, punctuated only by the occasional four-hour leave to descend onto a fuggy village pub for bitter ale or warm lager.

Then, one day, the passes to town ceased. The Rangers were confined to their quarters. Each man knew combat was near. But where? Over poker hands and the clicking dice of craps games that muted late-night conversations, one word dominated. Cliffs. Why cliffs? The cliffs played on their minds.

Five months earlier, on December 1, 1943, the men of the 2nd Ranger Battalion had debarked from the *Queen Elizabeth* in the Firth of Clyde, on the west coast of Scotland, their land legs quaking from the seven-day Atlantic crossing. Although largely uneventful, the voyage had managed to introduce the green American troops to a soupçon of real war when one night the ocean liner suddenly swerved and spun on its wake to outrun a wolf pack of German U-boats.

At the Scottish quayside they were greeted by a small U.S. Army band muddling through a set of martial tunes as well as a lithe and wiry American major who introduced himself to Lt. Col. Rudder as Max Schneider. Schneider, thirty-one, a veteran company commander in Bill Darby's 1st Ranger Battalion, had survived the amphibious landings in North Africa and Sicily before a concussion grenade felled him near Salerno. Placed on limited duty for recuperation and sent to London, upon his recovery he'd been reassigned to Rudder's battalion.

Rudder was taken aback at having an officer he had never met suddenly injected into his command—given the vagaries of wartime transatlantic communications, Schneider's official transfer orders had never reached the States. But Schneider was a combat veteran who had been decorated with a Silver Star before earning his Purple Heart, and thus the only trooper in Rudder's outfit who had "seen the elephant," in Ranger parlance, of live combat. Perhaps Schneider's experience would complement Rudder's organizational expertise. It even crossed Rudder's mind that, with the 5th Ranger Battalion scheduled to arrive in England soon, Schneider might fit as its commanding officer. By the end of his time with Darby, after all, Schneider had served as an executive officer. But first, of course, Rudder would have to observe him in action during training exercises.

Max Schneider walked by Jim Rudder's side as the 2nd Battalion marched the mile or so to the waiting troop train that would transport them to their new duty station five hundred miles to the south. Their destination was the quaint seaside hamlet of Bude, on the Cornish coast of western England, just south of the Bristol Channel. At Bude, all except Rudder's senior staff were billeted in private homes by the town's residents, who had seen their population of some five thousand swell with refugees from more eastern precincts fleeing the Luftwaffe's tender mercies.*

The Rangers were not the only Americans welcomed into Bude's cottages, pubs, fish-and-chips shops, and tea rooms. As part of the Allied buildup to the invasion of Adolf Hitler's "Fortress Europe," Great Britain's towns and cities were fairly bursting with soldiers from its former colonies. A howitzer unit from the U.S. Army's 190th Field Artillery Division had been posted to Bude a few weeks before the Rangers, and the cannoneers resented having to compete with the newly arrived special operators for the affections of local lasses.

The women, whose fighting-age men were either dead or departed, ostentatiously strolled the town's cobblestone streets in a nation where the constant threat of bombing and even German occupation had pierced the veil of prewar proprieties. It became a running joke among the GIs that Bude's ladies had been issued utility underwear—"One Yank and they're down"—and a music hall comedian noted that so many British girls had been impregnated by Americans that in the next war the United States need only send uniforms.

Each morning before dawn, Lt. Col. Rudder would assemble his Rangers for reveille not far from his temporary headquarters in Bude's venerable Links Hotel, a boxy, three-story structure with enough rooms to house his immediate staff. Roll call was followed by the familiar program of calisthenics, explosives training, and speed marches across boggy fields that reminded a few of the more

---

* Despite the enemy's concentration on more easterly British targets, western Great Britain was not completely immune to the destruction wreaked by their Heinkels and Junkers. On the train ride from Scotland to Bude the Rangers had glimpsed some of the damage done to the Devonshire town of Exeter, whose city center had been virtually flattened by Luftwaffe bombs.

literate Americans of Conan Doyle's great Grimpen Mire. Weapons drills were conducted on rifle ranges requisitioned from nearby golf courses. A twist was added to the exercises when flamethrowers were distributed to burn out faux pillboxes.

Rudder also implemented a new practice designed to ensure that each of his men would remain self-reliant in the fog of war. Every morning after roll call a few Rangers—officers as well as enlisted men—were pulled aside and handed a map of England with a location circled. They were given a certain amount of time— sometimes hours, sometimes days, depending on the distance to the target—to reach the site and return with proof that they had made it. Sometimes men were sent off alone, sometimes in pairs. How they accomplished their missions was left solely to their own shrewdness. In addition to a per diem of one pound to cover room and board, the Rangers had been receiving regular pay, and some rented vehicles or purchased bus or rail tickets. Others hitchhiked. Rudder's point: it was up to every man to hone his capacity for individual problem solving. One never knew when the exigencies of combat would force a buck private to take command of a squad or even a platoon.

As the days shortened and Christmas approached, the season induced a kaleidoscope of emotions. The vast majority of the Rangers had never been away from their families for the holiday, much less stationed overseas in a "foreign-speaking" land—to American ears, the peculiar Cornish accent lent the impression that the entire population of England's West Country was descended from Long John Silver. But nostalgia for sharing the rituals of Christmas with now-absent loved ones was compensated in part by the outpouring of generosity from the residents of the little resort town. The locals, descended from ancient Celtic tribes who predated the Roman conquest, organized nativity plays, held carol-singing competitions, and managed to round up enough musicians to fashion a dance hall complete with a giant Yuletide tree.

The Americans repaid the hospitalities by hosting a Christmas party for Bude's children wherein seven hundred boys and girls lined up to receive the hard candies, chocolate bars, and sticks of gum the Americans had collected and pooled from their C rations. They even distributed oranges, as rare as rubies to the youngsters living under Great Britain's wartime austerity programs.

Yet even as the year-end tide of good feelings lingered in each Ranger's memory, the war hit home for the Americans. By February a pall hung like an illness over the Rangers billeted in Bude as word filtered in that the stalled American landings at Anzio, in western Italy, had not only turned problematic, but written the coda for Darby's beleaguered Rangers.

In an attempt to break out from the Anzio beachhead, Lucian Truscott—now a major general commanding the 3rd Infantry Division—had ordered Lt. Col. Darby's 1st and 3rd Battalions to launch a push into the ancient crossroads town of Cisterna, southeast of Rome. On January 30, Darby and his men had walked into a trap when the Germans allowed the forward American scout patrols to pass unimpeded through their lines. When the bulk of the Rangers followed, they were encircled by a reinforced enemy buildup and cut to pieces. Of the one thousand or so Rangers involved in the fight, only eight—including Darby—managed to avoid being killed or captured. When the 4th Ranger Battalion embarked on a futile rescue mission, it proceeded to lose half of its combat strength.*

The men of the 2nd Battalion were restless and angry at the

---

* Following its annihilation at Cisterna, Gen. Truscott ordered what was left of Darby's Ranger force deactivated, while Darby was eventually reassigned to the 10th Mountain Division. As the U.S. Army's official history of the Rangers notes, even after observing the special operators' accomplishments during fifteen months of hard combat in North Africa and Sicily, "regular-army officers had yet to learn how to employ their unique abilities during the Italian campaign."

slaughter of their brethren, and news of the ferocious fighting in Italy was apparently having a similar effect on the 1.5 million American soldiers stationed across the length and breadth of Great Britain. As the weeks rolled on, more and more regular-army GIs turned up in Bude, eager to volunteer for an outfit that, rumor had it, was to spearhead the invasion of France. In scenes reminiscent of the early days at Camp Forrest, most of the newcomers were weeded out within days if not hours, unable to keep pace with the strenuous physical regimen. But some managed to stick. Among them was the twenty-one-year-old Bob Edlin.

At a glance it was apparent that the short and stocky Edlin was something of an enigma; beneath his thick thatch of jet-black hair he would flash a jaunty smile that offset a craggy face that brought to mind a hard winter breaking up. Born and bred in southern Indiana, Edlin was a child of the Great Depression whose father barely managed to feed his wife and nine children by building bridges, paving roads, and digging drainage ditches for President Roosevelt's Works Progress Administration. To help put food on the table, Edlin dropped out of high school in his mid-teens and found work shocking wheat and picking peaches. At seventeen he enlisted in the state's National Guard; a year later his unit was activated for federal service.

By this time Edlin was his platoon's staff sergeant, which made him eligible for Officer Candidate School despite his lack of a high school or college degree. In 1942 he graduated as a 2nd lieutenant and was assigned to the 112th Regiment of the 28th Infantry Division just as the outfit was deploying overseas. Stationed in South Wales, Edlin was among the few GIs selected to attend the elite British Battle and Commando School in Dover, England. The institute was an offshoot of the Fort William training site, and Edlin's ninety-day stint at Dover not only resulted in a promotion to 1st lieutenant but served to supercharge his fighting resolve—and his frustration. The Brits with whom he'd drilled had seen combat, some had lost limbs, and the sight of them had left an impression.

Upon his return to his regiment, he grew disenchanted with his fellow junior officers, who seemed more interested in the Welsh pubs than in fighting Nazis. Even his unit's senior command struck him as not truly grasping the gravity of what awaited them when they reached the continent. When Edlin learned about the Ranger battalion seeking recruits up the Cornish coast, he put in his transfer papers. He wasn't even quite certain what or who the Rangers were, but the notion of joining a select fighting outfit that only accepted volunteers piqued his curiosity.

Edlin's train pulled into Bude on a starless mid-February night in 1944. A cold wind blew sheets of rain in from the Celtic Sea as he paced the railroad siding awaiting whatever form his welcoming committee might take. As the minutes passed, however, his enthusiasm began to ebb. He thought of his brothers Sam and Marion, serving in the South Pacific, and then of the soldiers from his old outfit. Some had laughed at his decision to sign up for what they called a "suicide squad." Edlin didn't get that. If you were going to be a fighter, he reasoned, you may as well go into combat with the very best. Moreover, as he had no intention of making the army a career, he thought it practical to just get on with the damn war, help bring it to a close, and get back home to Indiana as soon as possible.

But now, dripping wet and shivering on the Bude rail siding, doubts crept into his mind. Could the vaunted unit that billed itself as a *special* force not even be bothered to send someone to greet a like-minded soldier? The large bag of fuck-it that Edlin had been toting since his return from commando school seemed to grow heavier with each passing moment. *Even these Rangers don't care either,* he thought. The notion entered his mind simultaneous to the appearance of a jeep with cat's-eye blackout slits muting its headlamps. The officer behind the wheel pulled over and stuck out his hand.

"You look like a Ranger that needs a drink and a hot meal," said Captain Ed Arnold, commanding officer of the battalion's Baker Company.

Capt. Arnold's "hot and a cot" took the edge off Edlin's railside misgivings. The next morning, during his formal introductory interview with Rudder and Cleveland Lytle, whom Rudder had placed in command of Able Company, both officers were impressed enough with the lieutenant's résumé, particularly his stint with the British commandos, to test his skills as a platoon leader under Capt. Lytle.

Edlin made an immediate impression on his new charges, not least because of the mastery of close-in fighting he had honed at Dover. He was also an able boxer, a Golden Gloves champion in his teens, but since those days had vowed to only fight opponents above his weight class. One day the enlisted men in his platoon put him up to step into a makeshift ring with Charlie Company's Sgt. Golas, the former navy middleweight champion—a fact they conveniently failed to mention to Edlin. When Golas finished bloodying Edlin, the new lieutenant endeared himself even further to his troopers by thrusting the victor's arm into the air and declaring that he would stand the entire platoon to drinks on its next leave.

Lt. Col. Rudder heard about the incident and silently approved. His outfit was taking shape much as he had hoped, a fine continuation of the Darby tradition. By the same token, as the North Atlantic's early spring breezes began to wash winter's gray from the Cornish seacoast, it was not lost on Rudder that his was now the U.S. Army's only special operations unit still functioning in the European Theater of Operations.

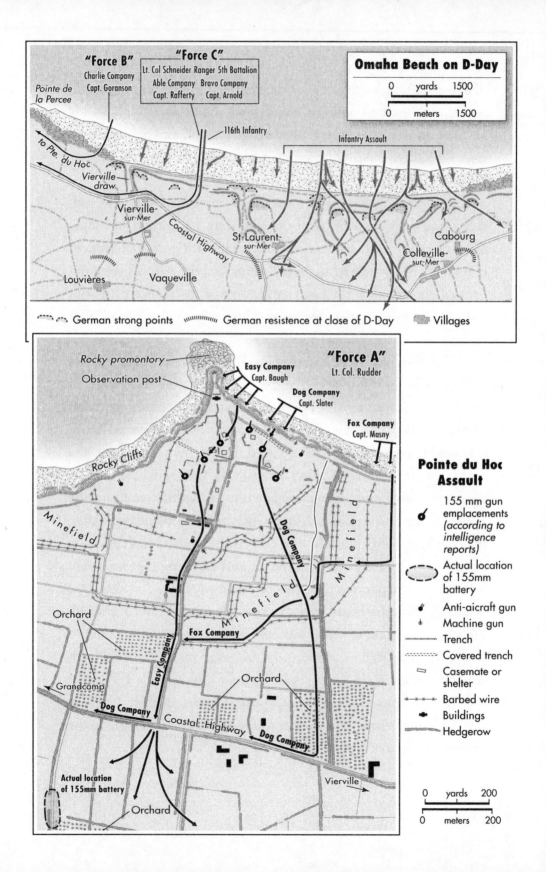

"Force B"
Charlie Company
Capt. Goranson

"Force C"
Lt. Col Schneider Ranger 5th Battalion
Able Company   Bravo Company
Capt. Rafferty   Capt. Arnold

Pointe de
la Percee

to Pte. du Hoc

Vierville draw

Vierville-sur-Mer

116th Infantry

Infantry Assault

Omaha Beach on D-Day

| 0 | yards | 1500 |

| 0 | meters | 1500 |

Coastal Highway

St-Laurent-sur-Mer

Cabourg

Colleville-sur-Mer

Louvières   Vaqueville

German strong points   German resistence at close of D-Day   Villages

Rocky promontory

Observation post

Easy Company
Capt. Baugh

"Force A"
Lt. Col. Rudder

Dog Company
Capt. Slater

Fox Company
Capt. Masny

Rocky Cliffs

Pointe du Hoc Assault

155 mm gun emplacements *(according to intelligence reports)*

Actual location of 155mm battery

Anti-aicraft gun

Machine gun

Trench

Covered trench

Casemate or shelter

Barbed wire

Buildings

Hedgerow

Minefield

Dog Company

Minefield

Minefield

Orchard

Easy Company

Fox Company

Orchard

Grandcamp

Dog Company

Coastal Highway

Dog Company

Vierville

Actual location of 155mm battery

Orchard

| 0 | yards | 200 |

| 0 | meters | 200 |

PART II

The Beach

We knew where France was,
but where in the hell was Normandy?

—LIEUTENANT BOB EDLIN

10

"The Most Dangerous Mission of D-Day"

While the 2nd Ranger Battalion continued to undergo weapons training, night maneuvers, and navigation and cliff-scaling exercises along the Dorset coast, in April they were joined in Great Britain by the more than 550 enlisted men and 34 officers of the 5th Ranger Battalion. To differentiate the units, the newcomers had the number 5 painted in the center of the horizontal orange diamond, or lozenge, on the back of their steel helmets. The new arrivals were folded into Rudder's overall command as part of what the army now designated the Provisional Ranger Group, with Rudder naming Maj. Schneider as the 5th's commanding officer.

Rudder had come to like and trust Schneider in the months since they'd met. Schneider's background as a descendant of nineteenth-century pioneers who had settled in Shenandoah, Iowa, lent him a flinty, western persona with which Rudder was taken. The lieutenant colonel also admired the way the major never complained when the grenade fragments that had been embedded in his body in Salerno worked their way out through his skin, causing painful and sometimes festering sores. Finally, he fancied the man's matter-of-fact approach to persistent newspaper reporters' attempts to turn him into a Daniel Boone cum Sgt. York. Schneider had been aboard the initial landing craft to make the beach at Salerno before he was wounded. As such, he was lauded by war correspondents as the first American soldier to set foot on the Italian Peninsula in World War II. When Rudder asked him about it, Schneider brushed off the story as mere press fodder. No one would ever really know, he said, whose combat boots first touched Italian soil until the dead Rangers he had left behind on that strand made their reports at the Pearly Gates.

Schneider, however, was carrying a secret. Prior to the war he had attained his pilot's license, but a stormy crash landing had ended his flying career when a metal plate was inserted into his skull to protect a section of his bleeding brain. Since his wounding in Italy, he had suffered a sense of overall anxiety as well as severe headaches, both of which he had managed to hide. He suspected that the concussive grenade blast might have disturbed the plate in his head, but never said anything about it to the army doctors in London who had pronounced him fit for duty. Unlike the shrapnel lesions, the latter maladies were invisible. Since so little was understood at the time about neurotic disorders in combatants, Schneider's boyish charm managed to obscure what was likely an acute case of combat exhaustion.*

As it was, Schneider had barely settled into his new assignment

---

* Prior to World War I, psychologically distressed American combatants were officially described as suffering from "hysteria." By the time Congress declared war on the Central Powers alliance in 1917, that descriptor was considered too feminine, and front-line soldiers suffering from neurotic disorders, often caused by the advances in heavy artillery, were deemed to be "shell-shocked." During World War II's 1942 Tunisia campaign, the phrase "shell shock" was officially replaced by "combat exhaustion," or, more colloquially, "battle fatigue." Over the course of World War II, the U.S. Army hospitalized close to one million soldiers—929,000 men, to be precise—with neuropsychiatric diagnoses.

as the 5th Battalion's commanding officer when Rudder and he were ordered to pack their standard brown-and-tans.* They had been summoned to London to receive their operational orders for the impending invasion. Both George Williams and Harvey Cook had previously journeyed to the British capital city, Williams to familiarize himself with the intricacies of resupplying the thousand or so Rangers who would be entering France, Cook to gather maps and aerial photographs of the French coast from his counterparts at SHAEF—Supreme Headquarters Allied Expeditionary Force.

Over a year earlier, Allied war planners had made the decision that the cross-Channel landing would take place across a sixty-mile front in the Baie de Seine, along the Normandy coast of northwest France. The invasion, code-named Overlord and commanded by the now five-star general Eisenhower, would involve a first wave of over 150,000 American, British, and Canadian troops assaulting the Wehrmacht infantry and armored divisions under the command of Field Marshal Erwin Rommel. Although France's Pas-de-Calais region, north of Normandy, was closer to England—only about twenty miles across the Strait of Dover—it was not only subject to stormier weather, but its narrower beaches were perhaps the most fortified positions along Hitler's Atlantic Wall under the command of Rommel, which stretched from France to the Netherlands.

In arguing for the Normandy invasion—the most prodigious expeditionary force into mainland Europe since Hannibal's crossing of the Alps—proponents pointed to several advantages. One was the landing site's proximity to the strategic supply port of Cherbourg, at

---

* Unlike the more formal pink-and-greens, a U.S. Army lieutenant colonel's brown-and-tans consisted of olive-shaded trousers, tan shirt, socks, tie, and field jacket, and brown shoes and gloves.

the tip of the Cotentin Peninsula, only thirty-two miles away from the westernmost D-Day beach. Further, the city of Caen, some thirty miles inland, was a major communications center as well as the hub for multiple rail lines and highways over which, it was anticipated, Allied armor could roll east.

Between Cherbourg and Caen, Allied intelligence analysts reported the presence of four German infantry divisions, perhaps sixty thousand men, with nearly as many Wehrmacht soldiers comprising a surplus infantry division and three to four Panzer divisions held in reserve farther inland. SHAEF strategists knew well that the reefs, tide cycles, and rugged contours of the Normandy coastline limited the areas where a sizable Allied force could come ashore. But, by eschewing Pas-de-Calais, they counted on catching the enemy by surprise while establishing a beachhead and moving inland before Rommel could call up his Panzers.

All this and more Rudder and Schneider learned at their London briefings. As they pored over topographical maps, it struck the two Ranger officers that the Americans had drawn the most harrowing assignments. British and Canadian troops under the overall command of the British general Bernard Law Montgomery had been assigned three landing zones—designated, from east to west, as Sword, Juno, and Gold. All three rose gently from the sands onto relatively flat terrain. The American thrust, on the other hand, would take place to the west of the British landings on beaches dubbed Omaha and Utah, which were far less hospitable.

Omaha Beach was a crescent-shaped strand stretching more than seventy-five hundred yards and separated from Gold Beach by a narrow inlet. It was backstopped by seawalls and steep bluffs supplemented by massive bunkers and concrete pillboxes along dunes laced with concertina wire. American intelligence reported that the grassy hummocks sheltered at least six mortar positions and some eighty-five machine gun nests. The gunners in what the GIs came to call these "murder holes" had been issued smokeless and flashless ammunition to further obscure their positions.

The enemy had situated their defenses to provide enfilading fields of fire across the length of the waterline, whose offshore surf had been studded with metal, concrete, and wooden *Tellermine*-topped pedestals designed to pierce the hulls of landing craft. They had also laid some ten thousand anti-personnel *Schutzendosenmines* in and around the beachhead.* Farther inland, another fourteen artillery pieces, ranging from 37 mm to 88 mm guns, were poised to theoretically annihilate any soldiers who reached the sands before driving the survivors back into the sea.

The second American landing zone, Utah Beach, lay seven miles to the west of Omaha. The two were separated by the promontory of Pointe du Hoc, which jutted into the English Channel like the blade of an ax. It was to this near-vertical cliff face and its sister headland, Pointe de la Percée, that Rudder's and Schneider's attentions were directed. The plateau atop Pointe de la Percée was interwoven with trenches and bunkers surrounding a fortified stone farmhouse almost certainly containing artillery spotters. It would take at least a company of Rangers landing on Omaha to climb that precipice and secure the high ground.

The pièce de résistance of the German defensive line, however, was the battery of six 155 mm howitzers that aerial photographs placed atop the slightly taller Pointe du Hoc, some three miles west of Pointe de la Percée. It was left to Rudder and his staff to devise a plan to ascend the heights, rising ninety to a hundred feet from

---

* The wooden and thus hard-to-detect "*shoes,*" as the Americans came to pronounce them, contained about eight ounces of TNT. Though unlikely to kill any man who triggered its detonator by stepping on it, the explosives were enough to blow away a foot midway to the shin and often maim penises and scrotums.

the Channel, and find those guns. The powerful howitzers, which Germany had captured from the French army, had a range of over thirteen miles, putting the invasion fleet in danger before it even closed on the beachheads to offload assault troops, tanks, vehicles, and artillery. The guns could also be turned on soldiers exiting landing craft and making for the sandy stretches of both Omaha and Utah as well as the western edges of Gold Beach. Capable of firing ten to thirteen rounds per minute, the howitzers' nearly one-hundred-pound shells had a kill radius of 150 feet and a casualty radius of double that.

Gen. Eisenhower had placed General Omar Bradley in command of the American invasion forces set to storm Omaha and Utah Beaches. While conferring with Gen. Bradley's chief operations officer at Combined Operations Headquarters in London, Rudder was told that silencing those guns was the most dangerous mission of D-Day.

Rudder was nonplussed. His first reaction was that Bradley's man was for some reason pulling a practical joke, or was at least "trying to scare me." In the brief, somber silence that followed the remark, however, Rudder realized that the operations officer was deadly serious.

Prior to the Normandy landings, Rudder was told, as two divisions of American paratroopers were being dropped inland from the beaches, the bunkers cross-hatching the tableland atop Pointe du Hoc would be subjected to massive aerial bombardments and naval shelling in an effort to take out the 155s. Yet even with that, only a direct infantry assault up the escarpment could ensure that the threat from the big guns had been eliminated as the bulk of the Allied troops came ashore. With casual understatement, the official Ranger history notes, "Destruction of the [155 mm] battery was critical to the success of the invasion."

It was the challenge of Rudder's Rangers to scale the fortified wedge of quartz to confirm and, if need be, to follow through with that destruction. The task would take all the traits that Rudder felt he had instilled in his battalion—leadership and audacity, guile and celerity, initiative and tenacity. Unlike at Baggy Point and the Needles, however, this time the gunfire would not be aimed over their heads.

11

Gin Blossoms

On the evening of June 4, 1944, each Ranger was issued twenty dollars' worth of emergency French francs and directed to one of the various troop transports berthed along Weymouth Quay, on the Dorset coast in southern England. Aboard the HMS *Ben My Chree*—"Girl of My Heart" in the Manx language—Lt. Col. Rudder and his staff held what should have been a final intelligence and operational briefing in the stateroom of the converted steam packet that would transport them across the Channel. They had only just learned that the invasion had been postponed for twenty-four hours due to worsening weather conditions. Rudder and his officers nonetheless continued to huddle over aerial photographs, maps of minefields, tide tables, weather reports, and a miniature clay scale model of Pointe du Hoc that Harvey Cook had mocked up. Geography, they knew, was destiny.

It was Capt. Cook, studying the spy-plane photographs, who had set the plan in motion. He realized that the Wehrmacht defenders atop the Pointe had never considered a direct attack from the sea. They had thus positioned themselves in a sort of self-contained fort designed to repel an assault from inland. Should any American

GIs make it off Omaha Beach, Utah Beach, or both, the Germans would be waiting for them with bunkers, concertina strands, and machine gun nests strategically placed to protect themselves from an incursion from the south. Even the enemy minefields were concentrated in this area, leaving the ground near the cliff's edge relatively unguarded except for one large bunker complex, likely used by artillery spotters. In Cook's planning sessions with Rudder, the two Ranger officers recognized that they might be able to make this small quirk work for them.

In the end, Rudder settled on a three-pronged assault that was as intricate as a bank vault's set of tumblers locking into place. If the scenario held, prior to the invasion proper the 230 Rangers of the 2nd Battalion's Dog, Easy, and Fox Companies, dubbed Force A and commanded by Rudder's newly promoted executive officer, Major Cleveland Lytle, would be the first Americans to set foot on French soil in a direct, seaside assault on Pointe du Hoc's towering rock face.

In their wake, the sixty-eight Rangers of Captain Ralph Goranson's Charlie Company—Force B—would make shore farther east on Omaha Beach, near the base of Pointe de la Percée, ascend the heights, and take out a string of German 88 mm batteries and mortar emplacements overlooking the beach.

Waiting in reserve would be the six-hundred-odd Rangers of Force C—assault teams from the 2nd Battalion's Able and Baker Companies as well as the also newly promoted Lieutenant Colonel Max Schneider's entire 5th Ranger Battalion. Rudder would command this Force C. After the initial wave of Rangers in Force A scaled Pointe du Hoc, they would radio Rudder's Force C to join the attack while Force A moved inland to reinforce Capt. Goranson's Rangers moving up the road from Ponte de la Percée that ran between Omaha and Utah.

Timing was everything, and Rudder and his staff had gamed out the landings to the minute. Force A was scheduled to hit the narrow shingle of scree and sand below Pointe du Hoc, designated "Beach Charley," at precisely 6:30 A.M. With this, the first of two code words—"Crowbar"—would be flashed to Rudder aboard the British troop transport HMS *Prince Charles*. That would be the signal for Rudder's reserve force aboard that ship to begin manning their landing craft. When the Rangers at Pointe du Hoc had attained the heights, a second code word—"Bingo"—would let Rudder know to follow on. If for some reason radio communications failed, rocket-fired red flares would be lofted.

If no radio transmissions were received or flares sighted by 7 A.M., Rudder was to conclude that the attack on Pointe du Hoc had failed. In this case, his landing craft would peel off and fold themselves into the general assault on Omaha Beach, joining the 116th Infantry Regiment of the 29th Infantry Division—the regular-army unit to which Rudder's Provisional Ranger Group was formally attached. Rudder and his men would then attempt to neutralize Pointe du Hoc with a flanking attack from the beach. It was a solid tactical plan. On paper.

It was nearing midnight and Lt. Col. Rudder had retired to his berth aboard the HMS *Prince Charles* when the tide tables and maps were pushed aside in the stateroom of the *Ben My Chree*. Someone uncorked a bottle of Scotch, and after toasting the success of the invasion, glasses were raised to Captain Joe Rafferty, who had replaced Cleveland Lytle as commanding officer of Able Company. Since arriving in England, Lytle's subordinates had continued their surreptitious night-watch assignments, drawing lots to keep an eye on the major when he was issued a pass to town. Through these back-channel sources, Rudder had determined that, with combat looming, Lytle had reined in his hard-drinking ways. Now, however, after the draining of the Scotch, he cracked open a quart of

British gin that Rudder had presented him as a congratulatory gift upon his promotion to major. It soon became clear that Lytle's labile personality was trending toward belligerence.

For weeks Lytle had subtly argued that a direct Channel assault on Pointe du Hoc far exceeded the Rangers' bite-chew ratio. A suicide mission, he called it, cooked up by a cabal of rear-echelon brass with no conception of Rangering. In addition, Lytle had recently picked up a rumor that infiltrators from the French Resistance had informed SHAEF intelligence officers that the Germans had moved the 155 mm howitzers from atop the escarpment. Good men, Lytle contended, were going to die for nothing.

As Lytle's face reddened and his voice grew louder, Doc Block stepped in to try to calm him. Lytle punched Block in the face. Fellow officers subdued the enraged Lytle, and Rudder was summoned. When he arrived, he relieved Lytle of duty on the spot.*

After Lytle was escorted belowdecks, Rudder was left to wonder if the battalion's entire enterprise was somehow jinxed. He had not told anyone, but Max Schneider had only recently confessed to Doc Block that he was experiencing what he called psychological "episodes." After an examination, Block told Rudder that he believed that Schneider was suffering from "a neurasthenic condition brought on by overwork and mental fatigue." Rudder had diplomatically put Schneider in for a stateside transfer—the man had paid his dues with Darby and deserved the rest. But Gen. Eisenhower himself had blocked the move, citing the need for Schneider's combat experience on D-Day.

First Max Schneider, now Cleveland Lytle. Rudder was well aware of the adage that no military plan survives first contact with the enemy. Still. His outfit had not even departed England.

---

* Lytle went on to a sterling combat career fighting with the 99th Infantry Division, for which he was awarded a Distinguished Service Cross and a Silver Star.

In any case, the Ranger brain trust confronted a dilemma. Lytle had been tasked with leading the eleven landing craft of Force A in the initial assault on the cliffs. It was too late to brief another officer on the specific logistics of the attack, even if one were available, which was not the case. Although Schneider appeared to have recovered his emotional stability, Rudder had planned to attach himself to Schneider's 5th Battalion as a precaution to better control the entirety of the Ranger landings. Now he determined that he would personally take command of the first three companies shoving off for Pointe du Hoc and leave Schneider in command of Force C.

It was a fraught decision. As overall commander of the two Ranger battalions, Rudder realized that even the slightest communications glitch could leave him out of touch with his counterparts in the 116th Infantry Regiment. He might also lose radio contact with the offshore command-and-control ships directing artillery fire in support of the Pointe du Hoc assault. But he saw no other option.

In the troop holds, the Ranger noncoms and enlisted men had no idea of the drama that had unfolded in the suddenly combative stateroom of the *Ben My Chree*. It was Herman Melville who observed that meditation and the sea are wedded, and as the transports plunged and rose through the choppy Channel waves beneath a sky as black as tar, soldiers dealt with the momentous weight on their shoulders in various manners. Some silently dealt cards or rolled dice on spread blankets, gambling away their French francs; others fell into that liminal state between waking and sleep in search of a brief respite of tender oblivion. Some cleaned and recleaned their weapons and sharpened their trench knives to a scalpel's edge, while several, many Rangers among them, shaved the sides of their heads into Mohawk haircuts for good luck. Not a few wrote poignant letters to families back home. A fair portion of them took Pascal's wager, betting with their lives on God's existence and prayed silently for their deity to "still the storm to a whisper."

General Erwin Rommel was confounded. If the Allied invasion was imminent, as all signs and reports indicated, his superior, Field Marshal Gerd von Rundstedt, was decidedly nonchalant about what it meant for the continued existence of the Third Reich. Perhaps Rommel wondered if he and the unflappable *Oberbefehlshaber* Rundstedt—commander in chief of German forces in the west—had reached the same conclusion. That is, if the Americans were allowed to establish a toehold in Europe, the war would become unwinnable, and Germany would be forced to find political compromise with the enemy to end the conflict.

Seven months earlier, on November 3, 1943, Adolf Hitler had issued one of his increasingly frequent "Führer Directives," Number 51, placing Rommel in command of Germany's France-to-Netherlands Atlantic Wall defenses, the entire length of which ran from Norway to northern Spain. Rommel would also shortly assume command of the German army's Group B, whose responsibilities included the likely Allied landing locations at either Pas de Calais or the beaches of Normandy. On his first inspection tour of the Wehrmacht's French coastal units, Rommel found their installations woefully deficient. Despite prodigious Nazi propaganda designed to both bolster home-front morale and cow the enemy, to Rommel the German army's effort to engage in two combat fronts resembled a Janus coin—fighting for its very existence in the Soviet Union while settling into a slovenly occupation of Norway, the Low Countries, and France. "In effect," observed one historian, "German troops in the west had been on vacation."

Rommel's observations led him to completely reverse the quick-strike strategy that had made him such a feared figure across North

Africa. Almost alone among Germany's senior officers, he had seen firsthand the massive airborne capability the Americans brought to the battlefield in Tunisia. He was also fairly in awe of their extensive logistical capabilities. Moreover, he was hamstrung by his own lack of air support, as most of the Luftwaffe's aircraft had been deployed against the Russians. So, now, the Desert Fox renowned for his lighting raids saw no choice but to rely on a static defense.

Across northern France he put into motion a whirlwind program of bunker and pillbox construction, had acres upon acres of minefields laid, installed beach obstacles between the low- and high-tide limits along the Normandy coast, and unspooled hundreds of miles of concertina wire barriers anchored by wooden or metal posts.* Multiple strands of this deterrent were designed to halt—and make easy artillery and machine gun targets—of troops even equipped with wire cutters. If the Germans could not stop the invasion at the water's edge and throw the English and Americans back into the sea, he argued to Rundstedt, Hitler's Fortress Europe would be lost. Rundstedt disagreed.

It was during these debates with his superior officer that Rommel realized that Rundstedt's insouciance stemmed not from any innate pessimism over the ultimate course of the war, but from an overoptimistic view of the Wehrmacht's superior operational and tactical doctrines. Like Hitler, Rundstedt had been unimpressed with the British army's performance from Dunkirk to Tobruk, and—again, like Hitler—he even denigrated what he considered the American army's ineffectualness in Italy. He subscribed to the theory that an Allied landing in northwest France was inevitable, but once ashore it would be crushed by a massive counterattack led by the Wehr-

---

* Commonly confused with barbed wire used to corral cattle or horses, or to top a ranch or farm fence to deter intruders, concertina wire—named after the musical instrument and its expanding and contracting bellows—was unspooled in massive coils similar to huge hay bales.

macht's nine Panzer divisions stationed in France. To that effect, Rundstedt wanted the tanks concentrated in reserve away from the coast until the location of the Allied invasion was certain. This strategy was also championed by the commander of German armored forces in the west, General Leo Geyr von Schweppenburg. Rommel, on the other hand, foresaw overwhelming Allied airpower making quick work of such consolidated armor, and preferred that diffuse German tank battalions be deployed forward closer to the beaches.

In the end, the arguments between the two defensive strategies proposed by Rommel on one hand and Rundstedt and Schweppenburg on the other became moot when Hitler ordered the reserve Panzer divisions placed under the aegis of *Oberkommando der Wehrmacht* (OKW, the German high command), which he alone controlled. When the time came to move against an invasion, only the Führer would decide the tanks' disposition.

Thus stood the situation when, on June 5, 1944, Erwin Rommel, convinced that the continuing bad weather would forestall any Allied invasion for at least a week, stepped into his Horch staff car and departed his Seine-side headquarters in the Château de La Roche-Guyon for his home in Heidenheim, Germany. The next day was his wife Lu's birthday, and he planned to stop in Paris to buy her a new pair of shoes.

12

Charon's Craft

I n rough soldiers' slang, it was TU from the launch. Tits Up. The four duck boats carrying the hydraulic ladders were floundering in the thrashing surf and the British LCA—landing craft assault—ferrying Duke Slater had already swamped and sunk over a mile from the beach.* It was Slater's Dog Company that had been tasked with finding four of the six German 155s while elements from Easy and Fox Companies established a perimeter atop the escarpment. Now, with Slater and a third of his effectives struggling to stay afloat in the frigid English Channel—eighteen Rangers in all—that objective had become exponentially more difficult.

Meanwhile, the soot-gray sky was spitting a cold rain that pelted like grapeshot and the cloud cover had lowered to one thousand feet. Visibility was so parlous that a navigational error had thrown the first Ranger assault wave—Force A—miles off course. Adjusting

---

* The Rangers had been assigned the twelve-by-thirty-foot British landing craft as opposed to the tens of thousands of American GIs who hit the Normandy beaches in the larger and more familiar American-manufactured LCVPs—landing craft, vehicle, personnel—popularly known as "Higgins boats" after their designer and builder, Andrew Jackson Higgins.

their approach and doubling back toward Pointe du Hoc had left the entire operation forty minutes behind schedule after nearly three hours at sea.

Had the Force A landing craft reached the beach on time—exactly five minutes after the Allied naval bombardment ceased at 6:25 A.M.—there was a small chance they might have caught the German defenders atop the headland still cowering in their bunkers. That opportunity had evaporated. The delay also meant that the entire plan for a coordinated second-wave assault on Pointe du Hoc was as underwater as Duke Slater's boat.

Still, the cliffs waited.

From the bow of his landing craft, Dog Company's 1st sergeant, Len Lomell, watched Duke Slater's "iron bathtub" pitch one final time and go under. There was nothing he or anyone else could do. The British coxswains helming the remaining LCAs had orders to stop for nothing. The wind was blowing at fifteen knots and the crosscurrents were causing the seas about Lomell's own bucking vessel to agitate and flow, like water coming to a boil. Lomell and the twenty or so Rangers beside him bailed furiously with their helmets as rolling waves washed over their bare heads. His epic journey had only just begun, but already it seemed to Lomell like the passage across the River Styx on Charon's craft.

A roster snafu had created a ripple effect in Dog Company's chain of command, and Lomell was now not only the company's 1st sergeant but had also assumed acting command of the outfit's 2nd Platoon, an assignment usually reserved for an officer. What had seemed like a big deal back in England, however, mattered little now as the bald cliffs hove into view through the mist and clouds obscuring the early morning's half-light. Lomell's platoon was still over a quarter mile from the headland, and the seawater in the landing craft, mixed with an increasing amount of vomit, had risen to knee level. Men who were not bailing were heaving extraneous packs overboard to lighten the vessel's load.

The naval "drenching fire" from the 138 warships among the nearly seven thousand vessels supporting the Allied invasion had long since ceased throwing great gouts of earth high into the air atop Pointe du Hoc when, at 7 A.M., the ramp of Lomell's LCA finally dropped some twenty feet from shore. A burst of gunfire tore through the boat and Lomell was spun in a circle. He felt a gooey substance oozing from his right side, just below his rib cage. The recognition took a moment—he'd been shot. The wound was through-and-through—it had missed bone and organs—and Lomell's first thought was that one of the men behind him had panicked and put a bullet in his back. He was disabused of the notion by the sight of the machine gun slugs leaving tiny trails of geysers among the Rangers struggling through the deep water. Within moments four of the Rangers from Lomell's boat had disappeared beneath the surface. Some were men who had entered a ten-dollar pool on who would be the first to reach a German howitzer.

The Ranger assault force had been issued heavier loads than they were accustomed to carrying. From the boots on their feet to the cigarettes and chewing gum in their pockets, stateside quartermasters had calculated that the average GI would go into combat hauling just over forty-one pounds of equipment. As a matter of course the Rangers had trained with sixty-pound packs. But, this morning, in addition to the usual tools of their trade—weapons and ammunition, field jackets, helmets, and gas masks—Rudder's men were also laden with the sections of extension ladders, boxes of coiled rope, grappling hooks, and the rocket tubes needed to fire them. Like much else during the assault on the Pointe, plans to launch the grapnels from the LCAs had been lost at sea when the waterlogged lines proved too heavy to reach the top.

Still the Rangers pressed on—dog-paddling, swallowing salt

water, searching for sea-bottom toeholds as they made their way toward the bomb-cratered littoral of gravelly sand, perhaps thirty yards wide, snaking between the waves and the sheer face of Pointe du Hoc.

The soupy weather and navigational errors that had delayed the landings at Pointe du Hoc also upended Lt. Col. Rudder's meticulous blueprint for a precision ascent of the cliff face. The original plan had called for Duke Slater, now missing and presumed dead, to make shore with his three Dog Company platoons on the west side of the promontory, while Easy and Fox Companies assaulted from the east. But the delay and the choppy seas had left all the landing craft disgorging men on the eastern salient. Moreover, the exploding potato mashers and the storm of rifle fire raining down from the clifftop concentrated the Rangers' climbing assignments into a single imperative—lunge for the nearest rope line and go. Some Rangers did not even wait for ropes, cutting handholds into the cliff face with their trench knives and clawing their way up.

Fox Company's L-Rod Petty was one of the outfit's most dexterous free climbers, yet three times he had lost his grip on a wet and muddy rope and fallen back to the beach. Next, he grabbed a rope ladder. In addition to the enemy hand grenades and small arms fire pelting from above, the Germans were swarming the American grappling hooks, chopping at the hemp lines with hatchets, knives, and entrenching tools. Petty was close to two stories high when his rope ladder was cut. He plunged back to the beach, the severed line twirling down atop him like a flying tree snake.

Petty looked up as a stream of curses pierced the shrieks of the wounded and the clamor of gunfire. A Ranger who had forgotten to doff his Mae West had stalled the line of climbers on another rope ladder when his yellow flotation device accidentally inflated halfway up the scarp. It was Sergeant Herm Stein, desperately trying to unhitch the life vest. Petty was agog. What the hell was Herm doing still wearing his life preserver? The line began to move again when Stein finally stripped off the vest and hauled himself over the outcropping. Petty tightened the strap of his BAR across his shoulders, reached for the same rope ladder, and touched fire to what was left of his candle. If Bubby Stein could make it wearing a damn Mae West, L-Rod Petty could damn well make it without one.

The vertical exodus included several Ranger squads that had been designated to remain on the beach to offload pallets of food, water, and extra ammunition stored on a supply craft trailing the LCAs. This was no longer necessary. The supply vessel had taken a mortar shell to her fuel tank. After lifting from the surface like a breaching humpback, she had come to rest at the bottom of the Channel.

Observing this chaotic scene were two paratroopers from the Army's 101st Airborne Division. Six hours earlier the C-47 Skytrain carrying them to their jump destination behind Utah Beach had taken antiaircraft fire and plunged into the English Channel. The two had ditched as the aircraft plummeted and managed to steer their chutes toward the beach. They had spent the night huddled between the cliff base and one of the many boulders that littered the strand. As the sun rose, they watched in horror as the Rangers making for shore were scythed like hay. The airmen had no idea that the bewilderingly bloody scene unfolding before them mirrored what was happening to their para brethren farther inland.*

• • •

---

* In one of those macabre sidebars that emerge from the fog of war, the two surviving paratroopers were rumored to have noticed that the sopping Rangers emerging from the flotsam-laced English Channel had been issued Corcoran jump boots. Normally this would have been an affront to any airborne soldier; the Corcorans were a distinguishing mark of unit pride heretofore worn only by troops who entered combat from the air. It is not recorded if either of the jumpers objected to the slight.

At precisely 7:09 A.M. on June 6, 1944, the communications officer aboard the HMS *Prince Charles* reported to the ship's captain, the Royal Navy commander Stratford Dennis, that he had received transmission of the code word "Crowbar." Lt. Col. Rudder and his Rangers had made the beach below Pointe du Hoc. With the news, Lieutenant Colonel Max Schneider exhaled. Rudder had originally set a 7 A.M. deadline for Schneider's Force C—if the Rangers on the troop ship had not received the code word by then, they were to abort the Pointe du Hoc assault and fall in with the GIs steaming for Omaha Beach. But as the minutes ticked away, Schneider had lobbied Commander Dennis for just a little more time. It was the British officer's decision whether to launch the LCAs ferrying Schneider's Force C in Rudder's wake or, as the backup plan called for, toward Omaha Beach. It appeared, for the moment, that Schneider's pleas and Commander Dennis's patience had prevailed.

Schneider now assumed that if Rudder had made land, it would be no longer than twenty to thirty minutes before the code word "Bingo" was received, signifying that Rangers were atop the promontory. Commander Dennis was sympathetic. He recognized that even if the first three Ranger companies of Force A managed to scale the cliffs, they could still be shredded without Schneider's reinforcements. Again, the Britisher agreed to wait. And wait.

At 7:54, forty-five minutes after Rudder's first and only dispatch, Commander Dennis approached Max Schneider. His ship's radio operators, he said, had picked up no more transmissions from Rudder's frequency. His lookouts pacing the *Prince Charles*'s bridge, their binoculars trained on the heights of the Pointe, had seen not a single flare. The British officer made the call. Force C was sailing for Omaha Beach.

· · ·

Dog Company's Sergeant Len Lomell had a vague sense that he had somehow mixed in with men from Easy and Fox Companies as he grabbed a rope and began to pull himself up. He had even noticed two American paratroopers as he'd crossed the beach; where they had come from, he hadn't a clue. The clay cliffs were slippery from the rain and wave froth, and footing was treacherous. Chunks of the cliff face had been dislodged by the naval shelling, and whenever Lomell spotted the barrel of a German gun extend over the precipice he tried to swing his rope toward the indentations for cover. Midway to the crest, Lomell saw a half dozen Rangers on a nearby rope suddenly free-fall back to the beach, still holding their severed line. He watched, horrified, as they bounced from ledges and rock outcroppings before landing with a series of thuds. He kept on climbing.

The first person Lomell ran into when he dragged himself over the precipice was an Easy Company Ranger standing on the lip of a thirty-foot-wide shell crater. The Ranger's BAR was "talking American" amid the clamor of Mauser rifle fire, exploding potato mashers, and the rat-a-tat reports from the new German machine pistols that GIs had dubbed burp guns. Beneath the BAR man, in the pit of the hole, sat Easy Company's commanding officer, Captain Gilbert Baugh. Nicknamed "Sammy" after the great Washington Redskins quarterback, Baugh was dazed, likely in shock, and attempting to bandage his right hand, which was dangling from his wrist by thin slices of flesh and sinew. Lomell paused only long enough to inject a syrette of morphine into Baugh's arm. Then he moved on, promising the captain to send a medic if he passed one. His paramount mission was the 155 mm howitzers.

Lomell had traveled but a few yards when most of his platoon, twenty-two Rangers in all, seemed to coalesce around him as if by osmosis. As Dog Company was now short the troopers from Duke Slater's sunken LCA, Lieutenant George Kerchner, the company's 1st

Platoon leader, had assumed command.* Lomell had last seen Kerchner and his men topping the cliffs using extension ladders that had somehow made it ashore. Kerchner—a twenty-six-year-old North Carolinian who bore an uncanny resemblance to the tough-guy Hollywood actor Robert Ryan—had headed off in search of their targets, the westernmost 155s.

Lomell took a moment to orient himself. Beginning in late May he and his fellow Rangers had begun to study the contours and defenses of these uplands in detail. Before and after training exercises—early in the morning and late at night—small squads of Rangers would be led into a tent to find the intel officer Harvey Cook surrounded by miniature rubber and plaster models conforming to overlays of the Pointe du Hoc terrain, down to the position of pillboxes and concertina-wire barriers. Lomell had tried to memorize aerial and topographical maps. Now he recognized nothing. Months of Allied bombing sorties topped off by the morning's naval barrage had given the plateau an otherworldly aura, as if the limestone and Precambrian schist that composed the crust of the Norman earth had been lifted, crumpled, and folded in on itself.

Lomell gathered his little group in a circle on the churned and pitted land. "Guys, look on this as a big football game," he said. "Hit them fast and hard and keep moving faster. Never stop, because that's when they're going to pinwheel you."

Lomell then led his platoon southwest, ducking enemy fire as they hopscotched from bomb crater to bomb crater.

· · ·

---

* Lomell, of course, had no way of knowing that only four of Duke Slater's Dog Company Rangers, as well as an army photographer accompanying them and their landing craft's British coxswain, had drowned before the survivors were picked up by empty LCAs returning from the beach. Despite Slater's pleas to turn back toward shore, he and the rest were ferried to a hospital ship sailing for England. They would not return to the 2nd Battalion for nearly three weeks.

As Lomell's squad drifted from sight, Rangers who had crested the summit behind them began sweeping the German hidey-holes and bunkers that catacombed the tableland. Enemy snipers took their toll, as did the machine guns the Germans had begun moving from near the inland highway toward the cliff edge. Individual heroism and, in some cases, recklessness were the order of the day.

Herm Stein had been assigned as an ammo carrier to the Fox Company BAR man Sergeant Jake Richards. When Richards took a slug to the throat that killed him, Stein picked up the gun and wiped out a German squad in what he described as "a turkey shoot." And when Sergeant L-Rod Petty ventured too far out in front of his unit while crossing a clearing, he saw too late the sign hanging from a strand of concertina wire: ACHTUNG! MINEN! Petty carefully retraced his steps, digging his Corcoran boots into the loamy soil as deep as possible in order to leave a path. He then led a contingent of Fox and Easy Company Rangers back through the minefield single file.

At one point the twenty-year-old aid man Frank South, following the plaintive cries of "Medic! Medic!" ventured out onto the tablelands to treat a wounded Ranger. Wondering all the while whether the German riflemen would respect the Geneva Convention articles protecting medics wearing the Red Cross armband, or brassard, South jabbed the trooper's bullet-riddled body with a morphine syrette. South assured the man that his wound was his ticket back to the States before draping him across his shoulders and carrying him back to the rim of the Pointe to be lowered down. He never noticed that his patient had taken two more slugs along the journey and was dead.

Back near the cliff face, Rangers from Easy and Fox Companies had carved out a small, if tight, perimeter at the edge of the promontory. Below them, Doc Block—using as cover several of the large wedges of cliff face that had been blown to the beach by naval fire—had thrown together a semblance of a triage station to treat the expanding cadre of wounded. A few yards from Block's aid center, Col. Rudder had established a small command post in a cave-like alcove offering some protection from the fire from above. From the dozen or so flimsy cots stacked against the reinforced concrete wall behind him, he figured it was probably a way station for German beach patrols. Near the mouth of Rudder's little grotto, Ike Eikner worked frantically to repair the field radio that had gone dead soon after he'd managed to transmit the first code word, "Crowbar." Somewhere on the seabed beneath the roiling waters off Pointe du Hoc sat the rockets intended to fire the signal flares.

"Bingo," Eikner shouted into the mouthpiece as his team hand-cranked the old radio's generator. "Bingo!"

He looked at Lt. Col. Rudder and shook his head. For his part, Rudder suspected that by now the point was moot. Rudder, blood trickling from a bullet wound in his thigh, was certain that Max Schneider's Force C was already steaming toward Omaha Beach. There would be no reinforcements. He told Eikner and his communications crew to pack up. They were heading up top. As Rudder reached for a rope, he was surprised to see two Army Airborne paratroopers fall in with Eikner's men.

When the 2nd Ranger Battalion's commanding officer finally pulled himself over the rim of the cliff face, he took stock of his outfit's striated positions. Rudder could only pray that, somewhere out in that wasteland, his Rangers had found the big German guns.

[13]

Charnel Ground

ust shy of three miles east of Lt. Col. Rudder's precarious command post atop Pointe du Hoc, Captain Ralph Goranson's Charlie Company—Force B—was slogging through a slaughterhouse.

Before even making the shore of Omaha Beach, Goranson's Rangers had been momentarily baffled when doughnutlike concentric circles began to appear in the rough seas battering their LCAs. Then a Higgins boat ahead of them ferrying a platoon from the 116th Infantry erupted like a flaming volcano. The realization dawned as body parts rained down on them. They were being shelled. For all their training, this was the Rangers' baptism—they were seeing the elephant. As they closed on the sands the whistling mortar and artillery shells became interspersed with the song of machine gun bullets ricocheting off the hulls of their craft.

When their ramps finally dropped in hip-deep water, the Rangers of Charlie Company found themselves facing a hellscape that measured the length of three football fields from the waterline to the headland leading to Pointe de la Percée. Men dropped to the left and right of Goranson as three mortar shells hit his LCA and great daubs of blood stained the sea in a Bosch-like tapestry of red. Those who made it to the waterline found that the wet sand engulfed their boots as they struggled through piles of American corpses washing back and forth in the ebb and flow of the tide. From somewhere up in the dunes a hidden battery of *Nebelwerfer* rockets—the dreaded screaming mimis—were raining metallic death. The smell of seared flesh was almost visible.

Over a millennium earlier, in the year 867, the French king Charles the Bald—grandson of Charlemagne—found himself in need of an ally. His treasury had been drained by a series of bloody wars in which he had defeated his brothers Lothair and Pepin for control of Gaul, and Charles lacked the military might to stave off the increasingly bold Viking raiders plundering the northwest coast of his kingdom. He turned to a Breton noble named Salomon for aid, ceding to Count Salomon control of Normandy's Cotentin Peninsula in return for an oath of fidelity and the promise to defend the territory from Viking incursions. One of the Count's martial innovations was the construction of low bridges spanning the peninsula's rivers in order to block the passage of the shallow-draft Norse *langskips*, or longships.

Now, in 1944, the Germans had also constructed impediments to repel an invasion from the sea. Among their contrivances was a small forest of wooden "mortar markers" studding Omaha Beach to provide Wehrmacht artillerymen with preregistered targets. On this morning another Salomon, the recently promoted 1st Lieutenant Sid Salomon, 2nd Platoon leader of Ralph Goranson's Charlie Company, found himself playing the role of invader instead of defender. And as Lt. Salomon exited his landing craft and raced across the sands, he was astonished to find a gaggle of GIs from the 116th Infantry huddled beneath one of the enemy's sighting beacons. He had heard nothing but tales of the 116th's fighting prowess, across both North Africa and Sicily. But these riflemen, pale and drenched, appeared paralyzed. Several of Salomon's Rangers streamed past him as he paused and screamed, "Get off the beach! Go forward!"

The combination of Salomon's penetrating, dark-eyed stare and the deep rumble of his New Jersey accent was usually enough to spark any enlisted man into action. In this case, however, the scrum of GIs remained motionless. Salomon finally gave up. Just as he turned to catch up to his men, a mortar shell detonated near the marker, killing the soldiers and knocking Salomon to the ground. For a brief moment he was sure he'd taken a lethal hit. He reached into his field jacket for his maps. They were precious, and he needed to pass them on before he died.

Then a string of machine gun bullets kicking sand into his face cleared his head. He forced himself to his feet and made for the base of the rock face that led west to Pointe de la Percée. Once under the lip of the limestone rise he glanced about for a medic. There were none. His platoon sergeant removed Salomon's jacket and shirt and began clawing out the chunks of shrapnel that had peppered his neck, shoulders, and back.

Salomon counted heads. He had ushered thirty-seven men from his platoon aboard his landing craft less than ninety minutes earlier. Nine now remained. In the distance, plowing in from the waterline, he thought he could make out the outfit's S-2, Harvey Cook, as well as the 1st Platoon leader, Lieutenant Bill Moody. Several of Moody's Rangers were hustling across the beach in his wake. Not far from Moody, Salomon also spotted Capt. Goranson. Behind Goranson was the oddest sight Salomon thought he might ever see. The 5th Battalion's Catholic chaplain, Father Joseph Lacy, seemed to be strolling—no, not strolling; waddling—along the waterline among the wounded, administering last rites.

Lacy, commissioned a lieutenant upon his enlistment, had volunteered to minister to the Rangers only a week earlier, straight out of chaplain school. At first the men had been incredulous. The forty-year-old Father Lacy stood barely five foot six and was a good thirty pounds overweight. One Ranger described him as "a small, fat old Irishman," and with his thick glasses and thinning white hair he indeed looked more like an overgrown leprechaun than a man who could keep up with the battalion when they finally hit the beaches of France. But the diminutive priest had shown a flash of his mettle as soon as he'd boarded the cross-Channel troop ship. "When you land and get in there, I don't want to see anybody kneeling down and praying," he'd told his new flock. "If I do, I'm gonna come and boot you in the tail. You leave the praying to me, and you do the fighting."

And now here he was, true to his word. Sid Salomon could only shake his head.*

When Ralph Goranson reached the cliff base, he dropped between his two platoon leaders, Sid Salomon and Bill Moody. He eyed Salomon's shirt, crusted with blood. Salomon waved it off; he was riding for the brand and gave no thought to dismounting. Moody flashed a thumbs-up and pointed to the wooden box of toggle ropes he had dragged across the beach. With the grappling hooks and the rocket tubes to launch them lost somewhere in the charnel ground of the landing, the ten-foot sections of climbing rope, with a loop at one end and a connecting wooden crossbar at the other, were the Rangers' last, best chance to make the top of the escarpment.

Only then did Goranson count the bullet holes. Nine. They had punctured his canteen, his first-aid kit, and his field pack. They

---

* Father Joseph Lacy would survive D-Day and the war. For his valor on June 6, 1944, he was awarded the Distinguished Service Cross.

had pocked the sleeves of his field jacket and shirt and the legs of his pants. One slug had lodged in the stock of his M1. None had found flesh. Luck? Divine intervention? There was no time for eschatological contemplation. Goranson surveyed his outfit's prospects.

The butcher's bill ran high. Of Charlie Company's sixty-eight Rangers, thirty-six still stood. These included Sid Salomon and four other wounded men who had refused evacuation.* With a nod, Bill Moody summoned Private First Class Otto Stephens, one of his platoon's most nimble climbers.

Stephens draped the toggle rope sections over his shoulders and stepped into a crevice that ran all the way to the top of the outcropping. He gripped bayonets in both hands, reached high, and drove one, then the other, into the cliff face. He began to pull himself up.

Several hundred yards to the east of Ralph Goranson's Charlie Company, the 2nd Ranger Battalion's Able and Baker Companies were taking the same murderous fire as they chugged toward the beach alongside the 28th Division's 116th Infantry Regiment. Dead and dying GIs littered the sands as they disembarked, and Baker Company's Captain Ed Arnold—the officer who had greeted Lieutenant Bob Edlin in Bude on that lonely February night that now felt like ages ago—could locate only thirty of his sixty-eight Rangers.

Astern of Ed Arnold's landing craft, Able Company's Lt. Edlin had been one of the thirty-four men forced to abandon their LCA some eighty yards from shore when a rocket shell blew off the head of the coxswain helming their boat into the English Channel.

---

* Goranson had no way of knowing that among the nineteen Charlie Company Rangers who had been killed on the beach—with another thirteen seriously wounded—was the former United States Navy's South Pacific middleweight boxing champion Sergeant Henry Golas. Prior to Salomon's exhortations, Golas had also slowed in an attempt to rally the soldiers from the 116th Regiment hovering at the base of the wooden mortar marker. As he yelled for them to move, a German machine gunner riddled his body.

The vessel, with the headless body of the dead British seaman still slumped over the rudder, had plowed into a sandbar. Struggling through the cold and swirling surf, most of Edlin's command either drowned or were killed crossing the sixty-yard strip of sand. Edlin zigzagged across the beach before taking cover on the pebbly littoral that ran beneath a seawall. It was then that he realized that his platoon was down to fourteen Rangers.

Across Omaha Beach, American viscera littered the sands. Like Bob Edlin, Joe Rafferty—to whom his fellow officers had raised a glass of Scotch less than thirty-six hours earlier in the stateroom of the HMS *Ben My Chree* to celebrate his promotion to captain—made the dash to the seawall unscathed, only to find himself alone. Running back toward the waterline to rally his Able Company Rangers, he was exhorting stragglers to get off the beach when slugs from a German machine gun raked both his legs. Falling to his knees, Rafferty continued to shout to his troops until shrapnel from an 88 penetrated his helmet and skull. He died in the arms of the medic attempting to treat him.

With Rafferty dead, Lt. Edlin was now Able Company's commanding officer. He had watched Rafferty's mad run. He followed suit. He was standing ankle-deep in whitewater when a bullet buckled his left leg. He spun to the ground. He attempted to stand, but another slug tore through his right leg. He fell again, the surf lapping against his cheek. The tide was coming in. Already the corpses of dead Americans were drifting out to sea. Instinctively he reached for his M1; he couldn't find it. At that moment Edlin resigned himself to drowning without ever having gotten off a shot. Then he felt a yank on the strap of his backpack. It was Sergeant Bill Klaus, dragging him to safety. Klaus, hopping on one foot, had also been hit in the leg. Back at the seawall, a medic jammed a syrette of morphine into Edlin's right thigh. The lieutenant, his face marinated in misery, begged for another in his left leg. The medic refused. He knew the battlefield maxim: "One for pain; two for eternity."

As the morphine kicked in, Bob Edlin realized that all of Able Company's officers, including himself, were either dead or wounded.

One thousand yards offshore, Lieutenant Colonel Max Schneider's LCA was out in front of the vessels carrying his 5th Ranger Battalion. Schneider watched in horror as the 2nd Battalion's Able and Baker Companies were cut to pieces. He had seen men die before, good men, friends. In North Africa and Sicily. At Anzio. But nothing like this. Omaha Beach was a meat grinder.

Schneider swung his binoculars and scanned the coastline. There had to be an alternative. He saw it. Thick smoke from a grass fire was obscuring the beach farther east, near the estuary that separated Omaha from the British landings on Gold Beach. Smoke meant cover. Even better, there were several stone breakwaters running out into the surf from the base of a five-foot wooden seawall.

Schneider raised his hand, waved furiously, pointed. The Britisher at the helm veered the craft east. The vessels ferrying the rest of the 5th Battalion fell into its wake like a row of ducklings.

Lieutenant Bob Edlin tried to concentrate as artillery shells and mortar rounds detonated about him. With no Able Company officers left standing, he ordered the scrum of troopers huddled about him to locate and retrieve any wounded Rangers from the beach. As the injured arrived, perhaps a dozen, he arranged them in a defensive line to fend off the counterattack he felt certain would come. He then placed his platoon's 1st sergeant, a wiry ex-jockey named Bill White, in command of what was left of the company's effectives, four or five men, from what he could tell. He ordered White to get them over the seawall and to head west toward Pointe du Hoc. With the morphine kicking in, he tried to drag himself after them. He couldn't.

From the bluffs above he recognized Sgt. White's voice. "Cover me." Then, the sound of a German burp gun, immediately followed by the rapid fire of an American Thompson machine gun. He heard Sergeant Bill Dreher yelling to Sergeant Bill Courtney to move out. And then nothing.

Edlin and the wounded Rangers, several of them bleeding out, would hold their positions for the next sixteen hours. The counterattack never came.

14

Thermite

Len Lomell was perplexed. He scanned his waterproof map yet again, wiping away flecks of his own blood. He and his platoon had picked their path carefully through the forty acres of Pointe du Hoc's uplands. The German howitzer they had been assigned to take out was supposed to be here, on the very spot where he and his twenty-odd Rangers were squatting. Instead, a bomb-blasted artillery casemate contained a long wooden pole. It was painted black, implanted in the ground like an angled stalk of asparagus. Fake gun. Quaker gun.

For months the Army Air Force and the RAF had pulverized this small patch of earth, dropping a total of 3,264 bombs. In addition, earlier that morning the USS *Texas* had loosed 255 14-inchers in just under thirty minutes on these coordinates—one shell every seven and a half seconds—while the destroyers USS *Satterlee* and USS *Thompson* had trained their 5-inch guns on the same spot in a mighty display of time-on-target fire. All told, more than ten kilotons of high explosives had been unleashed on Pointe du Hoc. It was equivalent to the bomb that fourteen months hence would be dropped on Hiroshima. To describe the denuded brown wasteland pocked with craters as a moonscape did an injustice to the moon. All to obliterate a sham artillery emplacement. There was a new expression beginning to gain purchase in U.S. Army barracks— pissing up a rope. Here was its manifestation.

Lomell gathered his men in a loose circle. "Okay," he said. "They're not here." He swept his arm from right to left, indicating the unseen Americans whom he knew were swarming onto the Utah and Omaha beachheads. "But we'll hear them soon enough."

At any moment, Lomell was certain, the German gunners manning the 155s would train their sights on the invasion force. The Rangers waited. One minute. Three minutes. Five minutes. The big guns remained the dog that didn't bark.

It was not long before Lomell's little group was spotted by a 44 mm antiaircraft crew off to their left. The battery had been directing flat-trajectory "crawling fire" toward the Rangers at the cliffs' edge. Now the gun barrel swiveled toward Lomell's platoon. There was no need for firing stakes; the gunner loosed his rounds over open sights. The shells roared over the Rangers' heads like flying diesel trains. Near simultaneously, a German machine gun nest some two hundred yards to their right began spitting slugs. Scylla and Charybdis. The Americans clawed deeper into the damp and muddy marl. Men about Lomell slumped, some wounded, some dead. *Digging our own graves,* he thought.

When the machine gun crew paused to reload, Lomell dispatched a small squad, including his BAR man, to flank them. A moment later he heard the staccato cadences of the Browning automatic. Silence from the machine gun. It was time to move.

During a lull in the fire from the 44s, they broke toward a nearby hedgerow. "Bocage," Harvey Cook had called it in the intel briefings.

The Rangers, Lomell on point, had nearly reached the elevated tangle of trees, shrubs, and prickly bramble when a Wehrmacht patrol emerged from a tunnel hidden in the earthen mound beneath the coppice. Perhaps a dozen riflemen. The lead *Landser* was so close that Lomell could make out the small swastika stamped into the barrel of his Mauser.

The Germans were shocked to find Americans this far inland. The Rangers opened fire first. A brief gunfight ensued. The Germans scattered. *Like rabbits,* Lomell thought, *right back into their holes.*

With the howitzers seemingly vanished, Lomell saw little choice but to move on to the Rangers' second objective—to secure the coastal highway that connected the Omaha and Utah landing sites. The road was only a half mile or so to the south, but it took the group close to thirty minutes to weave their way around and through uncounted sniper and machine gun positions. The firefights took a toll. The platoon, now down to a dozen men, had only just reached a bend in the blacktop highway when they heard the clops of heavy footfalls and the clanking of equipment.

The thoroughfare was bordered on either side by tall hedgerows. Lomell ordered his men into a ditch behind the thick overgrowth. The outgunned Americans watched silently as a unit of fifty to sixty Wehrmacht soldiers hove into view. They were moving toward Utah Beach, lugging heavy machine guns and mortar tubes and shells. The Germans, joking and laughing, passed within yards. Given their nonchalance, it occurred to Lomell that his tiny outfit had likely pierced the enemy's second line of defense.

Tense moments passed, long enough for the German troops to drop out of earshot. Lomell ordered several telephone poles lining the coast road dynamited. As the sappers placed their charges, he instructed the rest of his men to set up an ambush site in a shallow drainage ditch at the bend in the highway. He then motioned for his platoon sergeant, Jack Kuhn, and the platoon scout, Jack Con-aboy, to follow him across the highway. He made a fist, then raised his index finger twice. One at a time.

Lomell was relieved that Kuhn was still by his side. The fair-haired sergeant, three months younger than Lomell, was a former Pennsylvania National Guard cavalryman with the chiseled cheekbones of a Hollywood cowboy. Despite Kuhn's slight stature, Lomell knew him to be as hard as a wet sandbag; as the battalion's judo instructor, back in Camp Forrest, Kuhn had laid out the biggest men in the outfit. Where he had picked up the crazy Japanese hand-to-hand martial art techniques no one knew. Kuhn had only just reached the far side of the road when he motioned for Conaboy to follow. The scout was midway across the road when a single shot crumpled him to the asphalt. Lomell and Kuhn dashed out and dragged him behind a tree.

"How bad?" Conaboy asked. He wriggled to unhitch his pants and pulled down his three-button boxers. Lomell and Kuhn swallowed their smirks. Adrenaline and gallows humor have been wed since the advent of war. The sniper's bullet had passed through both of Conaboy's butt cheeks. The tip of the spent 9.6-gram slug was peeking out of the fatty flesh of his ass.

"Save the bullet! Save the bullet!" Conaboy said when Lomell described the wound. Kuhn unsheathed his trench knife, extracted the piece of lead, and handed it to the scout.

Kuhn was salting Conaboy's butt with sulfa powder when Lomell noticed a narrow farm track heading inland. The rough lane was somewhat sunken, and unpaved. Like the coast road, it too was bracketed by hedgerows—thick and tall, sprouting atop age-old earthen humps. But something was amiss. Deep ruts creased the little dirt road. Even a city boy like Lomell could not imagine farm equipment whose wheels would so chew up the loamy soil. He lifted his chin toward Kuhn. Together they disappeared down the lane.

Not far from Lomell's position, Fox Company's platoon sergeant L-Rod Petty had also reached the coastal highway. The Rangers he led through the minefield had only begun taking up blocking positions when machine gun bullets sprayed the dirt and gravel at their feet. Diving for cover, Petty glimpsed a wisp of smoke to his right. Apparently, the Germans defending Pointe du Hoc had not been issued smokeless ammo. The enemy was using a nearby farmhouse as cover. Petty took off, followed by the Fox Company staff sergeant Bill McHugh. The two used the ubiquitous hedgerows as cover to approach the enemy position from the rear.

Earlier, back toward the end of the Channel crossing, it had been McHugh who had snapped Petty out of a funk that turned his world sideways. The roaring sound of the pre-landing naval bombardment had seemingly squeezed Petty's brain to the size of a fist when McHugh sidled up to him and asked for a smoke.

"We haven't got a hope in hell of coming out of this alive," Petty said as he handed the staff sergeant a Lucky Strike.

"You're just a goddamn pessimist," McHugh answered.

"Maybe," Petty said with a shrug.

McHugh was unimpressed. "When you gotta go, you gotta go," he said. Petty laughed, his tension broken.

Now, as the two Rangers crept through the farmhouse's back fields, Petty was stunned when two Germans wearing camouflage uniforms popped up from a hole in the ground. They were so close that the barrel of Petty's BAR extended between them. McHugh leveled his M1. Both Wehrmacht soldiers threw their weapons to the ground and raised their hands above their heads. Then they shouted something in German. Two more enemy riflemen appeared from another hidden dugout. They, too, had their hands in the air.

McHugh stood incredulous at the turn of events while Petty collected their ammunition and weapons, including the machine gun. It was a feared German *Maschinengewehr* 42—"Hitler's buzzsaw," as Soviet soldiers had dubbed the heavy machine gun. The Rangers had landed with only several .30-cal. Lewis machine guns. Now Petty thought they might need the extra firepower of the *Maschinengewehr*. Petty was laughing, his mouth agape as he scooped up the enemy weapons.

Motioning to Petty's missing teeth, McHugh said, "Hell, L-Rod, that's a good way to save ammunition. Just scare 'em to death."

Len Lomell and Jack Kuhn, having assisted the wounded Jack Conaboy back across the highway, leapfrogged down the rutted farm lane leading inland. They had no idea that on that morning of June 6, 1944, they personified the deepest American infantry penetration into occupied France. The two Rangers estimated that they were two hundred yards south of the coast road—a mile or so from the cliffs of Pointe du Hoc—when they descended into a slight swale. It was just past 8 A.M. Peering up at the nine-foot hedgerow looming over his right shoulder, a bit of material caught Lomell's eye. The edge of a mesh camouflage net. *Splittertarnmuster*, the pattern was called. The netting was the type used to conceal artillery. Lomell wriggled into the thicket.

Using the sturdy branches as footholds, Lomell hefted himself and peeked over the top. His blue eyes widened. In a corner of an apple orchard, perhaps a football field away, sat five 155 mm howitzers. They were draped in the *Splittertarnmuster* netting. Bags of gunpowder and stacks of the one-hundred-pound shells were piled in neat pyramids at the base of each gun. Their twenty-foot barrels were pointed west, toward Utah Beach. Lomell assumed they could also be swiveled east, to target Omaha. There was none of the usual detritus scattered about to indicate that the guns had been fired. Nor were there any bomb craters or shell holes in sight.

Two disparate thoughts collided in Len Lomell's mind like the clang of broadswords. All the Allied bombing sorties to take out the guns had no clue as to their location. And the Germans had not left even a single soldier to guard their precious artillery.

· · ·

Beyond the German howitzer emplacement, perhaps another one hundred yards farther south at the far end of the apple orchard, two more farm tracks formed a crossroads. There, a German officer stood in the flatbed of an Opel Blitz addressing about seventy-five soldiers. Lomell could not hear what he was saying—and would not have understood at any rate—but assumed he was the chief artillery officer giving final instructions to his crews. Most likely telling them which invasion beach to fire on, Lomell figured. He clambered back down and described what he'd seen to Jack Kuhn. Both knew that Easy and Fox Companies had been assigned to take out the Wehrmacht observation posts back near the cliffs. If those outfits had done their jobs, the enemy manning the howitzers had no way of knowing that the Amis, as the Germans called the American soldiers, were so near.

"Let's take a chance," Lomell said. He drew a thermite hand grenade from his field jacket. "Give me your thermite, and you cover me."

Kuhn handed over his thermite grenade and squirmed to the top of the hedgerow. He zeroed his Thompson submachine on the scrum of Germans as Lomell belly-crawled through the swale toward the massive 155s. The muzzles were too high to reach, so, hidden behind the howitzers' head-high wheels, Lomell placed his first thermite in the traversing and elevation mechanism of one gun and pulled the pin. The grenade, resembling a tall can of soup, was an incendiary ordnance that relied on a chemical process between metal powders and oxides, known as vitrification, to create extraordinarily high temperatures. It made only a slight popping noise when detonated, and could burn underwater if need be. They had been issued to the Rangers precisely for the purpose of silently disabling artillery pieces.

Lomell moved to a second gun and did the same with Kuhn's

thermite. He watched the gears of the first two 155s melt and fuse into glass. He then wrapped his field jacket around the wooden stock of his Thompson submachine gun, crawled among the remaining three howitzers, and used his weapon as a club to smash their sights. For good measure he also wrecked the sights of the two guns he had disabled with the thermites.

Lomell and Kuhn tore back to the coast road, where the remaining Rangers—including Jack Conaboy, clutching his "lucky bullet"—were settling into ambush positions in the hedgerows on either side of the highway. The two collected another half dozen thermites and dashed back to the apple orchard. Incredibly, the 155s remained unguarded; the German officer was still talking.

This time Kuhn crept to the 155s with Lomell. He pulled the pin of a thermite and dropped it into the breech lock of one of the guns Lomell had already taken out. He then took a knee while Lomell not only disabled the traversing and elevation mechanisms of the final three guns but inserted his remaining grenades into their breech locks. Lomell glanced at his watch. It was eight thirty. Dog Company, in the form of Len Lomell and Jack Kuhn, had accomplished its objective within eighty minutes of making landfall on the scree below Pointe du Hoc.

As Lomell and Kuhn skittered back up the dirt lane, a deafening explosion knocked them both to the ground. Dirt, chunks of metal, and several giant metal ramrods rained down about them. They assumed that a round from an Allied ship, perhaps the *Texas,* had detonated a German ammunition depot somewhere behind them. They had no idea that a four-man scout patrol from Easy Company had not only discovered the ammunition dump used to store the powder for the 155s, but had also found a sixth howitzer not far from the apple orchard. On orders from their company commander, Captain Richard Merrill, the Easy scouts had lugged Bangalore torpedoes on their inland patrol and used the "bangers" to blow the ammo dump. Their thermite grenades had disabled the last howitzer.

When Lomell and Kuhn returned to the ambush site on the coastal highway, Lomell dispatched two runners by different routes—"in case one of them got knocked off"—to inform Col. Rudder that five of the six howitzers had been destroyed. Not far away, messengers from Easy Company were carrying to Rudder news of the sixth big gun's incapacitation.

Within a half hour the remnants of Len Lomell's 2nd Platoon were joined on the coast road by Lieutenant George Kerchner and the eleven surviving members of Dog Company's 1st Platoon. Counting Duke Slater's ill-fated component, the company had begun its morning with sixty-eight enlisted men and two officers. In a matter of hours, it had been reduced to perhaps twenty Rangers strung along the blacktop. The original battle plan, long since blown to hell, called for the battalion's Able, Baker, and Charlie Companies and the regular-army troops from the 116th Regiment streaming from Omaha Beach to consolidate with Dog, Easy, and Fox Companies atop Pointe du Hoc sometime that afternoon. Kerchner, Lomell, and their outgunned men could only wait and hope.

Throughout the remainder of the day, small groups of troopers from Easy and Fox Companies straggled onto the coast road. There were about sixty Rangers in all, spread out and hunkered down midway between the Utah and Omaha beachheads. Their orders were "to maintain and defend until relieved." They constituted the first and only continuous roadblock established on D-Day.

15

"No Reinforcements Available"

B y noon on June 6, 1944, Lt. Col. Rudder had established a command post atop the Pointe du Hoc cliff face in a crater behind the skeletal remains of a bombed-out German antiaircraft battery. What was left of the bunker's sixteen-foot, shell-pocked casement provided a modicum of cover. As Rudder stomped about the little perimeter checking defensive positions, his Rangers could not help but notice the bandages wrapped around his right leg and left arm. Both were stained with brown dried blood. The first was the result of the bullet that had grazed his thigh during the landings; the second covered splinters of shrapnel that had lodged in his arm and chest when a naval shell had fallen short of its target area. Rudder had been lucky—the same friendly fire had killed a young U.S. Navy fire control officer acting as the battalion's liaison to his fellow gobs on the ships offshore. After being patched up by Doc Block, Rudder never mentioned the incident.

An hour or so earlier, Ike Eikner had finally established sketchy radio communications with the outfit to which the Rangers were attached, the 116th Infantry Regiment. Eikner found that his still-balky SRC radio's transmissions could be picked up by the destroyers USS *Thompson* and USS *Harding* lying off Omaha Beach. The ships' communications shops, in turn, passed on any messages to the 116th's headquarters unit. It was a complicated electronic relay system. But it worked.

One of Eikner's assistants, Sergeant Lou Lisko, had also managed to retrieve from the surf one of two tripod-mounted signal lamps thought to have been lost during the landing. Lisko used the battery-operated beacon to blink out Morse code messages in case the radio transmissions did not get through. As a backup to this backup, Eikner had affixed coded bulletins to the legs of two carrier pigeons he had hauled ashore. So far, he had not needed to release the birds, although he was forced to rapidly unfurl a large American flag he'd carried ashore to warn off a squadron of American P-47 fighter-bombers which had previously bombarded the Pointe and were now sweeping over it to determine if the Germans still held it.

By this time each of Len Lomell's runners had made it back to Rudder with word that five of the howitzers had been destroyed; Easy Company's messenger arrived soon after with news that the sixth gun had also been disabled. Rudder's first radio communiqué to the 116th was not subtle: "Located Pointe du Hoc—mission accomplished—need ammunition and reinforcements—many casualties."

The reply was equally terse. "No reinforcements available."

Rudder would have to make do. Moreover, he could not be certain that every last German artillery spotter had been cleared from the vicinity. To leave his Rangers concentrated along the scarp was to invite an enemy barrage. As what was left of his squads and platoons gradually cohered out of the clashing bedlam, he'd dispatched them piecemeal to fight their way toward positions around the coast road to the south. He retained a small coterie led by Big Stoop Masny to defend his command post.

The bloody spectacle across the tablelands was "a new kind of warfare," wrote a correspondent for *Stars and Stripes* who had landed with the Rangers. "A crazy kind. The Jerries knew every inch of the terrain; they had long deep tunnels, through which they would dash, firing first from one spot and then another." Particularly irksome was a fortified German blockhouse presumably constructed to house spotters directing fire for the 155s. From the way enemy soldiers popped in and out of the structure, it appeared to be the hub from which weaved several spokes of underground warrens. A squad of Rangers had managed to barricade the bunker's only door, but the Rangers' mortar shells merely bounced off its reinforced concrete walls.

As the hours wore on, the scenes atop charred and chewed-up Pointe du Hoc took on the aspect of a back-alley gang fight as small American patrols haphazardly crossed paths with their disoriented and fragmented German counterparts. In one typical encounter, Herm Stein—still toting the dead Jake Richards's BAR—and the Fox Company private Cloise Manning peered over the edge of a shell hole and spotted a Wehrmacht squad of perhaps twenty riflemen pop up from one of the tunnels. As the enemy inched toward Col. Rudder's command post, Manning inserted a fresh eight-round clip into his M1. Stein stayed his hand. He sensed that a patrol of that size would not be moving forward without machine gun support. Sure enough, within moments Stein and Manning saw three more Germans settling into a crater to set up their *Maschinengewehr*.

The nest was some one hundred yards from the CP, and perhaps fifty yards in front of Stein and Manning. Both took careful aim and opened up. All three machine gunners fell dead. With that the remaining Germans disappeared into shell holes. At nearly the same moment, the Fox Company sergeant Murrell Stinnette slid in between Stein and Manning. Stinnette, who before the war had served a stint as a navy corpsman before volunteering for the Rangers, was considered the best mortarman in the outfit. Stein and Manning laid out the situation. Stinnette nodded and crawled away. Within moments a Ranger mortar began "walking" its shells toward the enemy position. Several Germans leapt from their dugouts and tried to flee. Only one escaped Stein's and Manning's concentrated fire.

Farther southeast, L-Rod Petty took a position on a patch of high ground near the farmhouse where he and Bill McHugh had captured the four prisoners and confiscated their weapons. Petty had sent McHugh back to Col. Rudder's perimeter with the captives and the German machine gun while he settled into a perch offering a clear field of fire along the coast road leading from Omaha Beach. Soon enough, enemy patrols began to appear in small groups. Petty allowed them to get to within nearly point-blank range before his BAR swept them to perdition. He mowed down a unit on bicycles, and even took out an enemy squad attempting to escape in the bed of a horse-drawn wagon stolen from a nearby farmstead. Ranger lore has it that Petty alone dispatched close to thirty Wehrmacht soldiers that day.

Yet despite the disorganized German defense on Pointe du Hoc, Lt. Col. Rudder's Ranger command was slowly being whittled to the bone. Company and platoon leaders reported men simply disappeared, presumed dead or captured. By this point, Doc Block and most of his aid men had ascended to the cliff top and established a medical station inside the bombed-out German antiaircraft installation. "Heinie prisoners made to assist as litter bearers," Block jotted in his journal. "Mostly young soldiers . . . Sure as hell don't look like a 'Master Race.'"

The bunker that Block and his aid men took over had two rooms; one was used to treat the wounded, the other to store the dead. As more and more of each were carried into the makeshift infirmary and morgue, Rudder estimated that his command had been thinned by a third. Master Race or not, the Germans were proving adept at knocking off his Rangers.

And still the question hung. Where were Max Schneider's reinforcements?

Lt. Col. Schneider's last-minute decision to redirect his landing craft to the less-deadly eastern fringe of Omaha Beach proved one of the savviest judgments of the D-Day invasion. It was precisely the kind of individual leadership skill that Lt. Col. Rudder had been striving to instill in all his officers and enlisted men over the past months, and certainly justified Gen. Eisenhower's refusal to allow Rudder to transfer Schneider back to the States.

With the British seamen expertly depositing Schneider's 5th Ranger Battalion behind the stone breakwaters jutting into the Channel, both the jetties and the smoke from the grass fire provided enough cover to allow his troopers to make and traverse the beach relatively unimpeded. Facing only sporadic fire, they swarmed over the timber seawall and onto the marshy bluffs beyond.

Schneider's six companies met pockets of German resistance as they moved inland but had taken only light casualties. Along the way, Schneider was able to sweep up the remnants of the 2nd Battalion's Able, Baker, and Charlie Companies and fold them into his command. The additional firepower not only allowed the Rangers to spearhead the American breakout off the beach to the west, but filled the gap left by the inexplicable disappearance of the 1st Platoon of Schneider's own Able Company. Also missing was Able Company's commanding officer, Lieutenant Charles "Ace" Parker, who had come ashore with the unaccounted-for platoon.

Twice—once near the waterline and again just past the bluffs—Schneider's Rangers had been joined by the fifty-two-year-old brigadier general Norman "Dutch" Cota, the gruff assistant commander of the 29th Infantry Division and perhaps the oldest Allied soldier to land with the first wave on D-Day. Cota, the son of a French Canadian railroad worker who had relocated his family to New England, had played football with Dwight Eisenhower as a cadet at West Point, and was instantly recognizable by his long, lupine face dominated by a downturned mouth set in a permanent scowl. This seemed appropriate, as he was known for his bite as well as his bark.

Cota, a keen student of history, well remembered the bloody fiasco that resulted from the failure of the Australian Expeditionary Force to move inland from the sands of Gallipoli during World War I. Eyeing Schneider's Rangers, he anticipated a way to keep from repeating that debacle. Thus the legend would soon circulate that just as General Omar Bradley was seriously considering plans to evacuate the bulk of the American invasion force pinned down on Omaha, Cota stood and roared, "We have to get the hell off this beach. Rangers, lead the way."

The truth was more prosaic.* Thanks to Schneider's quick thinking, his 5th Ranger Battalion as well as the surviving elements of the 2nd Battalion were already some of the first American soldiers to break through the German coastal defenses. The feisty Cota, as a matter of course and personality, had naturally attached himself to them, preferring to lead from the front. Once, when warned by a Ranger scout to take cover against snipers in and around the French coastal hamlet of Vierville, Cota scoffed, "There are no snipers. Get up and start moving. We'll never win this war on our tails."

When a bullet kicked up dirt near Cota's feet, he shrugged. "Well, maybe there is *one* [sniper]," he said.

Gen. Cota had no way of knowing that each German marksman had been promised a reward of one hundred cigarettes for every ten

---

* The folklore did not prevent the 75th Ranger Regiment from adopting "Rangers Lead the Way" as its motto three decades later.

Allied bodies he felled in the Norman hedgerows, twenty days' leave for twenty corpses, and the Iron Cross, 1st Class, and a wristwatch from *Reichsführer* Heinrich Himmler for fifty verified kills.

Bounties aside, Vierville was in fact proving to be a flashpoint. The village sat astride one of the five draws cutting between the bluffs of Omaha Beach that could provide the Americans with egress. The commander of the 29th Division, General Charles Gerhardt, rightly suspected that it was from Vierville that the Germans would mount a counterattack.* Despite Gerhardt's second-in-command's seemingly bulletproof bravado, Cota's indestructibility was the anomaly that morning. In the opening hour of D-Day, Gen. Gerhardt had already lost nearly 350 officers and enlisted men from his 116th Infantry, over 10 percent of the regiment. He now decided to replace those fallen soldiers with Max Schneider's Rangers.

In a sense, Col. Rudder and his landing force may have sealed their own fate by eradicating the threat from the German 155s in such short order. For, now, the military priority was to establish an inland foothold beyond Omaha Beach before the GIs were trapped between the incoming tide and Rommel's Panzers racing toward the invasion site. Reinforcing three stranded Ranger companies atop Pointe du Hoc was of secondary importance.† Lt. Col. Rudder's men would just have to find a way to hold out.

Max Schneider of course understood both the strategic and tactical necessity of securing Vierville. He and his officers thus immediately set to poring over maps of the French village and the roads

---

* Gen. Gerhardt had no way of knowing that Field Marshal Rommel had ordered the earth beneath Vierville honeycombed with a series of tunnels to allow counter-assaulting Germans to infiltrate at the point of an Allied attack. He only found out about the buried bunkers when scouts from Lt. Col. Schneider's Baker Company discovered the underground complex's main artery and caved it in with satchel charges.

† The German tank crews were fueled by the amphetamine colloquially known as *Panzerschokolade*—"tank chocolate"—a portion of the thirty-five million tablets of the methamphetamine Pervitin distributed to Wehrmacht soldiers along Hitler's Atlantic Wall in preparation for the Allied invasion.

leading into it from the south. The decision to halt the relief of Pointe du Hoc, however, did not sit well with the Ranger rank and file, particularly the surviving members of Rudder's Able, Baker, and Charlie Companies now under Schneider's command. They were incensed at having to leave their battalion comrades in such a precarious position, and were barely mollified when told that several destroyers had been positioned offshore to provide Rudder and his trapped men with an unlimited supply of naval gunfire. Shells from the sea, they knew, could in no way make up for Ranger boots on the ground. Somewhat ironically, it was fire from the USS *Satterlee*'s 5-inchers that did eventually reduce to rubble the troublesome German blockhouse atop the Pointe.

Meanwhile, the setting sun had purpled the western sky to the color of a mussel shell above the English Channel as Max Schneider's Rangers took up positions around Vierville. Simultaneously, some four and a half miles to the west, Big Jim Rudder's desperate and weary fighters dug in. It was only a matter of time before the Germans, cognizant of Rudder's dire prospects from intercepted radio transmissions, would attempt to sweep them off those cliffs and back into the sea.

It was close to dark as Len Lomell assigned positions to his Dog Company Rangers on the right flank of the American defensive perimeter hugging the coastal highway. Lieutenant George Kerchner and what remained of the company's 1st Platoon settled in to Lomell's left, abutting the shallow foxholes scraped out by Easy Company's troopers. Fox Company, digging in on the eastern flank, completed the defensive line. It had become obvious that no relief was coming from Omaha Beach. They were alone for the night.

Jack Kuhn counted himself lucky. A copse of trees anchored by the massive trunk of a spreading beech protected the little trough he had scratched out of the bottom of a drainage ditch. Anyone coming at him would have to negotiate the thick hedgerow on either side of the tree trunk. Suddenly, however, Kuhn was startled by a sound behind him. He whipped around and came face-to-face with Private Harry Fate, one of the runners whom Lomell had sent off to inform Col. Rudder about the destruction of the howitzers. To a former cavalryman like Kuhn, Fate looked like he'd been ridden too hard and long.

"Orders are to hold until officially relieved," Fate said.

Since George Washington had stood up his Continental Army, it had been drilled into every American soldier that the most serious dereliction of their duty was to abandon their post. Kuhn stuck out his right hand. "No surrender," he said.

Harry Fate shook on it.

It was on toward 11 P.M. when the 5th Ranger Battalion's Lieutenant Ace Parker abruptly appeared at Col. Rudder's command post. Rudder looked past Parker, expecting to see Max Schneider and the rest of the outfit as well as his wayward 2nd Battalion companies. Instead, he counted only the twenty-two Rangers of Parker's 1st Platoon. They held their guns on some twenty German prisoners they had captured along their journey to Pointe du Hoc. If Rudder was disappointed at the meager relief, he hid it well.

Parker explained that he and his men had become separated from Schneider's main force during the landings and had proceeded to a prearranged checkpoint beyond the seawall southwest of Vierville. When Schneider failed to rendezvous, Parker presumed that he was already moving west toward the Pointe and hied to catch up. He had no idea that Schneider and his Rangers had been redeployed to Vierville. He even suggested to Rudder that Schneider and the rest were surely not far behind.

Rudder could only hope. Meanwhile, he dispatched Parker's platoon to reinforce his own battalion's sixty-odd survivors spread

about the coast road. Specifically, Parker's troopers would but-
tress Fox Company's left flank. Although there were no majors or
captains left standing to coordinate the American defenses along
the battered front line, lieutenants and NCOs commanding small
squads had managed to cobble together a system of courier routes
to keep communications as open as possible. Each company had
also positioned two men in foxholes even farther south of the coast
highway as forward listening posts.

Now that the Rangers had established a foothold in the enemy's
rear, Rudder had no doubt that the Germans were reorganizing
from a defensive position into columns preparing an offensive assault toward the cliffs. His troopers, many of them wounded, were
tired and hungry. More dismaying, they were running perilously
low on ammunition. The battalion's mortarmen were down to their
final two rounds, and during the past sixteen hours of fighting more
than a few men had scrounged Mauser rifles, potato mashers, and
even the odd Luger to hold in reserve for a last stand. The fact that
all enemy sniper fire had ceased with the sunset only further racked
their nerves.

The silence atop Pointe du Hoc was broken just before midnight
by a cacophony of trills from dozens of Bakelite whistles. This was
followed by a rush of wraithlike shadows from a reinforced company of some three hundred German riflemen washing in from the
southwest, where Dog Company's line met Easy Company. Enemy
soldiers, their distinctive coal-scuttle *Stahlhelm* headgear silhouetted
against the three-quarter moon that had risen through the rifts,
popped from craters and from behind hedgerows. The initial torrent
of gunfire overwhelmed the forward Ranger listening posts. A hail of
potato mashers followed.

Dog Company's Lt. Kerchner sprang from his hole not far from
the highway and ran southeast along his outfit's defensive front. He

hollered for men to follow him, hoping to flank the enemy falling on Easy Company to the east. But in the noise and pandemonium only Harry Fate heeded his call.

Jack Kuhn shot off an entire thirty-round clip from his Thompson submachine gun before he realized that the muzzle flash had exposed his position. A spate of gunfire poured into the beech tree protecting him, scarring its trunk and snapping its branches.

And then, just as suddenly as the night had erupted, all was again still.

16

"All Rangers Down!"

Sergeant L-Rod Petty was still occupying his lonely roost overlooking the road from Omaha Beach. He had watched and listened almost blithely as the terrain to his west had lit up with flashes of gunfire and exploding hand grenades, and then just as rapidly fallen silent. All that remained was the lingering smell of cordite.

Petty had been granted permission by Fox Company's acting commander, Lieutenant Bob Arman, to station himself in no-man's-land on the lookout for German patrols. Fearing nervous trigger fingers, he had remained quiet and still while Ace Parker and his contingent of Rangers had passed within feet of his foxhole a few hours earlier. But now, suspecting that the gunfight he had just witnessed was merely a probe to determine the precise locations of the Rangers along the coastal highway, he began to pick his way back to his company. He had only just found the bomb crater where Lt. Arman had established a small command post when, at 1 A.M., the shriek of German whistles again rent the air.

This time they came like Norse berserkers, with rifle fire and hand grenade barrages accompanied by a cascade of mortar shells and the unnerving sight of tracer rounds emanating from several heavy machine gun positions hidden in the hedgerows. In an astounding display of fortitude, the Rangers again drove the assailants back, thanks in no small part to a steady stream of BAR fire from Petty and Herm Stein.

Two hours later the Germans attacked for a third time. Mortar rounds again peppered the American lines as the machine gun tracers flew from the dark like formations of deadly green hornets traveling at three thousand feet per second. But something was off. The gunners were firing too high. The reason became apparent when enemy riflemen who had belly-crawled forward beneath the curtain of bullets began dropping into Ranger foxholes. The hand-to-hand fighting was as confused as it was vicious. The discordance was amplified by shouts and screams in a variety of languages. The Rangers had been warned that the Wehrmacht division they would face atop the Pointe included scores of conscripted Russians, Poles, and Hungarians. Now, here they were, fighting as hard as any homegrown Aryan.

In the pandemonium, some Rangers fired on fellow Americans who, out of ammunition, had resorted to firing their captured German Mausers whose bolt actions' *clacks* distinguished them from the American M1 rifles. Conversely, Germans who overran foxholes and confiscated American weapons turned them on their former owners. Nineteen Rangers who had been wounded in the initial attacks and moved to a primitive aid station in the bottom of a shell crater recognized the sound of a BAR firing above them. They assumed one of their own had come to their defense. Instead, a German soldier appeared on the lip of the hole pointing the captured weapon. A few of the wounded reached for their weapons. They were killed instantly, the rest taken prisoner.

Petty, now sharing a dugout with Private First Class Carl Winsch, was reloading his BAR when he spotted someone crawling toward their position. Petty signaled for Winsch to fire, but the enlisted man's M1 jammed. Petty, out of fragmentation grenades, motioned for Winsch to roll one of his. Winsch complied. The crawling figure inexplicably rose to his hands and knees just as the grenade passed beneath him and detonated, shredding his torso. Petty finished reloading and peered over the edge of his hole. The swarm of bodies swirling toward him resembled a large human tumbleweed. Not knowing what else to do, he stood and screamed, "All Rangers down!" Then he emptied the clip of his automatic weapon into any figure still standing.

At one point a Ranger stumbled through the Easy Company lines shouting that Dog Company had been wiped out. Thinking their right flank exposed, what remained of the Easy Company Rangers began pulling back north toward Col. Rudder at the cliff face. Sensing there was no way to stop the retreat and fearing it would turn into a disorganized rout, Lt. Arman ordered Fox Company to follow. He sent a runner to advise Ace Parker and his platoon to do the same. Arman left Petty and three others to cover the withdrawal.

Midway to Rudder's position, Arman managed to halt and reform the outfits as best he could. He counted forty-eight effectives, including the bitter remnants of Ace Parker's platoon. They had straggled in last and accused the men of the 2nd Battalion of cutting and running while leaving them to fight. Before pulling farther back, Arman double-checked. There were no Rangers from Dog Company. The lieutenant had no idea that a dozen or so Dog Company troopers, including George Kerchner, Len Lomell, Jack Kuhn, and Harry Fate, were unaware of the pullback and still occupied defensive positions along the coast road.

Given the circumstances, the retirement across Pointe du Hoc's blasted tabletop was as orderly as possible. Arman and his Rangers arrived at Rudder's makeshift command post just as dawn was breaking. No one understood why the Germans had not followed.

But Rudder was certain they would. Surely the enemy was aware that between Arman's contingent and Rudder's small headquarters command, the Ranger force now consisted of perhaps ninety men still able to fire a weapon.

Earlier in the day, the *Stars and Stripes* reporter and a battalion photographer had discovered a crate of M1 rifle cartridges half buried in the sands at the base of the cliffs. They guessed it had been washed in by the tide from the blasted supply boat. They'd dug it out and lugged the ammunition up the steep crag. Rangers now lined up to receive handfuls of ammunition like congregants tramping toward a communion rail. When the ritual was complete, Rudder formed what was left of his battered troops into a thin defensive line anchored in the center by the enemy machine gun L-Rod Petty had captured at the farmhouse. After nearly twenty-four hours of blood and sweat, the entire American anabasis had resulted in control of a two-hundred-yard swath of bombed-out rock, dirt, and clay—the distance between the captured machine gun emplacement and the edge of the drop overlooking the English Channel.

Rudder knew that his battalion's effort had not been completely bootless; the 155s, after all, had been silenced. He also recognized that it would take but a nudge to topple his outfit over the rim of the cliff.

Lieutenant George Kerchner woke up and blinked at the sunlight. He peered over the lip of his hole at the same moment that Len Lomell's head popped up from his own nearby dugout. The two nodded to each other, and Kerchner began crawling a wide recon circle.

The previous evening, as Kerchner and Harry Fate sprinted toward Easy Company's position, Len Lomell had practically tackled the lieutenant. "George," he'd hollered over the gunfire and explosions, "what do you hope to accomplish? You don't know where they are. You don't know how many they are. Let's think this through."

Besides, Lomell reminded him, Dog Company had orders. *Hold until officially relieved.* Kerchner and Fate had stood down.

Now Kerchner wiggled across the highway, checking the posts where his Rangers had dug in. After recrossing the road, he dropped into Lomell's trench. "Thirteen," he said. What was left of Dog Company had fulfilled its orders. *Hold until officially relieved.* Then, a noise. Kerchner and Lomell swiveled simultaneously and leveled their guns. Two Rangers from Easy Company tumbled into the dugout. Kerchner looked at Lomell. "Fifteen," he said.

A few hundred yards east of Dog Company's position, L-Rod Petty again found himself alone. Remembering the minefields strewn across the Pointe, he'd decided to wait until first light before releasing the three other Rangers who constituted his small rear guard. Moments before dawn he had collected their spare ammunition and told them to pull back toward Lt. Col. Rudder's command post. He planned to cover them, and then follow. But just as his comrades were vanishing into the long shadows cast by the rising sun, he heard the creaking and rustling of a large German patrol. They were nearly on top of him. He burrowed deep into his foxhole, covered himself with a branch of broken shrubbery, and held his breath. They passed him by.

L-Rod Perry, the Ranger who was good-naturedly mocked for waddling like a duck, spent the better part of the next hour scampering from crater to crater with a pantherish grace while searching for a hole in the haphazard arteries of field-gray uniforms assembling for another assault. At one point he found himself near the same dugout from which he had told Carl Winsch to roll the fragmentation grenade. He paused to kick over the mangled body of the man Winsch had killed. The blood drained from his face when he saw the insignia of the 101st Airborne. He had ordered the execution of some wayward American paratrooper trying to reach the Allied lines. The realization sat in his stomach like a broken bottle.

Petty could not remember how long it took him to snake back through the jumbled terrain before he finally fell into a crater manned by several Fox Company enlisted men. Rudder's shambolic defensive line had spent the morning fending off sporadic attacks, with Ike Eikner calling in coordinates to the destroyers *Thompson* and *Harding* whenever the enemy was spotted gathering en masse. Despite the death raining down from the vessels' 5-inch guns, still the Germans came. During one onslaught Petty hefted his BAR to fire and began to shake uncontrollably. After the rush was repelled, he was urged to make his way to Doc Block's aid bunker. He refused to go until Big Stoop Masny ordered him.

Reaching the station, Petty picked his way among the wounded Rangers splayed across the concrete floor. Their faces were blank masks, revealing "not despair or terror," as the British poet-soldier Wilfred Owen had written over two decades earlier, "something more terrible than terror, a blindfold look, without expression."

When Petty found Doc Block, the surgeon was painting a brown "M" in iodine on the forehead of a wounded Ranger, indicating that the man had already received morphine. Petty told the doc that he felt frightened. "But I don't know of what," he said. "I didn't feel frightened yesterday, or last night when I guess I should have."

Someone had managed to heat a pot of soup; Block made Petty take a long swig. Then he handed the still-trembling BAR man a pill of some sort—Petty guessed it was a sedative—and ordered him to lie down on a tattered and muddy blanket. It was only then that Petty noticed the side room that the aid men were using as a mortuary. The bodies were packed tight and the smell was putrid. When Block's back was turned, Petty walked out and again took his place along Rudder's perimeter.

17

Graves Registration

The noisy arrival of two Higgins boats dispatched from the USS *Texas* could be heard up at Lt. Col. Rudder's CP. They rode low in the water, piled high with jerricans of water and crates of food and ammunition. Equally encouraging, the vessels also carried a platoon of Max Schneider's Rangers.

The relief party had been organized by Major Jack Street, a veteran Ranger who had fought with Bill Darby's 1st Battalion across North Africa and Sicily. Street was now serving as an army liaison officer on the staff of Admiral John Hall, the invasion's director of naval operations aboard the communications and command ship USS *Ancon* lying off Omaha Beach. Street, aware of Col. Rudder's tenuous position atop the headland, had talked himself hoarse convincing his naval counterparts of the strategic necessity of preventing the Germans from recapturing the high ground of Pointe du Hoc while the secondary landings on the Omaha and Utah beachheads continued. Adm. Hall agreed, and had in turn requested that Gen. Gerhardt shave off a portion of Schneider's unit as reinforcements.

A mighty cheer arose across the Pointe's plateau when the newcomers, carrying the precious supplies, appeared over the lip of the cliff. Within moments boxes of rifle clips and C rations—a step up from K rations—were being passed from foxhole to foxhole. Never had the jam sandwiches from the homely "C rats" tasted so good. Maj. Street departed with a wave and a thumbs-up, his LCVPs crammed with Col. Rudder's most seriously wounded as well as some forty German prisoners.

The fighting atop Pointe du Hoc continued for the rest of the day, the front lines drifting to and fro like accelerated versions of the tide washing the beach below. Doc Block had released several of his aid men, who'd discarded their Red Cross brassards, picked up weapons, and filled holes in the perimeter. At one point a Ranger assault pushed the Germans nearly to the coastal road. But then several companies of riflemen from a reserve Wehrmacht regiment swept the Americans back almost to the cliff's edge.

By late afternoon, however, a sense that the enemy's will had begun to ebb began to spread among the beleaguered Americans. The German attacks became more fragmented and desultory, and Rudder guessed that the combination of the murderous fire from his reinforced and rejuvenated battalion and the precise time-on-target shellings from the two U.S. Navy destroyers were taking their toll, particularly on the conscripted eastern Europeans.

It was not quite noon on June 8—D-Day + 2—when the Germans attempted a last concerted rush against the western flank of Rudder's line, the section closest to Utah Beach. Near simultaneously, Rangers manning foxholes farther east heard gunfire on the coast road leading from Omaha Beach—at first a soft legato and then a fierce and distinctive staccato. M1s and BARs. American guns. Soon the terrifying seethe of fifteen-pound Sherman tank shells joined the chorus, echoing across the uplands like basso organ chords.

Before the Rangers could celebrate, however, an awful realization set in. They were being fired on by their fellow GIs. The approaching relief force—Max Schneider's 5th Battalion, what remained of Rudder's Able, Baker, and Charlie Companies, and forward elements of Colonel Charles Canham's 116th Infantry Regiment—had recognized the idiosyncratic sound of the captured *Maschinengewehr* and assumed that Germans still occupied the edge of the Pointe. As American tank rounds dropped on his position, Col. Rudder screamed to the Rangers manning the machine gun to hold fire. They could not hear him.

Ike Eikner, meanwhile, was frantically trying to raise the tank commander to let him know there were still Rangers on the Pointe. He screamed into the radio receiver that he would send up orange smoke to mark their location. As soon as the orange smoke rose the tank shells fell even more furiously. Finally, Rudder sent two runners who reached the 116th Infantry's forward positions, and the friendly fire ceased. The halt came too late for the four Rangers killed and six wounded by their own countrymen.

Len Lomell was the first to hear the steel tank treads clanking across the blacktop. The thirteen Dog Company and two Easy Company Rangers hefted their weapons. Each man had the same thought— after two days of near continuous fighting with no food and little sleep, the German Panzers had finally arrived. Rifles, tommy guns, and grenades, they knew, were not going to stop them.

Tense moments passed wordlessly. Then a shout. Harry Fate's voice. "Hold fire. They're Americans." George Kerchner scrambled from his hole and ran forward. He recognized the commanding officer, Col. Canham. Canham sported a bloody bandage on his left hand and held an M1 in his right. Approaching Kerchner, Canham barked, "Where are the Germans?" Kerchner was at a loss for words.

· · ·

By midafternoon an eerie calm had settled over the uplands of Pointe du Hoc. While Lt. Col. Rudder huddled with the senior officers Schneider and Canham, his 2nd Battalion troopers wandered the battlefield searching for stray survivors. Some were amazed to see the fifteen Rangers from Dog and Easy Companies, presumed dead, mixing with Schneider's men. No one felt worse than Fox Company's Lieutenant Bob Arman, who sought out his counterpart George Kerchner to attempt to explain the snafu that had led to Kerchner and his small group's abandonment.

The Higgins boats from the USS *Texas* were making regular runs to evacuate the wounded when, toward the end of the day, the 2nd Ranger Battalion was reassembled by companies. Shortly thereafter Rudder was given a head count. Of the 450 officers and enlisted men from his outfit who had departed England on the morning of June 6, 77 were dead, 152 were wounded, and 38 were missing. Of the latter figure, over twenty were presumed captured per eyewitness reports. Max Schneider's 5th Battalion suffered 20 KIA, 51 WIA, and 2 MIA. Prior to the invasion, War Department statisticians— analyzing casualty reports from World War I—had predicted that front-line rifle-company casualties in Europe would amount to nearly two-thirds of all Allied soldiers killed, wounded, and missing in this conflict.* The losses suffered by the 2nd Ranger Battalion had proven them eerily spot on.

Lt. Col. Rudder, of course, was counted among the wounded. Col. Canham and Lt. Col. Schneider both urged him to report

---

* As the war ground on, the rosters of American infantry divisions would fluctuate widely due to attrition and a host of other factors. In general, however, an infantry division consisted roughly of fourteen to fifteen thousand soldiers divided into some two dozen front-line rifle companies, with close to double that number serving in ancillary and support units ranging from medical to communications to transportation to supply. But the beating heart of a division was the trigger-pulling riflemen—"745s," so named for their military occupational specialty, or MOS, number—of whom some four thousand were assigned to each division.

to the medical center being established in Vierville for the less-seriously injured. Rudder declined. He could still walk and fight, he said; besides, Doc Block had examined him and reported no incipient signs of infections. Canham was unconvinced and pushed harder. As a sop to the colonel, Rudder promised that for the next few weeks he would rest as best he could, delegating any physical tasks to Captain Ed Arnold. Canham was mollified.

As the 2nd Ranger Battalion marched south toward their new bivouac outside of the village of Osmanville, not far from Utah Beach, they passed what Hemingway brusquely called "deads"—the bodies of comrades who had given their last full measure of devotion at Pointe du Hoc. The Ranger corpses, their death masks the color of gray clay, their mouths often frozen in rictus grins, were laid out in respectful rows along the edge of the coastal highway. They awaited formal identification by the hundreds of officers and enlisted men from the army's Graves Registration service who were already combing the landing sectors, lifting fingerprints, and searching shredded uniforms for laundry marks. German bodies were stacked like haphazard cordwood, a distracted child's idea of bonfire kindling. They were destined for bulldozed mass graves.*

On June 10, two days after the Rangers had departed for Osmanville, General Omar Bradley and his staff came ashore at Omaha Beach. After scouting the sector, Bradley's team established his command post in the apple orchard where Len Lomell and Jack Kuhn had discovered and destroyed the German 155 mm howitzers. The hulking guns were still there, reminders of what could have been but was not.

---

* Kept hidden from the American soldiers of the D-Day Expeditionary Force was the fact that among the supplies bullied into the holds of the troopships sailing for Normandy were 260,000 grave markers.

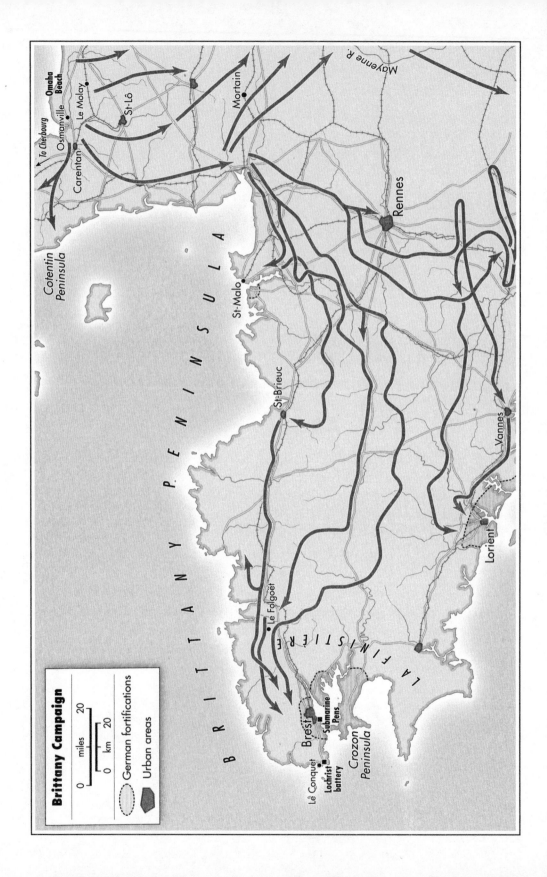

Brittany Campaign

0   miles   20

0   km   20

German fortifications

Urban areas

To Cherbourg

Omaha Beach

Osmanville   Le Molay
Carentan   St-Lô

Mortain

Mayenne R.

Cotentin Peninsula

Rennes

St-Malo

B R I T T A N Y   P E N I N S U L A

St-Brieuc

Vannes

Lorient

Le Folgoët

L A   F I N I S T È R E

Le Conquet
Lochrist battery
Submarine Pens
Brest

Crozon Peninsula

PART III

The Fortress

War is God's way of teaching Americans geography.

—AMBROSE BIERCE

18

Hurry Up and Wait

Asteel-gray sky was spitting hard rain when the Rangers reached their muddy bivouac on the edge of Osmanville on the afternoon of June 8. It did not matter. The billet might as well have been the Ritz. Awaiting them were rations and water cans, replacement weapons and ammunition, two-man pup tents and bedrolls, and the overstuffed packs the men had left behind on the troop ships. That night even the overhead drone of a single Luftwaffe Junker 88 bomber, scattering the men from their tents into roadside ditches, could not blunt the outfit's renewed spirit.

The next morning, a French farmer appeared at the Ranger camp excitedly repeating words that sounded to the Americans like *Le Boche, cinq, cinq*. Assuming that the local knew where five—*cinq*—Germans were holed up, a small squad led by L-Rod Petty, Herm Stein, and Bill McHugh followed the local back to a spinney of pines less than a mile away. There, huddled behind the trees in a long trench, they encountered an entire German headquarters company of fifty-five men. *Cinquante-cinq*. A brief firefight ensued. After several Germans fell, the remaining threw down their weapons. No Rangers were injured. Combing through a saddlebag, McHugh dug out a cache of reichsmarks likely intended for payroll use. He stuffed great handfuls of the bills into his field jacket. Although nineteen thousand tons of wood pulp had been shipped from the States to England to be converted into fifty million rolls of toilet paper, none of the precious commodity had yet reached France. The German money would do.

Also pending at Osmanville was the somber duty of sorting through the personal effects of the Ranger dead. As a prelude, Father Lacy conducted a prayer service. Any belongings deemed suitable for dispatch to grieving stateside families were recorded, stacked, and repacked. Per military custom, all personal weapons as well as perishable, fragile, or off-color items—condoms, pinup calendars, playing cards decorated with risqué pictures—were divvied up among the deceased man's company.

Someone found a bottle of White Horse Scotch among Duke Slater's possessions. Presuming Slater drowned, the whiskey was presented to Jack Kuhn, who celebrated his twenty-fifth birthday on June 10. Kuhn didn't go in much for hard spirits but took a swig before passing the Scotch around Dog Company. The next day, while exploring an abandoned Wehrmacht command post, a scout unit from Baker Company "liberated" several bottles of wine, champagne, cognac, and schnapps abandoned by the retreating Germans. With the return of the "booze patrol," wrote one Ranger, "things started to look up."

Following reveille and roll call on June 11, the battalion gathered its gear for the thirteen-mile march southeast toward the heavily forested former coal town of Le Molay. There, for the first time in a week, they wolfed down hot chow ladled from steaming pots and washed and shaved with the small bars of soap allocated to each man. More important, the Rangers were treated to a mail call. Some troopers grabbed their letters and searched for a secluded spot to read. Others eagerly ripped open packages and shared the potpourri

of newspapers, magazines, canned goods, and homemade cook-
ies that lent the foreign patch of earth a temporary taste of home.
When Herm Stein attempted to present Jake Richards's BAR to the
Fox Company commander, Big Stoop Masny, Masny told him to
keep the weapon. He was now the second platoon's new BAR man.
Masny also promoted Stein to section sergeant.

It was soon apparent that army strategists had given little thought
to future Ranger missions. With no direct orders from their parent
unit—Gen. Gerhardt's 29th Infantry Division—Lt. Col. Rudder
recuperated from his wounds while Capt. Arnold directed patrols
around the outskirts of Le Molay. Though harassed each night by the
lone enemy bomber—by now nicknamed "Bed Check Charlie"—
the Rangers encountered little human resistance. Caprine and bovine
engagements, however, proved irksome. One day, for instance, Sergeant Willie Clark and Sergeant Frank South, two of Doc Block's top
aid men, found themselves on an unexpected front line.

The bond between Clark and South had been forged a year earlier, during basic training at South Carolina's Fort Jackson. Despite
his youth, the twenty-one-year-old Clark had already served a hitch
in the regular army before reenlisting after Pearl Harbor. He was
fulfilling a refresher course in marksmanship on the camp's firing
range when he ran across the then teenaged South, who was training to become a medic. South confided to Clark that he planned
to volunteer for the new Ranger battalion he had heard was being
stood up in Tennessee. Clark was intrigued by both ideas—saving
lives as an aid man and becoming a special operator.

The more experienced Clark also knew a bit about the Rangers' physical and mental ethos and felt that young South was not
yet ready for the rigor. To that end he devised an after-hours regimen wherein the two would run and rerun Fort Jackson's obstacle
course, followed by sets of near-debilitating calisthenics. The drills
were topped off by ten-mile speed marches in full gear during which

Clark insisted that they both wear gas masks in order to increase their stamina. Each day at the conclusion of the regimen, the two would unfold a portable chessboard and play a match; they believed the game kept their minds as toned as their bodies.

The friends had been separated on D-Day, with South assigned to Doc Block's medical unit at Pointe du Hoc and Clark landing on Omaha Beach. Clark's memories of the day were mesmerizing, if horrifying. He told young South that he had rapidly depleted his kit of morphine, sulfa powder, and gauze bandages on the bloody sands, and when he finally spotted a medical unit coming ashore it carried typewriters and file folders but no triage supplies. His subsequent treatments came down to ripping sopping blankets off the bodies of the dead, shaking them out, and placing them over the soon-to-be-dead. When there was nothing else for it, he searched the corpses for handkerchiefs with which to cover their faces. A little dignity was all he could offer. Finally, he said, he'd shed his Red Cross brassard and picked up a discarded M1 rifle. After witnessing the horrors of the beach, he just wanted to kill Germans.

Now, a week later at Le Molay, the two were sharing cigarettes over hot coffee when a bearded billy goat stuck its head over the lip of their dugout. South began feeding the goat discarded cigarette butts, which the animal devoured. Then, with a movement as rapid as any blitzkrieg, the goat ducked its head into the hole and plucked a newly lit smoke from South's hand and swallowed it, drawing blood in the process. Howls from Willie Clark only added to South's embarrassment. He had escaped Pointe du Hoc unscathed, only to be wounded in action by a farm animal. It would take time to live the story down.

Not long after, a happier ending accompanied the battalion's confrontation with an ornery cow. One afternoon the animal, perhaps driven mad by a grazing gunshot wound, appeared out of nowhere and allegedly "charged" the area where Charlie Company was bivouacked. Two staff sergeants—one armed with a submachine gun, the other with an M1—hoisted their weapons. The Ranger and author Robert Black best describes the ensuing confrontation. "The cow was not supported by its herd, lost the engagement, and became dinner." Whether the chickens, potatoes, and onions that complemented the steaks had also assaulted the outfit is left unrecorded.

On June 20, Lt. Col. Rudder felt recovered enough to resume full duties as the battalion arrived at its new billet on the grounds of the magnificent Château de Colombières, some five miles northwest of Le Molay. The winged castle, a former medieval fortress, stood like a dragon guarding the entrance to the town of Carentan at the base of the Cotentin Peninsula.

For the Germans, Carentan had been looked upon as the key to preventing the American lodgments on Utah Beach and Omaha Beach from coalescing into an unbroken front, what the military author Rick Atkinson drolly refers to as "a black line on a war map." In the immediate aftermath of D-Day, the fourteenth-century château had been the site of a fierce firefight that decimated a regiment from the 101st Airborne. In the days since it finally fell to the Americans, the main house and its outlying buildings, rumored to have a room for each day of the year, had been converted into one of the many Allied medical stations ministering to the wounded of Gen. Bradley's First United States Army. Across the front, American casualties were exceeding eighteen hundred men per day, or one every forty-eight seconds.

By the time the Rangers arrived, however, all was quiet near the château—quiet enough for both the 2nd and 5th Ranger Battalions to be reclassified as reserve units. During Rudder's brief convalescence, Capt. Arnold had scoured the troop replacement centers, or "stockage depots," sprouting on the invasion beaches, seeking volunteers to fill out the battalion's diminished rolls. He had picked up 70 men during his quest; these were soon joined by another 180 volunteers from a "repo depot" in England.

Rudder had petitioned his superiors to allow the two Ranger battalions to return to England for refitting and retraining. He argued that his officers and noncoms needed time to discern the physical and psychological strengths and weaknesses of the replacement troops. The request was denied. Now, back in the saddle, he remained frustrated at having to plug the holes in his outfit while still so near to the front lines. He recognized that any soldier who volunteered for Ranger duty was likely to be a cut above the supply clerks, drivers, typists, and cooks being shoveled into regular-army regiments devastated on D-Day.

Nonetheless, he felt that division brass should have realized that special operators required a specific skill set, and that dropping new men piecemeal into already cohesive Ranger squads, platoons, and companies would compromise the outfits' unit integrity. As it was, there was nothing Rudder could do but attempt to fast-track the interview and training processes for the neophytes. As he expected, the battalion's physical curriculum on the grounds of the Château de Colombières soon winnowed out ninety of the newcomers.

The survivors were left to watch and learn when, in late June, the 2nd Battalion was assembled for an awards ceremony. Rudder presented eight Rangers—including Len Lomell, Jack Kuhn, George Kerchner, Ralph Goranson, and Big Stoop Masny—with Distinguished Service Crosses for their heroics on the Pointe and Omaha Beach. Doc Block, Sid Salomon, and twelve others were awarded Silver Stars. After the formalities were concluded, Rudder summoned his officers. There was work to be done and, more important, key battalion leadership slots to be filled.

With the transfer of the obstreperous Cleveland Lytle, the death of the Able Company commander Joe Rafferty, and the medical evacuation of Able Company's Bob Edlin, Easy Company's Lieutenant Gilbert "Sammy" Baugh, and Captain Fred Wilkins from Rudder's Headquarters Company, Rudder set about reorganizing the 2nd Battalion's command structure. Capt. Arnold stepped into Lytle's old position as executive officer, or XO, and Duke Slater—who had rejoined the battalion from England only a day earlier—was named operations officer, third in command. Slater took some ribbing for having missed so much time while being treated for *mere* hypothermia despite the condition's frequent fatal consequences. But beneath the jibes the men were happy to have him back. Slater was a tough guy; he'd been missed on the Pointe. Finally, rounding out the battalion's senior staff, Harvey Cook and George Williams remained in their S-2 (intelligence) and S-4 (logistics) positions.

At the company level, Ralph Goranson, Big Stoop Masny, and Richard Merrill retained commands of Charlie, Fox, and Easy Companies, respectively. Lieutenant Morton "Big Mac" McBride—one of the returning "ghosts" who had survived the LCA sinking with Slater—was named Dog Company's commander. And the newly promoted Captain Bob Arman—with whom L-Rod Petty had briefly shared a foxhole during the first German counterattack atop Pointe du Hoc—was placed in charge of Able Company. For his leadership on Omaha Beach, Sid Salomon was handed Baker Company and Ike Eikner, promoted to captain, replaced Fred Wilkins in Rudder's Headquarters Company.

With a concluding flourish, 1st Sgt. Lomell was named the battalion's sergeant major. There were rumors that Col. Rudder had filled out the paperwork putting Lomell in for the Medal of Honor for his heroics atop Pointe du Hoc. Though he and his parents could have certainly used the extra two dollars in monthly salary that came with receiving the military's highest and most prestigious military decoration, it would also have meant being shipped home early—the War Department did not risk MOH recipients being killed in action or, worse, captured.

Anxious to see the war out, Lomell was gratified enough to have the Distinguished Service Cross pinned to his chest along with the promotion. Per army tradition, the upgrade to battalion sergeant major also allowed Lomell to bypass the regular chain of command and go directly to Rudder with any suggestions or grievances from the enlisted men. The latter regularly outnumbered the former. The tougher the outfit, the louder the gripes.

For the restless Ranger battalions, the next several weeks provided the classic example of the age-old military saw—hurry up and wait. As the Allied Expeditionary Force slogged through the Norman hedgerows, Big Jim Rudder's and Max Schneider's warfighters were tasked with a series of mundane assignments that most felt were beneath their special-operator status. In late June they were ordered back to Utah Beach to guard the nearly forty thousand German prisoners, including 218 generals and admirals, awaiting transfer to POW camps in the States. The barbed-wire enclosures into which the Germans had been crammed—many constructed by the prisoners themselves—were built to hold twenty thousand men, and the primitive conditions were miserable. The Rangers, remembering dead friends, were not moved. *Vae Victis*. Woe to the conquered.

From there, Rudder's and Schneider's outfits were trucked farther up the Cotentin Peninsula to relieve a cavalry reconnaissance unit occupying a château that had formerly served as a Wehrmacht communications hub. The nearby port city of Cherbourg had fallen to the Allies on the first day of July, but the Germans still held the Channel Islands, including Guernsey, some forty miles off the tip of the peninsula. The ostensible Ranger mission was to prevent any heel-end sneak attack from the Channel. No one, however, truly believed that the enveloped enemy troops were about to move off those islands, and the Americans contented themselves with the luxury of hot showers that the Germans had installed in the estate's stables-turned-barracks.

By this time Lt. Col. Rudder had reinstituted the day-and-night training policy for his own battalion as well as Max Schneider's 5th. Rudder knew that he was overworking his men, but it was out of necessity. The intensity of the daily thirty-mile speed marches—interspersed with hand-to-hand fighting drills, instructions to the green recruits in the use of captured enemy weapons, and live-fire obstacle course exercises—were necessary to keep his new corn-plaster commandos alive.

To compensate, Rudder was generous with passes to Cherbourg, a mere twelve miles away. Despite the retreating Wehrmacht's largely successful attempt to raze the port city's harbor, the town's bistros and fleshpots survived, and the continent's first Red Cross clubs were beginning to spring up in the city. Rudder was well aware that Cherbourg's enticements were less R&R than I&I—intoxication and intercourse. But they proved a useful outlet for his overworked and randy troopers to blow off steam. Even when army MPs threw up checkpoints around the "fancy houses" to prevent anyone in an American uniform from entering, word passed among the Rangers that French sailors drinking in the town's wharf-side bistros were more than happy to rent out their blue-and-white *La Royales* uniforms in exchange for K rats and American cigarettes.

The dizzying merry-go-round continued through early August as both Ranger battalions were loaded onto two-and-a-half-ton trucks and transported over a hundred miles south in preparation to assist General George Patton's Third Army in repulsing a surprisingly strong German counterattack near the hilly village of Mortain, midway between the Cotentin and Brittany peninsulas. But they were recalled without explanation at the last moment; the Rangers joked that Patton was afraid of demoralizing his GIs with the sight of real fighting men. From there another caravan of olive-drab two-and-a-half-ton cargo trucks—the army's ubiquitous "Jimmy" deuce-and-a-halfs—hauled them thirty-two miles to safeguard the bridges spanning the Mayenne River at the base of the Brittany peninsula.* Along the way they were seemingly treated as afterthoughts by the American high command, attached first to a light tank battalion, then to the 4th Infantry Division, and then to the 9th Infantry Division.

By this time the Allies had landed well over a million men in Normandy as well as some seventy-seven thousand vehicles, ranging from tanks to halftracks to jeeps to the deuce-and-a-halfs. With the rolls of the entire United States armed forces about to swell to eight million soldiers, sailors, and Marines fighting across multiple theaters—a quarter of them serving in front-line assault units—it was not lost on Lt. Col. Rudder that his tiny band of several hundred special operators were barely keeping afloat in the countless eddies of the War Department's bureaucracy. Further, his outfit faced a serious tactical problem. American military strategists planning to push east through France, the Low Countries, and into Germany had failed to envision a doctrine that would dictate the Rangers' operational use beyond the immediacy of D-Day.

Lt. Col. Rudder himself did not lack for vision. From the outset he had conceived of his two battalions as stand-alone strike forces, lightweight and mobile, capable of lightning attacks on enemy positions behind the front lines. Nor did he lack an appreciation of military history. If the inspiration for Winston Churchill's Special Operations Executive was the prime minister's romantic view of Afrikaner Kommandos, Rudder's generation of Texans were not far removed from the frightful hit-and-run raids led by the legendary Comanche war chief Quanah Parker. But Rudder intimated

---

* The four-wheel-drive "Jimmy," made by General Motors and known phonetically by its G-508 Ordnance Supply Catalog number, was capable of transporting two and a half tons of cargo.

that his expectations had to be put on hold. His troopers took the cue. Sid Salomon's analogy was apt. "Being a separate battalion," he told one war correspondent, "we were like the runt of the litter."

Or, as the official history of the Rangers in World War II would observe nearly five decades later, "Having accomplished the task of eliminating the guns atop Pointe du Hoc as well as leading the breakout from Omaha Beach that had been the basis for their creation, the two Ranger battalions spent much of the rest of the war in search of a purpose."

Big Jim Rudder was determined to find and secure that purpose. All he could do for the moment, however, was to keep his men in fighting trim for when the opportunity presented itself.

Meanwhile, peppered among the new recruits entering the Ranger realm were a steady trickle of wounded veterans returning from British medical depots. Captain Fred Wilkins—the former commander of Rudder's Headquarters Company—was one of the earliest. One day Wilkins had simply sprung from his hospital cot in London, donned his uniform, and hitched a ride across the Channel on a supply ship. Upon his arrival at the Ranger billet near Cherbourg, however, Col. Rudder and Doc Block—who had opened up an ad hoc practice treating French children—examined the still-festering shrapnel wound running the length of Wilkins's back and ordered him returned into the British medical system.*

Lieutenant Bob Edlin, on the other hand, was more persistent.

---

* Block felt right at home in his new practice, as payment for his services came predominantly in the form of fresh eggs, red wine, and even the occasional lobster from a nearby fishing village.

19

The "Fabulous Four"

The first bullet Bob Edlin caught on Omaha Beach had left a bloody chunk of flesh as thick as a flank steak dangling from his left calf. The second had nicked his right tibia near the knee and sheared off several bone chips. Given the morphine coursing through his bloodstream, he only vaguely recalled being evacuated. He supposed he owed his life to the nameless American swabbie, a giant of a man with a thick mane of flaming red hair, who he hazily remembered tossing him over his shoulder like a rag doll and lugging him from the bottom of a Higgins boat onto a troop carrier returning to England.

But his first solid memory after watching the remains of his Able Company Rangers scurry over the seawall and disappear into the bluffs beyond the beach was riding a canvas cot and being carried by U. S. Navy corpsmen through the streets of Weymouth. He guessed from the cheering crowd thronging the thoroughfare that the invasion had been a success. That first night there were two dozen or so fellow Americans in Edlin's hastily thrown-up military hospital hard by the port city's docks. He thought the fresh paint on the walls would pucker from their nightmare screams. He watched as orderlies hustled from bed to bed administering sedatives. The next morning it was the eggs, real eggs, the first they'd tasted in weeks, that seemed to assure the wounded men that, yes, they were off the Omaha sands and safe.

From Weymouth, Edlin was transported by ambulance to a civilian hospital in Oxford, where a nurse finally helped him shed his uniform, filthy with sweat, blood, mucus, and vomit. The next day they operated on his left leg—"just pulling some of the ligaments together," the surgeon told him. He was certain that they had amputated the limb until he begged a nurse to hold up a mirror to show him the plaster cast. Two days later they wheeled him back into surgery to clean out the floating bone chips in his right knee. He had casts on both legs and was told to expect a two-month recovery. He was even offered the chance to return to the States to recuperate. He declined.

The cast on his right leg was removed shortly thereafter, and nurses cut the plaster from his left leg a week after that. Edlin spent the next ten days hobbling to and from the hospital's rehab room for painful workouts—two a day, three a day. The nurses told him he was doing too much, too soon. But he was determined to rejoin the battalion. By now he knew of their exploits both on the beach and atop the Pointe. Having never even fired his rifle during the invasion, he felt he owed the outfit.

On June 21, Edlin requested a meeting with the physician in charge of his ward. The medico was a Brit, and Edlin told him that he was ready to return to France. He did a little jig in the man's office to prove his point. It hurt like hell; he didn't let on. The doctor examined his left leg and told him that it was far from fully healed. If the wound became infected, he said, this time Edlin *would* lose the limb. Edlin said he'd take that chance. The doctor then said that his discharge papers weren't ready, and if he left the hospital grounds he would be considered AWOL. Edlin said he'd take that chance, too.

The medical man gave up; there were too many wounded soldiers pouring into his hospital to waste time parrying words with a lunatic. Edlin made him promise to forward all the proper paperwork to, well, wherever the 2nd Ranger Battalion might be in France. He then walked to his bed, shouldered the duffel bag he had packed before even seeing the doctor, and exited the hospital. He waited until he was around the corner and out of sight before reaching down to massage his left leg. It was killing him from that little dance.

It was mid-July when Edlin stepped from the jeep onto the gravel driveway of the château outside of Cherbourg. He headed straight for Doc Block's aid station, glowing as if he'd been polished for the occasion. The two men hugged wordlessly before Block removed the bandage from Edlin's left leg. He examined the wound with a gimlet eye. It was against his medical judgment, but he knew better than to argue with a Ranger who had just spent three weeks gimping his way through southern England, across the English Channel, and up the Cotentin Peninsula. He sent Edlin on to the room that Col. Rudder had commandeered for his headquarters.

Despite Edlin's noticeable limp, Rudder asked him if he wanted to command his own company. Edlin said no, he preferred to return to Able to serve in some fashion, even in his old role as a platoon leader. Rudder summoned Captain Bob Arman. He asked Arman if he had any problem with Edlin becoming his XO. Arman, who had grown up in Indiana just three hours north of Edlin's hometown, said he'd be delighted to have a fellow Hoosier as his number two. They shook on it and departed.

Although Rudder had greeted Edlin with the polite officiousness expected of a battalion commander, in private he was ecstatic. "This has been a very good day for me," he wrote to his wife, Chick, later that night. "Lt. Edlin returned from the hospital sooner than expected. It is a real morale booster to have him with us again."

He could not have guessed the half of it.

First Sergeant Bill White was giving a Ranger newbie a haircut when two hands clapped him hard on the shoulders from behind. "Whitey," as he was known, still as lithe and quick as in his jockey days, whipped around and brandished the scissors, ready for combat. Bob Edlin laughed so hard he nearly bent in half.

Someone found a jug and soon a half dozen of the "old timers," not one of them over the age of twenty-five, were reminiscing. It was a bittersweet reunion. Someone pulled out an old Able Company roster. They talked about those who hadn't made it off the beach. Donovan, Patterson, and Hart; Ware, Shanahan, and Sowa. Capt. Rafferty. Edlin asked after others. Dog Company's Lomell and Kuhn? Made it. The funny-looking BAR man from Fox, Petty? Him, too; too ugly to die. The boxer from Easy? Golas, Henry Golas? The room fell silent. That one hit hard; Edlin remembered throwing leather with him back in Bude. Fists of stone, that guy. Another jug was uncorked. The conversations continued well into the night.

The patrols began as a lark. Since rejoining the battalion, Bob Edlin had taken to personally inspecting Able Company's forward listening posts. One morning toward mid-August, with the battalion billeted along the Mayenne River, he and Bill White slid into a foxhole occupied by the squad sergeants Bill Dreher and Bill Courtney. The gangly Dreher, his six feet, three inches accentuated by a thick tuft of sable hair that made him appear even taller, towered over the beefy Courtney, half a foot shorter. Courtney's wrestler's nickname—"No-Neck"—was underscored by the heavy satchels of flesh that hung like parentheses beneath his close-set eyes. To-gether they brought to mind the era's popular comics-page charac-ters Mutt and Jeff, the cartoonist Bud Fisher's "two mismatched tinhorns" who became fast friends.

Courtney, like most of the Rangers, loathed the outfit's most re-cent assignments. Babysitting prisoners. Trucking about France pre-paring for missions that never happened. And now, policing a literal backwater far from front-line action. The men were getting sloppy. "The only casualties are men fooling around with mines and demo-litions," Doc Block jotted in his journal. The day after Block made that notation, an Able Company recruit accidentally shot himself in the head while cleaning his rifle. He died on the spot. This was not No-Neck Courtney's idea of Rangering, and he was not shy about letting anyone know it. That morning Edlin, White, and Dre-her were listening to Courtney gripe when he suddenly leaped from the hole and quietly declared, "Hell, there aren't any Germans out there."

Courtney began traipsing into no-man's-land. The other three stubbed their cigarettes and followed.

The quartet, edging forward in a classic diamond-shaped for-mation with Edlin on point, walked six or seven miles without en-countering any opposition. Edlin knew this would prove valuable intel to Lt. Col. Rudder. More profoundly, Courtney's headstrong frustration was also the genesis of what the Ranger historian Robert Black labels the legend of the "Fabulous Four . . . perhaps the most highly decorated patrol in the history of the United States Army."

Each morning thereafter the foursome would gather after roll call and chow to commence a new recon mission through the rolling farm plots, orchards, and dense oak forests of the Pays de la Loire—the lands of the Loire valley, which formed the base of the Brittany peninsula. Growing up in rural Indiana, Edlin had been an avid hunter, following the ancient Potawatomi Indian trails that laced the region known as Kentuckiana for its proximity to the state just across the Ohio River. A born lone wolf, as a youth he had preferred to pursue his prey by himself. Yet as the whitetail deer he'd stalked did not carry Mauser rifles and potato mashers, now he did not mind the company. When other Rangers asked to join the group, however, Edlin demurred. Four was the perfect number—the "magic number," someone called it—large enough to unleash plenty of firepower yet small enough to evade detection.

The patrols proved a mixed bag. On several occasions the Rangers found themselves easing into hamlets hurriedly abandoned by the Germans. They could judge how recently the enemy had departed by the closeness of the shaved heads of female collaborators who had been shorn as punishment. The locals would inevitably insist that the Americans remain for feasts of roast duck or goose accompanied by pots of boiled potatoes, carrots, and onions. It was not unusual for the Rangers to be serenaded by impromptu bands banging out "La Marseillaise" and off-key versions of "The Star-Spangled Banner." In one village they even "liberated" an old ambulance, which they presented to Doc Block.

Before departing they would inevitably be plied with flowers and fruit as well as bottles of wine, cognac, champagne, and the ubiquitous local liqueur, the apple-based Calvados. Some of this booty would later be distributed throughout Able Company, to the disquieting surprise of many a naïve young soldier prone to guzzling what they considered a form of French apple juice.

More often, however, their routes led to trouble. As in Normandy, the Germans had worked for years lacing the area with a crazy-quilt crosshatch of bunkers and trenches, usually anchored by sturdy pillboxes holding anywhere from forty to eighty soldiers. The pillboxes became the favorite targets of Edlin, White, Courtney, and Dreher, with each attempting to outstealth the others in creeping close enough to surprise the occupants. They killed scores and captured as many. When clandestine efforts failed, or if the enemy fortification proved too strong for four men to take, Edlin would radio their position to battalion headquarters and request mortar, tank, or even close-air support.

Lt. Col. Rudder approved of the off-book patrols—they not only provided the morale boost he had foreseen in his letter to Chick but embodied the incentivized critical thinking he had tried to inculcate in the battalion from its inception. At some point, however, he realized that having both the executive officer and 1st sergeant of the same company risking their lives on a daily basis might be walking a razor's edge. He summoned Edlin and asked him to "ground" Sgt. White and replace him with another noncom. White was disappointed, and briefly considered asking to be demoted to corporal or even private. Edlin talked him out of it.

In the end, the result of the personnel change could not have been more serendipitous. Not only was Edlin's choice—the twenty-year-old Louisiana native Sergeant Warren Burmaster—fluent in French, but he also bore a striking facial resemblance to the prizefighter Barney Ross, who in the 1930s had won championship belts in three separate weight classes. Edlin took that as a good omen. Even more fortuitously, Burmaster was a teetotaler.

As Edlin explained to Dreher and Courtney, "It's simple mathematics. With Whitey, none of us spoke French and all four of us drank what we could get. Now [with Burmaster], we get a guy that can speak French and doesn't drink. We only have to split the cognac and calvados [sic] three ways."

If past is prelude, Bob Edlin proved prophetic.

20

Brittany

As the 2nd Ranger Battalion trudged toward the seemingly endless convoy of smoke-belching deuce-and-a-halfs on the morning of August 17, 1944, the latrine scuttlebutt spread rapidly. They were moving west. While the bulk of Allied forces in France continued their push east toward Paris, the outfit was heading in the opposition direction, aiming for the tip of the Brittany peninsula. There, on the rugged Atlantic seacoast, rose the German-held city of Brest, France's second-largest port after Marseille, and home to the *Kriegsmarine*'s immense network of U-boat pens. Despite being encircled, German troops at Brest refused to surrender. The Rangers wondered if they were nuts. Adding to the troopers' surprise, for some reason—and for the first time since the Normandy landings—the 5th Battalion was not moving out in conjunction with the 2nd. There was, of course, a valid explanation for this that few of the rank and file were privy to.

Since examining Max Schneider back in England, Doc Block had kept a wary watch over the troubled officer. Block was relieved to report to Rudder that, having fulfilled Gen. Eisenhower's faith with his brilliant performance on Omaha Beach, Schneider seemed a new man and soldier, more affable and carefree than he'd been since reporting for duty in Scotland. This was understandable. Schneider's lengthy combat log made him eligible for rotation back to the States, and he was looking forward to the deployment. He would have departed already if not for his insistence on remaining to ease the transition of his replacement, the 5th Battalion's executive officer, Major Richard Sullivan. As it was, after a brief "shakedown cruise" under Sullivan's leadership, the unit was scheduled to move out for Brest in ten days.

Even in a war zone, especially in a war zone, Lt. Col. Rudder continued his modus operandi of keeping his men informed about the conflict's big picture. The evening before their departure for Brest he gathered his officers and told them that Gen. Bradley had reluctantly concluded that the damaged Cherbourg harbor and the Normandy invasion beaches could no longer handle the hundreds of thousands of Allied troops and the thousands of tons of equipment and supplies pouring into France. Thus, rather than bypass Brest and starve its German occupiers into submission, SHAEF had determined that it needed the city's deep-water anchorage. To that end the Ranger battalions had once again been attached to the 29th Infantry Division. The division was, in turn, but one component of General Troy Middleton's VIII Corps—nearly eighty thousand American GIs assigned to the Brest operation.

The 2nd Battalion's mission was to spearhead the effort to knock out a German battery of four 280 mm cannons protecting Brest's harbor. The massive 280s made the 155 mm howitzers atop Pointe du Hoc look like popguns. Dubbed the Lochrist battery by the Americans after a nearby French village, the Germans referred to the artillery complex as the Graf Spee battery, as their earthshaking firepower was equivalent to those aboard the *Kriegsmarine* battle cruiser of the same name, which the British had sunk off South America in 1939. In addition to silencing the big enemy guns, the

Rangers had also been deployed to act as the 29th Division's emergency "fire brigade," dousing any unforeseen conflagrations. Rudder was almost giddy. Finally, tasks that suited the expectations of his outfit.

The city of Brest was tucked into the lee side of a sixteen-mile spit of land jutting into the Atlantic that the French called Finistère—the end of the earth. Since medieval times it had been recognized as the key to the thumb-shaped Brittany Peninsula. "He is not the Duke of Brittany who is not the Lord of Brest" was a French axiom, and in the seventeenth century Cardinal Richelieu—the royal court's powerful *Éminence rouge*—convinced King Louis XIII to construct a harbor there that would become the primary base of French naval operations.

The seaport's inner core was the epitome of fastness, with walls up to twenty-five feet thick. Moreover, in the wake of the easily repulsed British amphibious raid on Dieppe two years earlier, the Wehrmacht high command had correctly surmised that any Allied assault on Brest would come overland. In expectation, the Germans had forcibly evacuated the city's population while German engineers had laced its suburbs with a checkerboard of minefields, trenches, and pillboxes supported by more than one hundred cannons and antiaircraft pieces. They had also constructed more than seventy mutually supporting citadels and fortresses strung like a pearl necklace around the city center and its harbor. The repurposed 280 mms at Lochrist—originally designed as naval weapons whose six-hundred-pound shells could reach targets up to eleven miles away—were housed in the strongest and largest of these bastions.

Prior to the Brest campaign, Gen. Patton had scoffed that "there aren't more than ten thousand Krauts in the entire [Brittany] Peninsula." He was off by a factor of at least four in Brest alone, where some forty to fifty thousand Wehrmacht defenders, anchored by the elite *Fallschirmjäger* 2nd Parachute Division, took deadly seriously Hitler's order to defend the port "to the last man, to the last cartridge." Their commanding officer, General Hermann Ramcke, a paratroop veteran of Rommel's Afrika Korps, took the Führer's command as gospel.

Following the two-hundred-mile truck trek to a billet in the village of Le Folgoët, some fifteen miles north of Brest, Lt. Col. Rudder designated specific tasks to his company commanders. Easy and Fox were charged with manning perimeter outposts around the village. Able, Baker, and Charlie would provide flank protection for the 29th Division as it prepared to move on the Graf Spee battery. Dog Company was to combine with a mechanized cavalry recon squad to form a roving tactical force for use wherever needed—to put out those fires. When Maj. Sullivan's 5th Battalion arrived toward the end of August, it would be assigned to take out a series of coastal forts farther to the northwest.

None of the Rangers quite knew what to expect when the fighting started. For all the Americans guessed, if Gen. Patton was correct, Brest—isolated, perhaps undermanned and demoralized from a lack of ammunition and supplies—might fall without a shot being fired. As it happened, it was not the first time that "Old Blood and Guts Georgie" Patton miscalculated.

Bob Edlin was steamed. It was his first morning in the new billet at Le Folgoët, and word had come down from Col. Rudder's headquarters in the village's grand basilica of Notre Dame that a patrol from Able Company's 1st Platoon was being formed up to scout the battalion's southern flank. Edlin naturally thought this was a job for the Fabulous Four. Instead, Rudder had tapped one of the company's recently arrived platoon leaders, Lieutenant Robert Meltzer, to lead the recon party.

Edlin had nothing against Meltzer. The thirty-year-old officer was one of the repo depot replacements who'd joined the outfit at Château de Colombières two weeks after the invasion. He seemed to Edlin a fine Ranger and a good man. He certainly didn't lack courage. Meltzer was the son of Russian immigrants who had incul- cated in him a hatred of all European dictators. Seven years earlier he had made his way to New York City from his home in North- ern California to enlist in the Abraham Lincoln Brigade, a unit of American volunteers organized by the Communist International to fight for the Republicans against Franco's Nationalists in the Span- ish Civil War. Meltzer, unwilling to hide his disdain for Marxism, was turned away.

With the onset of World War II, Meltzer was given a second opportunity to enter European combat. There was no little irony in the fact that he still detested America's ally Joe Stalin as much as its enemy Adolf Hitler. Bob Edlin recognized that Lt. Meltzer's heart was in the right place. It was just that his boots were about to be in the wrong place. Bob Edlin's place.

Edlin wanted an explanation, and sought out his company com- mander, Bob Arman, who happened to be conferring with Rudder. Rudder explained to Edlin that he wanted Lt. Meltzer to get a taste of combat. Besides, he said, as the XO of Able Company, now that they were facing concerted German defenders, Edlin's responsibil- ity was to both the company's platoons. Edlin understood—to a point. He disagreed with Meltzer's decision to take five men out with him, including Bill Dreher, Bill Courtney, and a medic. A six- man patrol? Everyone knew that four was the magic number. It was the inclusion of the medic that gnawed.

"I was pretty upset," Edlin wrote. "If you are three or four miles behind enemy lines, you sure as hell don't need a medic. If some- body gets hurt, you either have to pick him up and bring him back or you have to leave him out there."

But it was Lt. Meltzer's patrol to command however he saw fit, and he stuck with his decision. Edlin watched the men disappear through a hedgerow. He was pacing the same spot three hours later when Courtney and Dreher reappeared, running as fast as they could. They'd been ambushed. Lt. Meltzer and two other Rangers were dead. The medic, wounded, was still out there. Edlin organized a rescue party; he was not optimistic. When they reached the site of the firefight, the medic was gone.

If Lt. Meltzer's doomed patrol was but a trickle in the Ranger battalion's greater flow through Brittany, it was also indicative. A day later the aid man Frank South joined another patrol that found itself weaving through a minefield. Most of the unit had successfully navigated the field when one of the last Rangers in line tripped a spring wire. South watched in horror as the *Schrapnellmine*—the descriptively alliterative "Bouncing Betty"—shot three feet into the air before detonating, propelling a lethal spray of ball bearings in all directions. The shrapnel severed the Ranger's spinal cord, and by the time South reached him he was already bleeding out. He died within moments. Near simultaneously, three more Rangers were killed when their small patrol encountered an entire German rifle company probing out of Brest to scout Allied positions.

Meanwhile, in the immediate wake of the fiasco that befell Lt. Meltzer's scouting party, Col. Rudder acquiesced to Edlin's request to reconvene the Fabulous Four. Over the next fifteen days, he, Bill Courtney, Bill Dreher, and Warren Burmaster ran seventeen patrols into no-man's-land. There were no flowers or Calvados from grateful French villagers this time; most resulted in gunfights.

On one occasion the four paused in a small hamlet to enter a three-story tavern situated just before a bend in the lane they were traveling. For once it wasn't the booze that interested them, but a shell hole in the roof. Edlin figured he might be able to peek around that corner. Sure enough, from the attic aerie he spotted a crew manning a *Maschinengewehr* 42 hidden in a copse of trees on one side of the road and a camouflaged antitank gun on the other. A perfect ambush site. He could even see the bobbing head of an officer training his field glasses on the road from behind a wooden fence.

Edlin signaled for Courtney, Dreher, and Burmaster to guesstimate the distance. Each in turn peered through the shell hole in the attic. The consensus was that the enemy spotter was 475 yards away. Edlin hefted his M1 Garand. "I believe I can hit [him]," he said. His three companions knew well that five hundred yards was the rifle's effective firing range. They took Edlin's bet—a bottle of booze to be determined.

Edlin perched himself atop a stool and stuck the rifle barrel through the hole. He waited for the spotter to stick his head up and fired. The German officer went down. Later, when Able Company overran the ambush site, he, Courtney, Dreher, and Burmaster hopped the fence to check. The spotter had a bullet hole in his right temple.

Another foray behind enemy lines might have been mistaken for a Keystone Kops episode had it not been a life-or-death proposition. The Fabulous Four were picking their way along a hedgerow when a potato masher landed at their feet. Edlin grabbed it and threw it as hard as he could back through a large hole in the tangled shrubbery. Then he dived through the same opening. He landed on the back of a Wehrmacht sergeant crawling through a farm field attempting to flank the patrol. He knocked the soldier out with the butt of his rifle. A few feet away another German stood with his hands up while, at his feet, a lieutenant lay unconscious between a light machine gun and the enemy grenade, apparently a dud. A large welt was forming on the prone officer's forehead over his right eye. Edlin's toss had hit him in the face and knocked him cold.

As had become routine, after captured Germans were interrogated, most were handed over to one of the companies from the

Forces Françaises de l'Intérieur—French Forces of the Interior—which had attached themselves to various units of VIII Corps, including the Rangers. These were not trained resistance fighters, merely local farmers and villagers who knew the terrain and had been issued captured enemy weaponry. The Americans soon deduced that these ancillary outfits, identifiable by their armbands emblazoned with the letters "FFI," were more valuable as coalmine canaries than as fighters. If they suddenly dropped to the rear during a march, it was usually a sure sign that Germans might be up ahead. On most nights they departed around dusk to return to their homes and families. Sometimes they returned the next morning; sometimes they did not. In any case, the Rangers knew better than to inquire as to the fate of German prisoners transferred to Frenchmen who had lived for four years under the Nazi jackboot.

But perhaps the event at least three of the members of the Fabulous Four most liked to recount occurred when they were patrolling near the seacoast and happened upon an abandoned German tank whose tracks had been mangled by an artillery shell. Bill Courtney, seizing the opportunity to learn how to fire the vehicle's long-barreled 88 mm gun, clambered inside and blasted off several rounds into the Atlantic. He emerged from the tank with a feared *Panzerschreck,* or "tank scare," a larger and heavier version of the American bazooka.

Determined to learn to fire this also, he loaded it with a rocket and aimed toward the sea. He was unaware, however, that because of its size, the German weapon was meant to be used only with a large metal screen attached to protect the operator's face from the intense heat of its backblast. Bob Edlin, Bill Dreher, and Warren Burmaster were still smirking when they dropped Courtney off at Doc Block's aid station to have his bloody head treated. It was nearly as funny as Frank South's encounter with the hungry billy goat.

It was also around this time that Edlin had his first taste of what he called "the political part of warfare." It happened during one of the few occasions when the sixty-odd Rangers of Able Company were moving en masse to support the flank of the 29th Division's push into Brest. The company was edging along yet another hedge-row when Capt. Arman was radioed orders to halt and dig in. The Rangers were hollowing out holes in the raised berm when mortar shells began dropping around them. Edlin spotted the source of the fire, a German pillbox some two hundred yards off the company's point. He told the outfit's 60 mm mortarman to let loose. No sooner had the first mortar round stove in a section of the enemy bunker when Bob Arman's radio crackled again with urgent instructions to cease fire. Apparently, arrangements had been made for the Germans to surrender.

"They wanted to fire a few rounds at us to save face, then they would quit," is how Edlin described the incident. "We were sup-posed to let the damn enemy shoot at us until they . . . stick up a white flag and surrender. We didn't get a chance to get our licks in. That didn't seem quite fair."

Payback would come soon enough.

[21]

Festung Brest

On August 25—the same day that American troops paraded beneath the Arc de Triomphe through a liberated Paris—General Troy Middleton's VIII Corps launched its assault on what the Germans called *Festung* Brest. Fortress Brest. Multiple Army Air Forces bombing runs and heavy shelling from the 15-inch guns of the battleship HMS *Warspite* failed to daunt the occupiers, particularly after the 280 mm cannons from the Lochrist battery forced the British vessel out of coastal range. Gen. Patton's prediction notwithstanding, with the enemy's resolve finally dawning on the Allies, weeks of house-to-house carnage was to ensue.

One day later, on August 26, while moving to screen the 175th Infantry Regiment's slow and calculated assault southeast across Finistère, the 2nd Ranger Battalion's Baker, Dog, Easy, and Fox Companies, led by Duke Slater, ran into lethal resistance in Brest's northwestern suburbs. An hours-long firefight ensued before darkness stilled the engagement. Digging in that night, Slater issued a single order: "Stay in your hole. Anything moving gets shot."

Although the Rangers were never to enter Brest proper, over the next ten days they were called upon to douse multiple fires on the city's outskirts. At dawn on August 28, Bob Arman's Able Company and Ralph Goranson's Charlie Company—under Captain Ed Arnold's overall command and attached to a tank-destroyer battalion; fast, lightly armored vehicles designed specifically to disable German Panzers with their powerful 76 mm guns—swarmed a large pillbox, killing nine Germans and capturing another ninety-four. Later that same day, Slater's task force conducted stealth recon runs west of the city, locating and marking German strongholds for the 29th Division's artillery batteries. In the process, Lieutenant Morton McBride's Dog Company surrounded a building housing about three dozen Wehrmacht riflemen. Following what appeared a perfunctory showdown to save face, the enemy surrendered.

It was also around this time when forward elements of the 2nd Ranger Battalion ambushed a Wehrmacht work party herding 168 Russian prisoners of war. The Germans scattered after a brief gunfight, leaving the Russians behind. These were hard-edged Red Army veterans who refused to be conscripted by the Nazis. As such they had been put to work as slave laborers fortifying Brest's defenses. Col. Rudder, perhaps aware of the saying that you can't buy a Cossack but you can certainly rent one, armed them with surplus enemy weapons and formed them into yet another supporting unit. Between the FFI and the Russians, Rudder's outfit was taking on a decidedly international flavor.

Ike Eikner spoke a little Russian and was tapped as the liaison officer. That evening, after feasting on American C rats, the Russian contingent ambushed an eight-man German patrol. Their captain apologized for not keeping anyone alive for interrogation. He tried to sound sincere. Eikner asked him if he looked forward to returning to the Soviet Union at war's end. An incredulous look darkened the man's face. "Communists?" He spit the word out like an epithet. "Hell no!" He then ran his finger across his throat in a slashing motion. The late Lt. Meltzer, burning with his hatred for Stalin, would have been proud.

On August 29, Dog and Easy Companies teamed up with the tank-destroyer unit along the south coast of Finistère to assault another pillbox, killing eight Germans and capturing seventy-two. The next morning the same outfits overran and held a small rise overlooking Brest dubbed Hill 63—the designation reflecting the hummock's height in meters. They left two dozen enemy casualties littering the slope, while one Ranger was wounded. They were joined on the hill at dusk by Baker and Fox Companies.

As night fell on the Ranger position, so too did a barrage of artillery shells launched from a battery of the dreaded Czech Skoda guns. Their shells were accompanied by a rain of German mortar fire. The heavy "blaze," in Ranger lingo, left one trooper dead and another ten wounded. The next morning at dawn, Able Company flanked the Skoda battery and took it out, but the mortar shelling only intensified, wounding another eleven Rangers.

For the next several days the little rise occupied by the Rangers became the locus of some of the most intense shelling since Omaha Beach. Despite the street fighting farther south reducing Brest to rubble, the Germans seemed intent on driving the Americans from the high ground north of the city. More of the mobile Skodas were moved into place to complement the enemy's mortarmen while the Americans retaliated with 75 mm and 105 mm cannon as well as the tank destroyers' 76 mm guns. Lt. Col. Rudder even called in air support via the 29th Division's General Gerhardt. But the Rangers watched incredulously as two P-38 fighter-bombers mistakenly dumped their payloads into the harbor.

On September 3, attempting to administer the coup de grâce on the American special operators, Lochrist battery gunners manning the 280 mms trained their sights on Hill 63. The Rangers were all too familiar with the firepower erupting from the thirty-four-foot barrels. The battery had been hyperactive against VIII Corps since the onset of the Brest campaign, tearing holes in the thick hedgerows like steel rivets puncturing papier-mâché. Every time one fired off, a Ranger recalled, "the muzzle blast alone would lift us out of our holes." Taking a cue from the songwriter Harry Warren's recent stateside hit, shells passing overhead were nicknamed "Chattanooga Choo Choos" for the sheer intensity of their earth-heaving vibrations.

Now, however, those Chattanooga Choo Choos were not flying overhead, but slamming into the Ranger position. After the first salvo, Doc Block and his medics dragged twenty-three dead, dying, and wounded men to the lee side of the knoll. The next barrage tore so deep into the hillside that it set off an avalanche that rolled over an entire squad. As Rangers braved mortar shrapnel to claw at the earth to disinter the buried, the shelling abruptly ceased. Veterans of Pointe du Hoc scrambled to warn the new recruits of what was coming. As if on cue, the deafening reverberations of the big guns were replaced by the sounds of scores of Bakelite whistles.

Lt. Col. Rudder arrived at Hill 63 at the same time as the Germans. Leaping from his jeep, he ran from company to company, re-forming the battalion for a counterassault. When all was ready, the Rangers charged. "Rudder commanded personally the attack," reads an oddly translated eyewitness account from a French historian working with the FFI. "Bullets were whizzing by and the gunfire was very dense."

The Germans were driven off; the shelling began anew. Rudder concluded that his battalion had but one option before it was incrementally devoured. Move forward off that damn hill.

The advance began on the miserable morning of September 6. By dawn what had begun as a cold drizzle had hardened into buckshot bursts of rain falling from a livid sky awash with blinding white lightning. Some Rangers could not tell the accompanying thunder from the shellfire. On Lt. Col. Rudder's signal, Duke Slater led what remained of Baker, Dog, and Easy Companies toward the German mortar positions while the remnants of Fox Company formed a rear guard. Simultaneously, Captain Ed Arnold launched a diversionary flanking assault with Able and Charlie Companies. Their objective was a point several miles distant on the highway connecting Brest to the seaside village of Le Conquet. There a battalion from the 116th Infantry Regiment had temporarily halted to regroup before continuing its drive toward Brest's inner city.

It took the greater part of the day for Slater's force to advance one thousand yards, killing and capturing scores of Germans along the way. As night fell, the outfit's company commanders counted heads. One Ranger was dead; nineteen others were wounded. Slater and his small task force resumed their attack early the next morning. By late afternoon, having rendezvoused with Arnold's contingent, they'd reached the highway. Slater sent out patrols to scout their perimeter and make contact with the 116th. Within moments he heard gunfire. In time the patrols returned with 144 captives. They reported leaving at least thirty more German corpses to the rats and crows. Most of the FFI contingent had vanished from Hill 63 not long after the 280s had opened up, so the Russians were enlisted to guard the POWs. Then the Rangers dug in to prepare for the inevitable counterattack.

By this point the battalion line was so thin that only one man was assigned to each foxhole. Slater and Arnold worried about the replacements, troopers who had not seen the elephant at Omaha or atop the Pointe. The fight on Hill 63 had been primarily an artillery affair, and the advance over the last two days had taken place during the day. Now, for the first time, the newcomers faced night combat, likely hand-to-hand. Alone in their holes.

It was near midnight when the Germans attacked. First the ubiquitous whistles, then the machine gun tracers. This by-now-familiar opening act was followed by screeching whoops and Teutonic battle cries, the bark of Mausers, and explosions from scores of potato mashers. The Rangers held, and within moments all went quiet. No Ranger dared leave his hole lest he attract friendly fire. The Germans, to the Americans' surprise, did not come again. At dawn, Slater and Arnold inspected the defensive perimeter, paying special attention to the positions taken by the new men. They had acquitted themselves honorably, even the dead. Private First Class Walter Lukovsky had only just joined the battalion before it moved into Brittany. No one could say they knew Lukovsky well. Duke Slater discovered his bullet-riddled body slumped in its dugout. Six German corpses were arrayed about the hole, like petals on a daisy.

In the end, the 2nd Ranger Battalion's aggressive, thirty-mile offensive from Le Folgoët to Le Conquet hard by the Atlantic not only broke the Germans' main line of resistance north of Brest, but cut off from the city most of the enemy forces still roaming Finistère. Despite the Rangers' achievements, the 29th Division's Gen. Gerhardt was annoyed. The seed of his discontent may have occurred weeks earlier, when Rudder dismissed the general's suggestion that his Rangers prepare to attack the Brest harbor from the sea. Rudder informed the general he had neither the equipment nor the experienced troops to carry out what was essentially a Pointe du Hoc redux. Word soon spread of Rudder informing a seething Gerhardt that he'd face a court-martial before loading his greenhorns into rubber boats to get murdered.

Apocryphal stories notwithstanding, Rudder *was* a gruff officer, and his out-of-hand rejection of Gerhardt's plan had to sting the general. Since the rebuff, Gerhardt complained that he could seldom pinpoint Lt. Col. Rudder's whereabouts as the special operators swept across Finistère. And when Rudder did make radio contact, it was to hector Gerhardt for increased artillery and close air support. In just one twelve-hour period, Gerhardt's headquarters journal records Rudder requesting support on six separate occasions. Tellingly, the same journal reports Gerhardt admitting to one of his staff officers, "I would just as soon can [Rudder] if I could."

The animosity reached such a pitch that on September 4, Gen. Middleton removed Rudder's Rangers from Gerhardt's command and attached the 2nd Battalion directly to his own VIII Corps. Perhaps out of spite, the 29th Division's newsletter, *29 Let's Go*, gave credit for the breakthrough to Le Conquet to Gerhardt's GIs. When Rudder took umbrage, a small correction appeared in the next edition.

However, one enemy outpost that still had open supply lines with Brest was the Lochrist battery. The *Kriegsmarine*'s version of the *Graf Spee* may have been rusting under the Atlantic's swells off the coast of Uruguay. But the Wehrmacht's iteration was still spitting fire.

[22]

The "Fool Lieutenant"

Men in combat delight in bestowing nicknames. These were, of course, ubiquitous throughout the 2nd Ranger Battalion, from Big Jim Rudder on down. Joining Bill "No-Neck" Courtney on Bob Edlin's Fabulous Four patrols, for instance, were Bill "Stoop" Dreher—to differentiate him from Big Stoop Masny—and Warren "Halftrack" Burmaster, the moniker elided from the "half-cracked" way in which the Louisianan casually handled high explosives. Some Rangers had dubbed Bob Edlin "Fire Eater"; others went with the simpler (and perhaps more to the point) "Crazy." But the sobriquet that eventually stuck had its genesis months earlier, in what seemed like another lifetime.

During the Channel crossing, mere hours before the Normandy landings, Edlin had been straddling his bunk belowdecks on the HMS *Prince Charles* when his 1st sergeant, Bill White, sidled up next to him. "Whitey," as he was known, could tell something was eating at the lieutenant; he hadn't even touched the piles of flapjacks and the gallons of coffee laid out in the galley. Edlin couldn't lie, nor could he tell White the complete truth: he was scared. He decided to split the difference.

"I'm just a little down," he'd said.

White grinned and repeated the Ranger mantra drilled into the men since Camp Forrest—"Well, what the hell, you volunteered, didn't you?"

Edlin smiled, and in that moment his fears, if not his worries, fell away. He strode the hold of the troopship and gathered his platoon to go over their invasion assignments one final time. As he headed back to his bunk, he heard one of his sergeants say, "That damn fool lieutenant ain't afraid of nothin'."

The sobriquet stuck.

Now, over three months later, on September 9, 1944, the sun had barely cleared the eastern horizon when the Fool Lieutenant was again out in front of his usual four-man scout patrol. They were squatting behind a garden wall some eleven miles northeast of Brest's inner city and eyeballing the fifty-acre Lochrist battery complex. At its center sat a three-story fortified bunker—"the fort," to the Americans—housing the German command center and the observation post from which range finders spotted targets for the 280 mm cannons. The four German naval guns were located in a camouflaged depression in a pastureland about seven hundred yards to the east. They were encased in ten feet of concrete, thick enough to withstand both shelling and aerial bombardments. Three of the guns were set in open ring positions whose bases could rotate 360 degrees. The barrel of the fourth was fixed permanently, pointed toward the harbor and the sea beyond.

The German base also included a smaller outlying building, nearer to the coast, overlooking the harbor's U-boat pens. This was connected by tunnels to the fort, which rose like a landlocked battleship amid the former potato fields, strawberry patches, and dairy farms seized from the French in 1940. Allied intelligence reports indicated that beneath the structure the Germans had dug out barracks large enough to house nearly one thousand soldiers. Pocking

the surrounding acreage were innumerable concrete pillboxes reinforced with "lugged" steel bars, sandbag-protected antiaircraft bunkers, garages, warehouses, and even a laundromat and blacksmith's
shop. Marked minefields—ACHTUNG! MINEN!—were everywhere. As
the four Rangers took in the compound, they were stunned by its
breadth.

Edlin, Courtney, Dreher, and Burmaster had been tasked with
charting the locations of the pillboxes, machine gun nests, and
minefields shielding the perimeter of the fort. If possible, they were
also to snatch prisoners. Lt. Col. Rudder and the intel officer Harvey Cook wanted to gauge the morale of the Wehrmacht soldiers
occupying the grounds. Meanwhile, three Ranger companies—
Able, Baker, and Charlie—had dug in a quarter mile or so to the
rear of Edlin's patrol. Dog, Easy, and Fox had taken up blocking
positions along the adjacent roads in the unlikely event the enemy
took flight without a fight. Behind them, an additional task force
of nearly three thousand GIs and Frenchmen—two infantry regiments from the 29th Division supported by two tank battalions,
as well as several units of the FFI—had been diverted from the
Brest assault to assist the Rangers in overrunning the complex.
Major Richard Sullivan's 5th Ranger Battalion, which had arrived
on Finistère ten days earlier, had moved farther east, poised to take
a string of occupied coastal villages. The coordinated attacks were
scheduled for the next day.

Edlin's reconnaissance patrol had moved out from behind the garden wall and reached the edge of a minefield protecting one of the
battery's large pillboxes when he signaled to pull back; it was a dead
end. But Bill Courtney sidled up to Edlin and whispered, "I think
I see a way through." With that, Courtney broke into a dead run.

Bill Dreher hissed, "Stop, Courtney! Stop!" But Courtney, once
again displaying a rum attitude toward peril, plunged ahead. The

others followed. For the first time since the Channel crossing, Edlin was frightened. Then he saw the method to No-Neck Courtney's apparent madness. Gen. Middleton's VIII Corps artillery outfits and Army Air Forces bombers had been softening up the Lochrist battery compound for weeks, and Courtney was following a path of bomb craters that had disabled the mines.

Hopping from hole to hole like jackrabbits, the four Rangers found themselves crouched near the open door of the large pillbox. Incredibly, no guard was posted. Above them, hanging by the neck from a thick rope knotted to a stanchion, was the rotting corpse of a German soldier. Likely a deserter, left to dangle as a message. His boots were missing.

Edlin weighed their options. If they snuck away now, back through the minefield, they possessed a trove of information to deliver to Lt. Col. Rudder, not least of which was a lightly guarded pathway onto the base. On the other hand, if they attempted to capture the pillbox, a gunfight would alert the entire German contingent to their presence. Even if they cleared the enemy outpost, there would be no way out after that. The four would have to hold out against God knows what for nearly twenty-four hours and hope the next morning's assault found them alive.

Edlin looked to Courtney, who nodded. He turned toward Dreher, who did the same. Burmaster wordlessly dropped back to the edge of the minefield, the getaway man ready to bolt if the plan went south. Halftrack knew that it was his responsibility to report what had happened.

Edlin took a deep breath and dove through the doorway. Courtney and Dreher followed. Electric lights were blazing in the windowless bunker, silhouetting perhaps twenty stunned German paratroopers. A few of their Mausers were scattered about the floor; the rest were stacked in a corner. Two unmanned heavy machine guns sat mounted at slit embrasures facing the minefield. The three Rangers hollered in unison, *"Hände hoch!"* Every soldier raised his hands.

Bill Courtney started to say something in his high school German. An officer stepped forward. Eyeing Edlin's lieutenant's bars, he said, "Sir, I speak fluent English." He added that he'd gone to college in the United States.

Edlin suspected that Col. Rudder would bust him to buck private, but he asked anyway. "How do we get into the fort from here and to your commander?"

"I can take you to the commander," the German said.

Edlin glanced at Courtney and Dreher. Again, both nodded. Edlin moved to the door and waved in Burmaster. He and Courtney, he'd decided, would accompany the guide. Dreher would remain to guard the prisoners. Burmaster was to hie back to Able Company's position and radio Lt. Col. Rudder to call off any planned artillery fire.

It took Burmaster but moments to retrace his steps and reach Bob Arman's radio operator. When Burmaster raised Ike Eikner, Rudder and Len Lomell happened to be in the coms bunker talking to the book reviewer turned *New York Herald Tribune* war correspondent Lewis Gannett. All four heard Burmaster relay his message to hold fire. "That Fool Lieutenant," Burmaster said, was heading into the fort. Gannett scribbled furiously.

A long, well-trodden path traversed the middle of the German compound. The two Rangers, their tommy guns slung over their shoulders, kept the Wehrmacht officer between them. They walked as casually as their racing hearts allowed. They conversed informally with the German, the subjects ranging from his university experiences in the United States to Edlin's memories of growing up in Indiana. Bill Courtney tried to practice his German language skills, such as they were. They passed several armed soldiers. None challenged them. All the while Bob Edlin fingered the hilt of his trench knife.

At the base of the fort they descended a long tunnel. It reminded the Americans of the chute from which college football players ran onto the field. A set of large doors opened automatically. They were the first electric doors either Ranger had ever seen. They found themselves in an underground hospital. Half of the three hundred or so beds held wounded soldiers. Doctors in white coats and female nurses gaped. Bill Courtney hollered, *"Hände hoch!"* The medical staff, and even some of the wounded, complied. Their German prisoner asked if he could speak. Edlin warned him to talk slowly, so Courtney could follow. The officer announced that everyone should sit and remain calm. The Americans, he said, were on their way to the commandant's office to negotiate a surrender. Everyone sat.

Leaving the infirmary, they paused at an elevator. Edlin shook his head, "No," and pointed toward the stairs. Armed sentries were posted on the landing above. The German from the pillbox spoke to them—slowly—and they immediately lowered their rifles. They passed down a brightly lit corridor and stopped in front of an ornate wooden door. The commandant's office, the German said. He raised his fist to knock.

Edlin pushed him aside, threw open the door, and rushed in. Courtney was on his hip, slamming the door behind him. Edlin raced across the large office and pressed the barrel of his gun into the commandant's throat. Lieutenant Colonel Martin Fürst, wearing his *Fallschirmjäger* paratrooper's uniform, barely blinked. Edlin's first thought was that he resembled the popular comedian Joe E. Brown. It was the German's wide mouth.

Lt. Col. Fürst pushed his swivel chair away from a mahogany desk large enough to accommodate several craps games. As he stood, Edlin removed the Mauser HSc pistol from the holster on his hip. Fürst stood, walked to a side table, and poured himself a cognac. He took a sip and looked at Edlin. Neither of the Rangers had shaved or bathed in weeks, and Edlin felt the contempt in the paratroop officer's stare.

"What do you want?" Fürst said, in English.

Courtney began to say something in German. Fürst, his eyes still on Edlin, held up a hand, palm out. "You don't need your interpreter, Lieutenant. I speak excellent English."

"Fine," Edlin said. "Why don't you just surrender your fort and get this whole thing over with?"

"Why should I do that?" Fürst asked.

Bob Edlin was becoming impatient. The arrogance in the German's voice grated.

Edlin told the colonel that the compound was completely surrounded. An exaggeration. Then he lied outright. Even as they spoke, Edlin continued, Rangers were infiltrating the grounds. Fürst picked up his telephone receiver. Edlin thought about stopping him. He looked to Courtney, who said nothing.

The German spoke too fast for Courtney to catch most of the conversation. When he cradled the receiver, he told the Rangers, "They'll call back in a few minutes." In the meantime, he asked if the Americans would care for a drink. Bob Edlin could not recall the last time he would *not* care for a drink. His stomach was churning again. When the telephone rang he nearly jumped out of his skin.

Lt. Col. Fürst listened for a moment, then said something in German. Edlin looked at Courtney, who frowned and shook his head.

Lt. Col. Fürst hung up and grinned. "There are only three of you," he said. "You two, and one in the pillbox. You are my prisoners now."

Edlin's mind raced. They could kill the cocky bastard right here, push his big desk against the door, and empty their tommy guns at whomever managed to crash through. Or.

"Courtney," he said, "hand me a grenade." Edlin took the fragmentation grenade and shoved it, hard, into the colonel's crotch. "You're going to die right here," he said.

"Well, so are you," the German said. His voice sounded less smug.

Edlin pulled the pin and released the lever, pressing the grenade deeper into Fürst's nutsack. Each man in the room knew well that within five seconds, fifty-eight pieces of shrapnel would obliterate them. "One," Edlin counted, "two . . ."

The German shouted, "Okay!"

Edlin stuck the pin back into the grenade's hammer. He asked if the office contained a public address system. Lt. Col. Fürst pointed with his chin. Courtney picked up the microphone and passed it to the colonel. Edlin instructed him on what to say. Fürst flicked a switch and began speaking in German. The Rangers raced to the window. German soldiers were pouring from buildings and underground passageways across the complex, walking to the courtyard below the fortress, stacking their weapons to the side, and falling into formation. Surrendering.

To Edlin it looked like thousands of men. It was, in fact, 814.

Lt. Col. Fürst had a final request. He would prefer to surrender to an officer of higher rank than a lieutenant. Edlin and Courtney looked at each other and shrugged. Fine.

Credentials

To the Ranger rank and file it was all too decorous; too, well, National Socialist. A large white sheet billowed from a makeshift flagstaff above him as Lt. Col. Rudder waited in the town square of the small village of St. Mathieu. The hamlet, where Rudder had agreed to conduct the formal surrender ceremony, lay in the shadow of the Lochrist battery fortress. On his drive to the village, Rudder had passed close enough to see the long barrels of the 280 mm guns. Once so menacing, now gone silent.

The battalion sergeant major, Len Lomell, stood to Rudder's left. Behind both men, arranged as an ad hoc honor guard at Rudder's specific request, were Bob Edlin, Bill Courtney, Bill Dreher, and Warren Burmaster. To their rear, Able Company stood at parade rest. Facing the American contingent were more than eight hundred sullen Wehrmacht prisoners. A few army photographers and newspaper correspondents circulated, Lewis Gannett among them. He had already filed his seven-hundred-word story, which would appear on the front page of the *Herald Tribune*. His editor in New York, taking into consideration the journalistic etiquette of the era, had changed one word of Gannett's report in the sub-headline:

"'Fool Lieutenant' Breaches Bastion," it read, "Holds Grenade to Nazi Colonel's *Midriff*."

When Lieutenant Colonel Martin Fürst strode into the square with his pet German shepherd, Asgaard, loping at his heels, his soldiers snapped to attention. Rudder in turn called the Rangers to attention with a bellowing "Ten-hut!" Fürst, his boots buffed to a sheen, the sun glinting off his gleaming belt buckle and the silver buttons of his tunic, halted before the American commander. Fürst saluted and reached for his Mauser to present it to Rudder. His holster was empty. Fürst looked flustered. Rudder turned to the honor guard. "Where's his pistol?"

Trying not to look abashed, Bob Edlin withdrew the gun from his waistband beneath his filthy field jacket, and handed it to Rudder, who in turn passed it to the German commandant. With a Teutonic formality, Lt. Col. Fürst holstered the weapon, half bowed and clicked his heels, drew the gun out, and handed it back to Rudder. As Edlin watched the exchange he wondered how many bottles of whiskey such a souvenir might have brought in a trade.

Edlin was anxious for the whole officious rigmarole to be over. Prior to Lt. Col. Rudder's arrival, the Rangers had swarmed the enemy compound and discovered a warren of underground storehouses as large as bus depots. Two held scores of fifty-gallon wooden beer kegs. Another was stacked with shelves of cognac and whiskey. A deeper repository, cool and dank as a cave, contained thousands of bottles of French wine. There was even a room devoted to cigars and chocolate. A few hungry Rangers—joined by teetotalers like Halftrack Burmaster—had peeled off in search of hot food from the subterranean German kitchens. They found beef stew still simmering on oven burners. But the majority descended on the stockpiled alcohol like locusts drawn to fields of green clover.

Adhering to the truism that whiskey is for drinking and water is for fighting over, canteens were emptied and refilled with the amber and red liquids, while more than a few helmets were put to use as beer steins.

Finally, with the official surrender complete, Col. Rudder invited the German commandant back to a bunker he had commandeered as his headquarters. His aim was to talk Lt. Col. Fürst into contacting Gen. Ramcke in Brest to press home, paratrooper to paratrooper, the futility of fighting on. Before the two departed, however, Rudder—aware of the discovery of the alcohol cached beneath the captured compound—told Captain Bob Arman that he was pulling Able Company off the line for the remainder of the day. The battalion's remaining companies would secure the area. Arman's troopers made beelines for the booze.

Then Rudder called Edlin aside. For several moments Edlin endured an expletive-filled lecture. The gist was that the lieutenant was one of the saddest-sack, order-disobeyingest, dumbest-ass soldiers that Rudder had ever encountered in this man's army.

When Rudder appeared talked out, Edlin ventured a question. "What would you have done if you were in my position, sir?"

Rudder took a moment. "I hope I'd have had the nerve enough to do what you did," he finally replied. Then he slapped Edlin on the back. "Now get back there and drink that damn beer."

The fall of the Lochrist battery complex marked the beginning of the end of the German defense of Brest. Lt. Col. Fürst had not only ordered his troops in the compound to surrender, but all German troops across Finistère. "Sully" Sullivan's 5th Ranger Battalion had spent twenty-four hours marching from village to village along the coast and collecting them. Over the next week, while the dogged and weary soldiers of VIII Corps continued to shed rivers of blood pushing into Brest's city center, Rudder's and Sullivan's troopers hopscotched precincts of the Brittany peninsula south of the city mopping up what army intelligence officers believed to be pockets of enemy resistance. The Wehrmacht defenders rarely put up much of a fight, to the point where it became a wagering proposition as to which company could tally the most prisoners.

In one town, Sid Salomon's Baker Company collected thirty after a showy launch of but a single 60 mm mortar shell into a German fortification. Not long after, what had begun as Baker Company's cautious approach toward a building suspected of harboring an enemy rifle platoon became an all-out foot race when Salomon spotted Easy and Fox Companies nearing the position from the opposite direction. The Germans, watching three companies of screaming Americans bearing down on them at full gallop, tossed their weapons into the street without firing a shot.

Outside of a small village a dozen miles south of Brest, Major Ed Arnold thought he had a fight on his hands when Able and Charlie Companies were ordered to attack a Wehrmacht garrison that had held out for days against multiple American howitzer barrages and several waves of Army Air Forces fighter-bombers. The Germans were holed up in a well-fortified bunker atop a steep, denuded hill on the outskirts of town. Arnold decided that his most auspicious approach was to pick through a minefield, rush at top speed across a waist-deep stream, and dash up the rise, which offered no cover. The Rangers, their uniforms and gear still sopping from the watercourse, attacked so rapidly that the German mortar shells fell behind them. As they approached the bunker, a white piece of cloth tied to the barrel of a Mauser rifle emerged from a machine gun slit. Seventy-four Germans exited with their hands on their *Stahlhelms*.

On September 14, the 2nd and 5th Ranger Battalions were officially designated VIII Corps reserve units attached to the 8th Infantry Division. Rudder fretted over how to replace the more than sixty casualties his outfit had taken during its nineteen days of fighting around Brest, while Sullivan's battalion had suffered a 30 percent depletion rate, including twenty-four troopers killed in action. A fleet of deuce-and-a-halfs ferried the survivors to a billet west of Brest for rest and recuperation. This included not only hot showers and hot chow but blessed fresh socks. Passes were issued to the nearby towns of Lesneven and Landerneau, where, as one Ranger put it, "romance overcame language [barriers.]"

After three days of R&R, Rudder's battalion was ordered back into combat, tasked with clearing the thin Crozon peninsula, which formed the southern salient of the Brest harbor. "Combat," however, may have been too strong a term.

The Wehrmacht had constructed a vast military hospital on Crozon, and a modus vivendi had been reached between the opposing armies declaring it a sort of sanctuary area. When the Rangers arrived, sixteen hundred German soldiers, including over one thousand wounded men, were rounded up without a fight. The closest the affair came to reaching a boiling point was when the Americans, bivouacked in a frost-covered field without tents, learned that their "prisoners" had been given free run of the local brasseries.

As both Ranger battalions prepared to redeploy east, Bob Edlin took the occasion to jot a short note to his mom and dad back in Indiana. He assumed that his parents had by now seen the newspaper stories about his role in the fall of the Lochrist battery. He wrote that he was still "dazed" by how events had played out. He closed his letter by asking his folks—with a tentative "if possible"—to send him a box of candy bars. After signing off with "Love to all," he added a postscript:

"I have been recommended for the [Distinguished Service Cross]. I hope this doesn't sound like I am bragging, I am not. I was just lucky as the devil and I will admit I was a very scared boy."

Early on the unusually brisk morning of September 18, 1944, the 2nd Ranger Battalion lined up at a Brittany railhead to board a string of World War I *quarante-et-huit* boxcars—built to hold either forty humans or eight horses—pulled by an ancient French loco-motive. Though twenty-four hours earlier the Allies had launched a huge combined air and land invasion of the Netherlands, and the U.S. Seventh Army continued to push toward Germany from southern France, the Rangers were destined to join neither. Instead, while Maj. Sullivan's 5th Battalion was ordered attached to Gen. Patton's Third Army—already a mere twenty-five miles from the German border—Big Jim Rudder's Rangers were heading to the Ardennes region of Belgium for two additional weeks of rest and recuperation that would give Rudder and his staff an opportunity to restock the outfit's thinned roster.

Near simultaneous to the Rangers' departure, General Hermann Ramcke sent word to General Troy Middleton that he was prepared to surrender Brest. After nearly a month of fighting that cost close to ten thousand American casualties, including an estimated two thou-sand killed, Ramcke's defensive enclave, surrounded and outgunned, had been reduced to a two-by-five-mile jackstraw refuge by the sea.*

Gen. Middleton chose the 8th Infantry Division's assistant com-mander, Charles Canham, to accept the official German capitula-tion. In the eighty-four days since Canham had led his troops to the relief of the Rangers atop Pointe du Hoc, he had been promoted from colonel to brigadier general. On the afternoon of the cere-mony, Canham, flanked by hundreds of officers and enlisted men, was waiting outside the Wehrmacht general's headquarters when Ramcke emerged from his bunker. If anything, Ramcke's submis-sion superseded Lt. Col. Fürst's for Teutonic pomp.

Ramke greeted Canham in his finest *Fallschirmjäger* uniform, apparently freshly pressed and festooned with ribbons and medals, including the Iron Cross, 1st Class, that he had been awarded in

---

* In a final, ironic indignity, Brest's deep-water harbor had been so damaged by Allied bomb-ing and the half-million American artillery shells fired on the city that for the remainder of the war not a single cargo ship or troopship was able to berth there.

World War I. There was much boot-heel clicking, half bowing, and *Seig Heil!*-ing. When Canham finally read aloud the unconditional surrender terms, Ramcke, his face as pinched as an ax blade, demanded to see the American general's credentials. Canham had had enough. He hooked a thumb over his shoulder toward the throng of exhausted and dirty GIs.

"These are my credentials," he said.

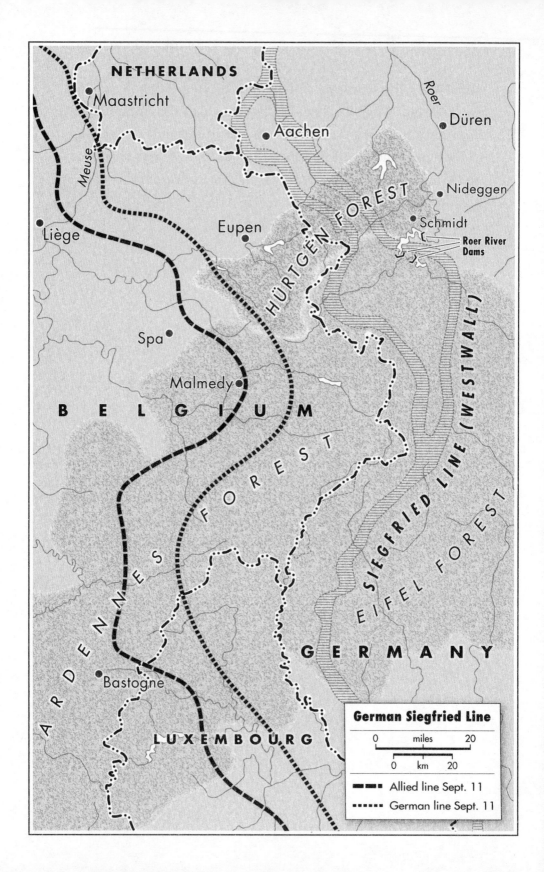

NETHERLANDS

Maastricht

Roer

Düren

Meuse

Aachen

Nideggen

Liège

Eupen

Schmidt

Roer River
Dams

HÜRTGEN FOREST

Spa

SIEGFRIED LINE (WESTWALL)

Malmedy

B E L G I U M

A R D E N N E S   F O R E S T

EIFEL FOREST

G E R M A N Y

Bastogne

L U X E M B O U R G

German Siegfried Line

0   miles   20

0   km   20

▬ ▬ ▬ Allied line Sept. 11

•••••• German line Sept. 11

PART IV

The Forest

Thinking of the Hürtgen now . . . It was
Passchendaele with tree bursts.

—ERNEST HEMINGWAY

[24]

"End the War in '44"

n the days after the Ranger battalions were pulled off the front
line in Brittany, a hypnotic valence of optimism pervaded the
seven Allied armies chasing the retreating Germans across continental Europe. "Pursuit warfare" is how the War Department's
official history dryly describes the movements. To Americans on
the ground, however, it was more like a carnival of routs.

While GIs packed Parisian movie theaters and wolfed down
hamburgers and Cokes in American Legion posts lining the Rue
de Rivoli, a Canadian army secured the port of Dieppe and the
British drove the Germans from Brussels. American warships ruled
the Atlantic, grounded Luftwaffe pilots from Germany's degraded
air fleet watched helplessly as American and British bombers obliterated their cities, and, on the ground in the west, Hitler's Reich
faced an unbroken Allied front deployed in an advancing arc from
the North Sea to the Swiss Alps.*

---

* Lest one be deluded by the plethora of movies and television shows that for decades after
depicted the war in Europe as a strictly Caucasian affair, it should be noted that Navajo code
talkers were also employed in the theater, the Japanese American 442nd Regimental Combat Team was integral in capturing the Italian fortress of Monte Cassino and subsequently

In the liminal dusk of September 11, 1944—D-Day + 97—Birnam Wood came to Dunsinane when a five-man reconnaissance patrol from the 5th U.S. Armored Division forded the turbid Our River from northeast Luxembourg to stamp the first American footprints on German soil. They had beaten by mere hours two separate scout units also vying for the honor of being the first GIs into Germany. The swiftness of the advance had not only stunned the Germans but astounded Allied strategists who had not planned on reaching the frontier until May of 1945. The Americans had arrived 243 days ahead of schedule.

By November, the German city of Aachen had been reduced to rubble and the Rhine River was a mere twenty-five miles away. It was all but a certainty that the smokestack corridor along the Rhine's eastern bank—the industrial beating heart of the Third Reich's war machine that wound elliptically through the fifty-by-seventy-mile Ruhr valley—would be dealt a final and fatal blow. Incredibly, despite the decimation of Germany's population centers by an Allied strategic bombing campaign, by the fall of 1944 Hitler's factories were manufacturing more armaments than at any point in the war. If Gen. Eisenhower was to fulfill his orders—"to rapidly starve Germany of the means to continue the war"—the elimination of the Ruhr's steel mills, chemical plants, coal mines, and munitions factories was his next step.

Though a cautious Eisenhower fretted over supply-line shortages created by the whirlwind advance, to many war planners it was as if

---

rescuing the Texan "Lost Battalion" surrounded by German troops in the Vosges Mountains of eastern France, and of course several distinguished African American units—including the Tuskegee Airmen and the 761st Tank Battalion of General George Patton's Third Army—saw major combat on the continent. Similarly, French Polynesian, Algerian, and Senegalese colonials were among the troops fighting their way north from the Mediterranean toward Germany with the First Free French Army, and the British field marshal Bernard Law Montgomery's command included Kenyan, Indian, and Nepalese Gurkha warriors whose chilling battle cry, "Repent, for the Gurkhas are upon you," surely gave pause to proponents of the Master Race theory.

the red circle that Roosevelt, Churchill, and Stalin had drawn around Berlin at 1943's Tehran Conference was now pulsing a bright scarlet.

In accordance with the mood, cities across the United States planned victory celebrations while the U.S. Army's chief of staff, General George C. Marshall, began designating which of his nearly sixty European divisions would be transferred to the Pacific to fight the Japanese. Among the reinvigorated GIs on Germany's doorstep, the adage "End the War in '44" had been repeated so often that many had come to consider it divine prophecy.

The feeling was particularly strong among the eight new officers and forty-nine NCOs and privates who had arrived to replace the 2nd Battalion Rangers killed and wounded during the siege of Brest. Yet their buoyant notions had also infected battle-scarred veterans who had grown the hardest bark over the preceding campaigns. "It looks like the war will be over before long," the "Fool Lieutenant" Bob Edlin wrote to his parents. "The Germans are on the run now."

The dank and dark Hürtgen Forest shattered such illusions. After months of "pursuit warfare," the enemy had apparently completed a remarkable reorganization.

By the time the 2nd Ranger Battalion arrived at the western edge of the Hürtgen Forest on November 14—a week after German defenders had turned the woods surrounding the crossroads town of Schmidt into an American charnel house—their mood had turned bleak.*

The intimidating trees that had escaped artillery damage, their trunks covered in black moss, seemed to climb into an expansive white mist, while eerie patches of the forest floor were also lost in the frigid fog. Draped in their sopping overcoats and lugging bedrolls

---

* What the Americans identified as the sixty-square-mile Hürtgen Forest was technically a series of densely packed and interconnected woodlands, each carrying its own local German name.

and full packs as well as heavy machine guns, bazookas, and mortar tubes and ammunition, Lt. Col. Rudder's men struggled through sleet and "pea soup mud" that mired jeeps to their bumpers.

The psychological toll was as weighty as the physical. As the U.S. Army's history of the Hürtgen campaign notes, "A soldier's mind obviously had to make tremendous adjustment from the exhilaration of the pursuit to the depression of stabilized warfare." The five-mile slog through the dank pine wasteland to their next objective—a bald saddleback ridgeline deep in the woods that ran between the American-held hamlets of Vossenack and Germeter—was the battalion's most grueling tramp since they had stormed the Normandy beaches. "One of the severest speed marches we had ever taken," noted Private First Class Morris Prince, Able Company's prolific journal writer. "We were bitching and cursing, angry at the enemy for causing us all these agonies." Prince and his fellow Rangers took solace in the fact that at least humping through the fast-running creeks chasing off the forest's ubiquitous ridges—their banks armored with flood wrack—had the salutary effect of washing the mud from their new shoepacs.

By now, however, even such small amenities had steeled the Rangers to the reality of their situation. This was driven home by a burnt-out jeep straddling a dirt road running parallel to one of those streams. The vehicle's dead driver, an unlucky GI whose uniform had been scorched black by a direct hit from a German 88, still wore his helmet at a jaunty angle. His mottled hands remained on the wheel, and his bluish death mask displayed an upper and lower set of brilliant white teeth, as if he had dressed as a skeleton for Halloween.

Vanishing into the Rembrandt gloom of the Hürtgen woodland, such scenes erased the ambrosial memories of cold beer and hot showers in billets few American civilians could have found on a map. Longuyon, France. Arlon, Belgium. Esch, Luxembourg, where the Walloon women and barkeeps had competed so fiercely for

American cigarettes and dollars. Yet as the battalion became fully enveloped by the Hürtgenwald, the memories of those easy bivouacs had become as dim as the forest at twilight.

Had it really only been weeks since the ingenue songstress Dinah Shore had serenaded them from the back seat of her USO jeep on the banks of the Seine, each Ranger certain that her love songs were meant only for him? Since Doc Block had organized the raucous boar hunt through old King Leopold's private game preserve in the Ardennes? Since they had raced captured BMW and Zündapp motorcycles down cobblestoned Belgian streets? In those heady days the battalion's biggest concern had been the unaccounted-for disappearance of Sgt. Maj. Lomell one morning in early October, only to have him return the following afternoon sporting a gleaming new brace of lieutenant's gold bars.

Even their gaping astonishment at the arrival of Gen. Eisenhower at their most recent staging area, in the tent camp between the Belgian towns of Eupen and Raeren, felt as if it had taken place in another world. Eisenhower, his heavy overcoat hiding the fashionable, waist-length uniform jacket that would soon bear his name, was on a tour of the front and accompanied by a bevy of brass that included Omar Bradley. He had turned up on a cold, rainy day to introduce himself to Lt. Col. Rudder and mingle with the Ranger officers and enlisted men who were racking up commendations faster than any unit in the theater. Two years earlier the War Department establishment had fought hammer-and-tongs against standing up an American commando force. Yet here was the Allied supreme commander come to congratulate them on their rolling heroics. It would not have been a Ranger outfit, however, without a wise guy in the crowd.

As Eisenhower stood beneath a makeshift canopy shaking hands and making small talk, he asked in the manner of military commanders from time immemorial, "Is there anything you men need?"

A disembodied voice—its owner, alas, lost to the ages—piped up. "Yeah. How come you're wearing shoepacs to keep your feet warm and dry and you don't get out in the rain or anything and we don't have any?"

Eisenhower peered down at his waterproof cold-weather foot-wear, and then to the worn and tattered summer combat boots the Rangers had been wearing since D-Day. The general was no doubt aware that trench foot, a condition that destroys blood vessels and tissue overexposed to cold rain and snow, was responsible for nearly a third of all recent GI hospital admissions. He promised on the spot to have new supplies delivered forthwith. True to his word, a shipment of rubber-and-leather winter shoepacs arrived at the Ranger camp just prior to the battalion's departure for the Hürtgen. As a bonus, the supply train also included winter over-coats and even wristwatches.*

With the 2nd Ranger Battalion now attached to the 28th Infantry Division, Col. Rudder was initially confounded by the last-minute change of orders he had received from the division's commander, General Norman Cota. In the wake of Dutch Cota's daredevilry on Omaha Beach, he had been placed in charge of the 28th, which had only recently seized the Belgian rail-and-road hub of Bastogne, a little town unknown at the time but destined to become part of World War II lore. Subsequently, on orders from the First Army commander, General Courtney Hodges, Cota had originally tasked the Rangers with capturing the Roer River hydroelectric dams on the Hürtgen's southeastern fringe.

---

* By spring of 1945, forty-six thousand American soldiers would be pulled off the line to be treated for trench foot. Most would never return to combat. By contrast, British and German infantry commanders, carrying vestigial memories of World War I's trench warfare, ensured that constant infusions of dry wool socks were delivered to the front lines, inspected soldiers' feet continuously, and even taught foot-massage techniques to keep blood flowing in lower limbs.

Inexplicably, Gen. Hodges and his strategists had not given the dams much thought, and Hodges had only begrudgingly handed the assignment of taking them to what he considered the peacock commandos who called themselves Rangers. Hodges had not been happy when Gen. Bradley had foisted Rudder's unit onto his command. Unlike Cota—or even Gen. Eisenhower, for that matter—Hodges had not come around to valuing the special operators for their unique skill sets. He was an old-school "soldier's soldier" who held little truck with troopers who were not regular army. The way he saw it, after his real GIs smashed through the forested portion of the German defenses, the dilettante Rangers could make themselves useful by rushing through the opening and seizing the dams beyond.

The staggering losses suffered in the Hürtgen by the 28th Division, however, had altered Hodges's calculations. In consequence, Lt. Col. Rudder was now simply informed that the dams were no longer a priority. He was to lead his men into the forest and "hold ground against enemy counterattacks." Or, as George Williams sardonically interpreted the order to the combat historian Master Sergeant Forrest Pogue, "to act as moving targets for the German artillery."

Once again, Rudder's mobile, quick-strike outfit—unaccustomed to waiting for the enemy to come to them—was being misused. "He was flabbergasted that anyone would place a highly trained unit such as the Rangers [in a position] to be wasted in an eroding defensive position," noted the communications officer, Ike Eikner. "We couldn't even get anyone [at Division Headquarters] to give us accurate data on the enemy's position, the minefields, theirs or ours."

Rudder and his company commanders had been issued old 1/25,000-scale French-made topographic maps of the forest—one centimeter equaling 250 meters—as well as more recent aerial photographs. But because of the woodland's treetop canopy, in most instances the recon pictures failed to pick up the enemy positions. The photos were nonetheless of more use than the field manuals the Rangers had been issued, which Bob Edlin noticed were dated 1914.

After witnessing firsthand the sorry wreckage of the 28th Division his battalion had come to relieve, however, Rudder's umbrage was somewhat assuaged. Hit hardest was the division's 112th Regiment, Bob Edlin's old outfit.

Eleven days previous, on the chill, foggy morning of Friday, November 3, the 112th had assembled in the forest hamlet of Vossenack. Exhausted from nearly twenty-four hours of fighting to take the village, its GIs were now tasked with spearheading the assault on the crossroads town of Schmidt, which sat astride one of the Hürtgen's highest ridgetops two miles to the southeast. There were no roads between Vossenack and Schmidt. The American attack route would be a single narrow and muddy cart path that ran down one side and up the other of the steep Kall River valley.

Flanked by two supporting regiments making their way through the woods, the 112th's troopers had splashed across the icy Kall as scores of enemy machine guns hidden in camouflaged bunkers buried in the facing hillsides spit enfilading streams of bullets. The point platoons had been ordered to spread out on the far side of the waterway. Yet once past the line of beech trees that screened the river, they found themselves touching off scores of wooden *Schümines* that blasted their legs off at the knee. As screams and plaintive cries rent the air—"Is all of me still there?"—raking artillery fire cut down those who followed.

Despite their flanking columns being either stalled by minefields or repelled by artillery broadsides, scattered elements of the 112th nonetheless managed to reach the outskirts of Schmidt's churchyard by midafternoon. Startled Germans eating lunch or strolling nonchalantly along the sixteenth-century town's main thoroughfare fled, and three depleted American rifle companies anchored by a machine gun platoon set up a loose perimeter. Then, at dawn the next morning, the enemy counterattacked from three directions with a fresh division that included Panzer tank support. It was a slaughter.

Over the next four days the remnants of the American regiment retreated back into the Kall River gorge, "thrashing through the underbrush like blind cattle," in the description of the U.S. Army historian Charles MacDonald, who as a twenty-one-year-old infantry captain fought through the Hürtgen. He described the orange American distress flares arcing high over the pine trees, crossing paths with the crimson parabolas of German artillery shells. The thundering enemy salvos were relentless; at one point some two hundred panicked GIs fled east, deeper into enemy territory and into the waiting arms of a German rifle company lying in ambush. All but three were either killed or captured.

Some Americans went underground, hastily digging foxholes which just as rapidly became inundated with rainwater and melting snow. As unrelenting enemy shells pranged day and night, soldiers too terrified to lift their heads urinated on the ground and defecated into their helmets. The few breaks in the barrage while the enemy gunners reloaded were opportunities to heave the shit out of the holes and restrap their helmets, sans liner, back onto their heads. Many didn't bother rebuttoning their flies for fear of pissing their pants.

Other desperate GIs, seeing dug-in comrades entombed by the drumfire, tried to outrun the unrelenting salvos. They were inevitably hemmed into tight groupings that were then cut down by enemy riflemen and machine gunners firing down from the snow-frosted ridgelines of the Eifel Mountains. Sherman tanks sent to rescue the infantrymen threw their tracks trying to negotiate the narrow and slick mountain trails, while impromptu aid stations were so overwhelmed that litter carriers were forced to stack the wounded like firewood outside in the rain and snow. An assistant division commander sent to reconnoiter the front discovered an entire battalion consisting of fifty-seven men, little more than platoon size.

The mauling was so gruesome that a Wehrmacht physician, Captain Günter Stüttgen—a dermatologist before the war—pleaded with his commander to halt the carnage in order to be allowed to evacuate the wounded. Although American casualties far outnumbered felled Germans, the officer reluctantly agreed, and signaled for a short truce. With that, Capt. Stüttgen's medics swarmed the valley, saving untold American lives for prisoner-of-war camps.* The show of mercy notwithstanding, the 112th Regiment would never be the same. Nearly a week earlier it had set off from Vossenack with twenty-two hundred men. Three hundred would eventually return. The Germans hailed the fight as the righteous *Allerseelenschlacht*— the "All Souls Day Battle." It referred to the date, not the Americans dispatched.

Not privy to division strategy sessions, Col. Rudder could only assume that Schmidt remained the Americans' penultimate target. The town was for the moment thought to be the strategic key to the forest, the stepping-stone that guarded the village of Bergstein, which in turn protected the key Hill 400. The medieval castle atop that rise may have been gone now, wiped out by centuries of erosion and Napoleon's 12-pounders. The Germans were not.

At an elevation of over thirteen hundred feet, the observation tower atop Hill 400—described by one Ranger as resembling an "upside-

---

* On several occasions Capt. Stüttgen and his medical team found themselves working side by side with American aid men treating wounded GIs trapped behind the front lines. "We had respect for one another, respect that only soldiers who know the horror of war can have for one another," the aging dermatologist told a German newspaper reporter long after the war's end. Months after the Hürtgen fight, Stüttgen was sentenced to death in absentia after surrendering an entire military hospital to the advancing Allies without a fight.

down ice cream cone"—offered an unimpeded vista of the entire Hürtgen woodland. It was from the promontory's pinnacle that enemy artillery spotters using state-of-the-art Zeiss optic lenses had directed the barrages from the amassed batteries in and around Schmidt and from beyond the hill in the Roer River valley. It was said that the Zeiss optics, more reliable than anything the Allies possessed, could target a squirrel a mile away. The survivors of the multiple American forays into the forest would testify to the accuracy of both the statement and the German guns.

In September and October, before Aachen had fallen, it had been the 9th Infantry Division that had twice been turned back from Hill 400. Now it was Dutch Cota's 28th that had been cut to pieces attempting to clear Schmidt and take the high ground. It was quite evident that the reenergized enemy had dug into the Hürtgen for an unexpected last stand. One U.S. Army historian compared the turn of fortune to the mythological Greek giant Antaeus, who regained his strength merely by touching his mother, Earth. In the mid-twentieth-century iteration of the analogy, it was not the mother who succored the Wehrmacht soldier, but the father, or, more precisely, the *Vaterland*. And protecting this Fatherland was a string of long-standing defensive fortifications built precisely for the purpose.

The Germans called it the Westwall.

25

The Green Hell

The Third Reich's military engineers were nothing if not inventive. Beginning in 1936, they had secretly begun overseeing construction on a defensive line that limned the country's western frontier for some 390 miles, from the Dutch border in the northwest to the High Rhine abutting Switzerland in the southeast. Such was this massive impediment's perceived value to the country's defense that by 1938 over a third of Germany's annual production of cement was being poured into its construction.

This Westwall—what the Allies dubbed the Siegfried Line—consisted of over three thousand pillboxes and bunkers encased in concrete up to eight feet thick and reinforced with steel girders, hardy enough to withstand the most powerful bazooka and mortar shells.* Some, in deference to potential air strikes, were designed

---

* The name the Allies had given the Reich's defensive fortifications derived from the fifth-century legend of the knight Siegfried—"Sigurd" in old Norse—who heroically slayed a dragon before being murdered. The German composer Richard Wagner reanimated Siegfried's romantic mythology in his nineteenth-century operas *Siegfried* and *Götterdämmerung*, when the paladin became synonymous with German nationalism.

to look like dilapidated barns, with fake haystacks that housed hidden gun emplacements. Others were built to resemble abandoned electrical substations complete with sham power lines.

Moreover, thousands of rows of pyramid-shaped concrete tank barriers were studded before the pillboxes. These obstructions, a dry-land version of the "dragon's teeth" planted in the waters off Normandy, were canted forward and surrounded by mazes of concertina-wire barriers intended to funnel enemy troops and tanks into myriad minefields and ditches up to eight feet wide and twenty feet deep. The larger blockhouses, often topped by steel observation cupolas, were equipped with fireplaces, kitchens, storerooms, and bunk beds. If clustered close enough, they were connected by underground tunnels. They had also been strategically placed to ensure their defenders interlocking fields of fire.

Nowhere were these lethal modifications more evident than in the Hürtgen Forest, where every open glade had become a kill zone for MG42 machine gun nests secreted in stout log bunkers. Range finders had also presighted the forest clearings for mortar and artillery barrages directed from Hill 400. The trails and firebreaks that German forest managers had so meticulously maintained for centuries were now sown with hundreds of thousands of mines, while scores of the woodland's thickest trees had been felled across switchbacks on the steep and winding logging roads in order to slow the advance of American armored vehicles. Given the meticulousness of the defensive preparations in the Hürtgen, it is no wonder that German soldiers were said to welcome any incursion into what they termed *Grüne Hölle*—Green Hell.

In the heady days since the blitzkrieg of western Europe, however, the Westwall had fallen into disrepair. Much of its weapons and equipment, down to the concertina wire and the case-hardened steel doors of pillboxes, had been scavenged and repurposed for use along the Atlantic coast to repel the expected American-led invasion. The deterioration was such that local farmers had bridged over rows of dragon's teeth for easier travel among fields and taken to using abandoned bunkers as vegetable cribs.

But by August 1944, with the Allies approaching the German border, Hitler had ordered a rapid rehabilitation of the Westwall. Preteen boys from the Hitler Youth and girls from the League of German Maidens were conscripted for tasks ranging from cutting back vegetation that had engulfed pillbox embrasures to forging new keys to fit rusting locks on bunker doors. In Hitler's increasingly febrile mind, this was only the first step of a large-scale operation designed to regain the initiative in the west.

By this point the increasingly delusional Nazi leader, having survived a July assassination attempt organized by several Wehrmacht officers, had nominally wrested supreme military leadership from his general staff. As such he had ordered twenty-nine infantry divisions and twelve armored divisions supported by artillery—hundreds of thousands of troops—to secretly begin assembling behind the Westwall to fulfill his dream of a massive counterstrike against the encroaching Allies.

The retaliatory drive was code-named Operation *Wacht am Rhein,* after a Germanic anthem, and was soon to go down in American history as the Battle of the Bulge. Its intent was to blast through the Ardennes Forest, capture the Belgian town of Liège, a major railroad center and the heart of the Allied supply system, and proceed across the Meuse River to seize the port of Antwerp. The offensive would bisect the American and British forces and, in Hitler's mind, force the Allies to sue for peace.

The Führer's eleventh-hour scenario turned on playing for time, particularly in the Hürtgen Forest, which was projected to be a major pathway toward the Ardennes. For if the Abwehr operatives from German military intelligence were correct, the Allies were near to outrunning their five-hundred-mile supply lines, which still originated on the Normandy beaches.* Thus, with the American drive stalled against the refurbished Westwall, they would be ripe for the counterassault.

Hitler recognized that if even one of the Allied armies surging toward the German heartland managed to ford the Roer River, his secret plans would be dashed. The pull and tug between the Führer and his recalcitrant generals also led Hitler to summon from retirement the sixty-eight-year-old Gerd von Rundstedt to begin his second tour as commander in chief of the Wehrmacht's western defenses, replacing his fellow field marshal Walter Model. In conquered nations across the eastern and western fronts the names Rundstedt and Model had only a few years earlier been as synonymous with misfortune as Smith and Wesson. But now, as the once-devastating blitzkrieg backwashed across Europe like a receding tide, an equally desperate Model—an ardent Nazi—recognized that his energies were best devoted to the planning of *Wacht am Rhein* while Rundstedt's primary assignment would be to reestablish the efficacy of the Westwall and hold his position "until annihilation."

"The fight in the west has spread to the German Reich," Hitler thundered in his orders to Rundstedt. "The situation no longer permits any maneuvering. Stand your ground or die!"

This was a refrain Rundstedt had heard too often since the failed July coup, to the point where he had ceased all personal interactions with Hitler in order to avoid being subjected to the Nazi chancellor's increasingly manic monologues. Yet despite Rundstedt's disdain for Hitler—whom he privately dubbed "The Bohemian Corporal"—the field marshal was descended from a centuries-long line of patrician Junker military officers, and thus viewed his recall as a patriotic duty.

---

* Though the great port of Antwerp was in Allied hands, Wehrmacht holdouts still controlled the mouth of the Scheldt River's Westerschelde estuary, which linked the city to the North Sea. Its wharves were thus useless to SHAEF.

On paper, Gen. Rundstedt's forty-eight infantry divisions and fifteen Panzer divisions were the near equal of the American, British, Canadian, and Free French forces commanded by Gen. Eisenhower. In reality, the Normandy invasion and its five-month aftermath had rocked and demoralized the Wehrmacht. The German army had suffered such severe losses—over four hundred thousand casualties since D-Day—that the field marshal recognized that units remaining in the field and fighting at reduced strength were destined to endure an even higher casualty percentage. In the end, Rundstedt sensed that he would be fortunate to muster half of the firepower employed by the Allies now closing the circle on the Reich.

Nowhere was this disparity more evident than in the Hürtgen, where even October's "victory" over America's 9th Division had come at a steep cost—over three thousand German soldiers killed, wounded, or captured, nearly 50 percent of the forest's defenders.

Although Hitler had lowered the draft age to sixteen and raised it to fifty in an effort to ship more "rear-area swine" to the Western Front, Rundstedt considered this acne-afflicted and potbellied "bow and arrow infantry" as no better than cannon fodder. Simultaneously, in a further, frantic bid to scrape the last ounces of manpower from the country's dwindling pool, the German *Reichsführer* Heinrich Himmler began press-ganging stray men and boys into what Hitler dubbed his *Volks-Grenadier* division, or People's Grenadiers. These units were answerable only to Himmler's feared Nazi paramilitary *Schutzstaffel* (SS), and not the usual chain of German military command.

As distasteful as Rundstedt found Himmler's methods, in reality he had no choice but to accept the *Volks-Grenadiers* being folded into his existing units manning the Westwall. The general did take some solace in the fact that the *Volks-Grenadier* units were salted with veterans such as sidelined *Kriegsmarine* and Luftwaffe personnel, dismounted Panzer crews, border-patrol officers, policemen, and ambulatory hospital returnees—those, that is, who did not purposely tear open their stitched wounds in rear-area hospitals "out of sheer terror of being sent back to the front."

Several regiments of these new divisions were deployed to the Hürtgen to be absorbed by the German 275th Infantry, the same division that had repelled the American 9th Division in September and October and Gen. Cota's 28th in November. Before taking their defensive positions in the forest, the *Volks-Grenadier* detachments were employed uncoiling miles of new concertina wire and laying thousands of additional antitank *Tellermines* and the maiming *Schümines* rushed to the front from Westphalian munitions plants in charcoal-fueled Opel trucks. Should the Americans again attempt to take Hill 400, they would now be facing a force of some sixty-five hundred enemy soldiers armed with a daunting assortment of artillery tubes, motorized assault guns, and 75 mm antitank weapons.

Some Wehrmacht strategists were perplexed by the American fixation on the forest, and considered the Hürtgen buildup extraneous. Successive waves of GIs, after all, had already been whipped badly attempting to break through the Green Hell. Further, if the long-range weather forecasts were accurate, storm clouds would continue to keep grounded all Belgium-based Allied planes. With the rugged forest terrain neutralizing the overwhelming American armor and artillery advantage and no close air support available, one captured German after-action document boasted, "in combat in wooded areas the American [infantryman] showed himself completely unfit." Why in the world would the Amis even think of trying again?

Not a few American war planners found themselves pondering the same question. The answer, Rundstedt knew, lay in the mind of the officer he faced across the Siegfried Line—Lieutenant General

Courtney Hodges, commander of the American First Army, the largest Allied fighting force in Europe.

Flunking out of West Point near the turn of the century had not dimmed the young Courtney Hodges's martial ardor. In 1905, within months of his defeat at the hands of the military academy's Euclidian geometry courses, Hodges had enlisted as a buck private. Over the ensuing thirty-nine years he had risen through the ranks to become the proprietor of the three stars he now wore on his shoulders, what the army called a mustang officer—the only such to assume command of an American army in World War II. Tall, gaunt, and sporting a graying mustache so close-cropped that it was barely visible, the fifty-seven-year-old Hodges was no stranger to combat with man or beast. He had twice been gassed in the trenches of World War I, and had bagged tigers, caribou, and elephants on safaris around the world.

The son of a small-town Georgia newspaper publisher, Gen. Hodges was known to affect the drawling mien of a Southern gentleman farmer in casual conversation. In fact, he was an insecure commander ever alert to rivals, particularly Academy graduates, receiving credit he felt was his due. Perhaps this insecurity was responsible for Hodges's doleful countenance, which prompted even the decorous Gen. Eisenhower to remark that "God gave him a face that always looked pessimistic."

By November 1944, the chain-smoking, bourbon-drinking Hodges had much to be pessimistic about. He was surrounded by what his immediate supervisor, Gen. Bradley, described as a "temperamental" ring of subordinates, and there was a sense among fellow officers and war correspondents who visited Hodges's headquarters that the art of modern warfare had passed him by. Like many of the general officers of his cohort, Hodges viewed the battering-ram strategy of Ulysses Grant as his inspiration. Hodges invariably used one of his two favorite phrases in answer to most tactical questions: "Smash ahead" or "Straight on."

Yet despite this outward bravado, even Hodges's own assistant chief of staff privately questioned his superior's disconcerting lack of aggressiveness. "[Hodges] was pretty slow making the big decisions," wrote Major William Sylvan in his diary. "He would study them for a long time and I would often have to press him before I got a decision." In a coda to his epic official army history of the Siegfried Line campaign, even the usually imperturbable Charles MacDonald admitted, "Surely [Hodges's] approach to the question of the Roer River dams was lacking in vigor and imagination."

More demoralizing, certainly from a GI's dirt-flecked perspective, was Hodges's habit of rarely venturing to the front lines to personally gauge the combat situation. He preferred, instead, to oversee the First Army's condition and efforts via the reports he received at the villa he had commandeered in the eastern Belgian town of Spa, a good forty miles from the front. While he and his staff dined formally each evening clad in jacket and tie, the generals commanding his divisions would often go weeks without seeing him.

Most frustrating, however, was Hodges's espousal of a military strategy many found completely unfit for fighting across such a confined and unconventional terrain as the Hürtgen Forest. With three armored divisions and three mechanized cavalry groups at his disposal, Hodges either would not or could not acknowledge that his rolling stock had no business attempting to negotiate the sharp highlands and ravines of the muddy and bloody woodland.

Despite all this, Gen. Eisenhower had little choice but to designate Hodges's First Army as the tip of the Allied spear to be thrust into the German heartland. Field Marshal Montgomery had lobbied hard for the same assignment. And with thousands of V-1 buzz bombs terrorizing London, Eisenhower was cognizant of what a morale boost to Great Britain it would be to appoint one of their own to lead the assault into Germany. But Eisenhower simply did not trust Montgomery. "At a moment when strategic harmony was needed in the Allied high command," the author Rick Atkinson notes, "dissonance and puerile backbiting obtained" between Monty and Ike's American generals.

Thus, with Montgomery's army still licking its wounds in the wake of the failed attempt in late September to forge a bridgehead over the Rhine from the Netherlands, and with Gen. Patton's Third Army stalled farther south for want of gasoline, the assignment fell to Hodges. But the general was hesitant. Regarded as a "calm and dependable, painstaking tactician," he now wavered, insisting that a dash from the captured city of Aachen to the Rhine would lay open his right quadrant to a flanking counterattack from within the Hürtgen Forest—hence his hesitation to move until the town of Schmidt was taken and a clear pathway was opened to the village of Bergstein, which guarded the artillery spotters atop Hill 400.

A cadre of Hodges's staffers argued with him, in vain. The Hürtgen proper, they pointed out, was of little strategic or tactical value. Moreover, the topography inhibited armored movements for the Germans as well as the Americans. Without Panzer tank support— currently and inevitably limited to the paved ridge roads around Schmidt and Bergstein—the Germans in the forest could hardly amass enough firepower to slow the entire First Army's eastward momentum. With the Wehrmacht on its heels, they contended, a dilatory slog back into the dark woods would further delay the November push to the Rhine for which Gen. Eisenhower was pressing. Eisenhower suspected that without an early-winter foothold on the far side of that key river, the war might be extended by months. It never entered Hodges's mind that a detour into the Hürtgen was precisely the sideshow that Field Marshal Rundstedt was counting on. Like a cosmologist, the general was often wrong but never in doubt.

Hodges also brushed off warnings from army engineers that in the unlikely event his "Smash ahead" strategy succeeded in the Hürtgen, the Roer River's floodplain could rapidly be submerged by the Germans who controlled the seven hydroelectric dams near the watercourse's headwaters. The Roer was already in spate from the inordinate autumn rain and snowfall, triple the monthly average. Should the enemy throw open the dams' floodgates, one engineering report warned, forty billion gallons of water—one hundred million metric tons—would sweep down the Roer River valley in a mile-wide torrent reaching twenty-five feet high, washing away bridges and further stalling the Allied offensive. If American forces north of the dams managed to cross the Roer before such a flood tide was loosed, they would be trapped between the Roer and the Rhine.

A fellow American general, the Ninth Army commander William Simpson, suggested to Hodges that if he remained adamant about eliminating the threat from the forest, perhaps he should alter his method of assault. In lieu of another frontal attack from the northwest, Simpson asked, would not a flanking, artillery-led offensive from the southeast, exploiting the flat and open terrain of the so-called Monschau Corridor, surprise the defenders concentrated in the Hürtgen? Such a gambit just might allow Hodges to sweep up both Bergstein and Hill 400 as well as the dams with a minimum of casualties before the levees could be breached.* But Hodges demurred. He was convinced that Dutch Cota's 28th Division would make short work of the woodland's enemy holdouts.

Hodges made it plain in a communiqué to Gen. Bradley that the fall of Aachen had altered the equation since the 9th Infantry Division's dismal showing in the forest in September and October. Unlike the Germans who had repelled the 9th, he reported, the enemy now defending the Hürtgen redoubts would put up no more than

---

* Simpson had personally addressed the Ranger battalions after the fall of the Lochrist battery, and several recalled one sentence from his otherwise anodyne speech: "I will send no soldier where a shell will do."

token resistance "for reasons of prestige" before either surrendering or falling back. With that, the dams would be left wide open for the Ranger assault.

In theory, Hodges's strategy appeared sublime—until, that is, elements of Cota's division actually attempted to implement it and were drowned in a steaming hellbroth of enemy resistance. What Hodges had not counted on, of course, was the zeal with which the typical German soldier would hold a fixed line to defend the Fatherland, particularly when he needn't worry any longer about French, Belgian, or Dutch partisans sabotaging his supply lines. In Hodges's defense, like almost all Allied commanders the general was completely in the dark regarding Rundstedt's orders to protect at all costs the Wehrmacht's ongoing secret buildup behind the Westwall.

Finally, in a colossal stroke of bad luck for the Americans, Field Marshal Model himself happened to be in nearby Cologne conducting a map exercise for the upcoming counteroffensive with his top staff officers just as Dutch Cota's regiments moved against Schmidt. When word of the attack reached Model, he assumed command of the town's defense and ordered the immediate counterattack that pushed the Americans back.

Thus, in the aftermath of the rout—those GIs who survived were driven back to the edge of Vossenack—Hodges now felt that an immediate second Wehrmacht counterassault was almost certain. His forest-fighting forces needed every gun available to hold the line in the Hürtgen while he aligned his divisions for the even larger operation of moving on the Rhine. Those guardians included the Rangers. The dams, and Hill 400, would have to wait.

26

The Queen's Gambit

Black clouds scudded past a crescent moon when, in the gloaming of November 14, 1944, the 2nd Ranger Battalion officially assumed the defense of the twin villages of Germeter and Vossenack. Lt. Col. Rudder divided his outfit between both hamlets in perimeter and reserve capacities while he established his forward command post in the cellar of a bomb-ravaged house on the western rim of Germeter, which rose on an open ridge several hundred yards northwest of Vossenack. Though the home's owner, a forest master, had long since fled with his wife and three daughters, there was a welcoming committee of a sort to greet him—the headless corpse of a German rifleman whose boots remained inexplicably clean, even pristine. Rudder was momentarily too mesmerized by the dead man's spotless footwear to notice the scrawny black cat gnawing at the soldier's open neck. He kicked the animal away, and he and Harvey Cook deposited the body in a coal bin.

The next morning Rudder and Cook attended a coordination meeting with the commanding officers of adjacent infantry and tank units to hash out the Ranger battalion's immediate prerogatives.

A company from the neighboring 4th Division's 12th Regiment had taken a forward position on an exposed ridgeline five hundred yards northeast of Vossenack, and German radio operators had located and jammed the American frequencies. The Rangers were needed to run patrols out to the GIs every six hours. Their mission was to relay information and orders, deliver food, water, and ammunition, and buck up morale as the only contact the outlying troops had with "friendlies." If necessary, they were also to assist in fending off enemy probes against the company's perimeter. Rudder divvied the tasks between Bob Arman's Able Company and Sid Salomon's Baker Company.

The haggard and departing veteran officers from the 28th Division also issued a warning to Rudder and Cook. The looming ridges to the north, east, and south of both Germeter and Vossenack, they said, were occupied by the Germans who had chased the GIs from Schmidt. Random shells from enemy 88s, 120 mm mortars, and captured French 75 mm cannons fell regularly on the enveloped GIs. Despite the fifteen-foot screening nets that American engineers had thrown up in an attempt to conceal the main streets running through the two villages, Wehrmacht artillery spotters atop Hill 400 could still see most movements. Any man or vehicle moving during daylight was fair game. One particular road junction linking Germeter to Vossenack, they added, was shelled so frequently it was known as Purple Heart Corner.

More concerning, Rudder and Cook learned that the enemy counteroffensive out of Schmidt had only finally been halted on the northeastern edge of Vossenack. Cannoneers from both sides had so devastated this section of the village that the Americans had taken to calling the area the Rubble Pile. Wehrmacht rifle squads had dug deep into the basements below the collapsed buildings after laying a semicircular minefield around their position. There they remained, impervious to repeated infantry attempts to root them out.

Rudder left the meeting perplexed. As he saw it, the capture of Aachen had presented the Americans with an ideal opportunity. Since Roman times the relatively open plains northeast of the city, the "Aachen Gap," had formed a natural gateway across the Rhine and into the German interior. That thoroughfare now beckoned the Allies like a flashing green light. Moreover, given the successive beatings the Germans had inflicted on American forces in the Hürtgen, bypassing the forest altogether, or at least leaving a small screening detail behind, made the most tactical sense. Considering the circumstances, Rudder suspected that his Rangers, once destined for the hydroelectric dams, were in fact to be used as that outnumbered and outgunned screening unit. "Don't worry if you don't hear from me very often," he wrote to Chick that night, affecting an insouciance far from his true feelings. "The news is rather scarce from here."

Rudder had good reason to fear that his outfit was once again being sidelined, if not sacrificed. To his north, he knew, the offensive he envisioned—what General Omar Bradley optimistically called "the last big assault to bring Germany to her knees"—was in fact already in the works. Bradley had finally lost patience with Gen. Hodges's equivocations, and in early November had ordered a full-scale attack across the Roer River and toward the Rhine by Hodges's First American Army and Gen. Simpson's Ninth American Army, supplemented by elements of the fifty-thousand-man British XXX Corps. Dubbed Operation Queen, the plan was to surge east along a fifty-mile front stretching from the industrial corridor north of Aachen to the northernmost fringes of the Hürtgen.

Prior to jump-off, the largest air-support operation employed thus far on the continent—thousands of heavy bombers, medium bombers, and fighter-bombers—was primed to pulverize the German defensive positions. But because of the worsening weather beclouding the frontier, Operation Queen had already been post-poned for several days. Running short of patience, Bradley had finally set November 16 as a deadline date, with or without air support. By the evening of November 15, Americans on the ground were left scanning the leaden skies in the hope of spotting a star. Their searching eyes may as well have been seeking the Second Coming. The Queen's gambit proved an unmitigated disaster.

Although by noon the next day holes had indeed opened in the skein of clouds over the battlefield, German troops, outnum-bered by a factor of five, seemed only to stiffen under the Allied bombardments designed to soften their resistance—just shy of ten thousand tons of ordnance dropped by over forty-five hundred American and British aircraft jinking through a flak-spangled sky. By midafternoon another cloud cover had blown in, retarding air support, and a freezing rain engulfed GIs thrown into house-to-house fighting east of Aachen. Allied lines of communications dis-solved, entire battalions were trapped in newly laid minefields, and an unforeseen Panzer division spitting fountains of orange flame from their extended barrels moved forward to fill any breaches. In the tracks of the German tanks followed shrilling battalions of *Panzergrenadiers*—mechanized infantry—which threw the advanc-ing GIs into a panic.

The Allied push south of Aachen fared no better. Two regiments from Gen. Hodges's 4th Infantry Division—the 8th and the 22nd—stalled almost immediately upon entering the northern fringes of the Hürtgen. The 22nd Regiment was particularly hard hit by artil-lery, taking more than three hundred battle casualties across the first three days of fighting. These included the loss of all three of its bat-talion commanders and close to half of its company commanders.

The weight of German metal falling from the sky took its toll in manifold ways, and the battle casualty list did not include the numerous GIs evacuated from the line suffering from combat exhaustion. Some of these unfortunates were sent to the rear through standard medical channels, while others were merely helped to a nearby rest tent and issued coffee, a shot of whiskey, and a sleeping pill. Ranger scouts, hunkered down a mere two and a half miles from the 22nd Regiment's southern flank, watched as addled Americans released from the rest tents after a day or two of recuperation passed through their ranks on the return trip to the front.

By the fifth day of Operation Queen, with the 4th Division's casualty toll approaching fifteen hundred, battalions had been reduced to the size of companies, companies to the size of platoons, and some squads had simply evaporated. During that same period, the two American regiments fighting in the Hürtgen had penetrated less than two miles into enemy-held territory. The division's objective had originally been to burst through the forest, cross the Roer, and fall on the German city of Bonn, some forty miles to the east. That was now a pipe dream.

Meanwhile, as the First and Ninth Armies slogged on, on November 19 the Rangers saw what remained of the battered 28th Division, per the official army history's theatrical description, "stumbling off the stage, having completed its tragic role in the drama of the Hürtgen Forest." That role, in fact, remained calamitous to its final moments, as the division's rear guard was decimated by artillery fire as they fell back from the Vossenack-Germeter area. The gory scene was such that after wading for hours "knee deep in bloody bodies" while treating the wounded, the heretofore stoic Doc Block lost his composure and vomited on the muddy road.

Gen. Hodges supplied the coda to the performance when, in a rare excursion from Spa, he motored to Dutch Cota's headquarters on the French-German border to meet with Gens. Eisenhower and Bradley. During the conference he pulled Cota aside to deliver what one witness described as a "crimson tirade" of opprobrium.

Cota took the dressing-down with equanimity. To err is human, he well understood, to blame it on someone else is politics. Hodges concluded the reproof with a typically terse dictum. "Roll on," he said. The 28th did indeed roll on, back to Belgium for rest and recuperation.

If the 28th Division's departure was an emotional exit, the arrival of the full-strength 8th "Golden Arrow" Infantry Division to replace them was baffling. Most bewildering was the Golden Arrow's assignment—to follow the same bullheaded battle plan through the forest that over the past two months had left a succession of American outfits shredded. Three regiments from the 8th Division found themselves fighting back and forth over the same stalemated ground that had so stymied Cota's troops. Observing the infantry movements, Rudder and his chief lieutenants—now officially attached to the 8th Division as reserve units—could not have been faulted for contemplating the famous definition of insanity: doing the same thing over and over again and expecting a different result.

Hodges's hope that fresh troops from the 8th might alter the equation was rapidly dispelled as the new GIs—cold, tired, and hungry, confused by the unfamiliar woods, and appalled by the uncollected, swollen corpses of their American predecessors—stumbled into the seemingly endless *Schümines* fields, were confronted at close range by bristling automatic-weapons fire from the well-disguised log bunkers, or were chewed up by pinpoint artillery salvos directed from Hill 400. As the War Department was to later sum up the episode, "Attempts by American artillery to silence the enemy's big guns and mortars might as well have been made with peashooters." And then the freezing rain turned to snow.

Although sporadic fighting would continue for weeks up and down the ragged front of Operation Queen, efforts to break through the Westwall ground to a deadlock, spent by the force of lethal inertia. Together the First and Ninth Armies suffered over thirty-eight thousand casualties without sniffing the east bank of the Roer, much less the Rhine. Bonn may as well have been the far side of the moon.

As the GIs involved in Operation Queen dug in to recover from the mauling, the 2nd Ranger Battalion continued to adjust to the unfamiliar foibles of forest fighting. One primary lesson quickly absorbed was to beware the enemy's nightly "infiltration patrols," which included sharp-eyed Wehrmacht snipers. As the Hürtgen's floor was laced with flare wires that could light up the leaden sky in an instant, moving about after dark was tantamount to suicide.

Nearly as important was learning to protect yourself from the treetop shell bursts that German artillerymen had honed to such an art. Unroofed foxholes offered little to no safeguards from the rain of steel shrapnel mixed with deadly wooden splinters, and each Ranger dugout was soon covered with timber and layers of frozen sod.* If trapped in the open during a fusillade, lying flat on the ground was an invitation to death by a thousand cuts, while diving into the nearest ditch risked detonating enemy-laid booby traps. Best to find the nearest tree trunk and crouch against it, exposing as few body parts as possible. It is doubtful that any of Rudder's Rangers had read Orwell's *Homage to Catalonia*.† But what had been a truism during the Spanish Civil War remained as accurate in 1944: "In trench warfare, five things are important: firewood, food, tobacco, candles and the enemy . . . with the enemy being a bad last."

Given the denseness of the Hürtgen's foliage, calling in friendly artillery or mortar fire with any degree of certainty was nigh on

---

* So frozen was the soil covering the forest floor that the Rangers resorted to detonating quarter-pound charges, about half the power of a wooden *Schutzendosenmine,* to break ground before digging deeper.

† Likely because what is now considered an Orwell classic sold less than one thousand copies in his lifetime.

impossible, even with the aid of smoke shells. Visibility was limited to no more than twenty-five or thirty feet, and even firing on a confirmed target risked endangering friendly troops with tree bursts. Moreover, the French maps that had been distributed to the battalion were fairly useless unless a scout team stumbled upon one of the prewar cement survey markers sometimes found at firebreak intersections. As one army historian observed with a barely concealed metaphorical sigh, "Without a map, you had to depend on a compass—if you had a compass. There was a lot to learn in the Hürtgen Forest."

On the other hand, the Rangers were nothing if not apt students. They used the cohesion and tactical proficiency they had acquired since D-Day to rapidly accustom themselves to this new form of combat, settling into a daily routine of patrolling, fighting, and finding nighttime cover. This included acclimating to the ubiquitous pressure-activated enemy mines. Every man in the outfit was soon adept at crawling on his hands and knees to probe the cold, soupy soil with his trench knife, searching for either the devastating antitank *Tellermines* or the maiming wooden "shoes." The Rangers discovered that often the former had been stacked like two pancakes in a deadly ruse—lifting the upper would ignite the lower. They also noticed that many of the "shoes" had been laid at intervals of precisely eight yards. They were thankful for the Teutonic precision.

When more rapid movements were required, company commanders assembled point squads whose sole task was to lob heavy logs and branches onto the trail ahead in order to set off the buried explosives. Each outfit developed its own means to cope. Charlie Company's Captain Ralph Goranson, for instance, consistently employed one particular sergeant to walk point. The noncom had the nose of a bloodhound and could pick up the distinctive scent

In mid-1942, General Lucian Truscott was tasked by the U.S. Army's chief of staff, General George C. Marshall, with standing up a force of American special operators modeled after British commandos. *Courtesy of the Library of Congress.*

Growing up in Concho County, Texas, "Big Jim" Rudder's competitive spirit was honed as the starting center for both the Eden High School Bulldogs and the Texas A&M Aggies. *Courtesy of Dr. Thomas Hatfield/University of Texas.*

The West Point graduate Captain William O. Darby was chosen by Truscott to lead the first Ranger contingents into North Africa, Sicily, and Italy. *Courtesy of the National Archives.*

Rudder and his new bride, the former Margaret "Chick" Williamson, looking sharp during their wedding in June 1937. *Courtesy of Dr. Thomas Hatfield/University of Texas.*

Among the spoils of war was Captain Harold "The Duke" Slater's confiscation of the German shepherd named Asgaard, who had belonged to the Wehrmacht commander of the captured Lochrist battery outside of Brest. *Courtesy of Leon Bombardier.*

Captain Ralph Goranson, commander of the 2nd Battalion's Charlie Company, is said to be the model upon which the Tom Hanks character was based in *Saving Private Ryan. Courtesy of the U.S. Army.*

The B Company commanding officer Captain Sidney Salomon's beaming smile belied a brusque New Jersey accent which, one Ranger said, "could scour a stove." *Courtesy of the U.S. Army.*

The oft-wounded Lieutenant Len "Bud" Lomell's exploits across Pointe du Hoc and atop Hill 400 earned him the honor of being a member of the first class chosen for the U.S. Army Ranger Hall of Fame. *Courtesy of the U.S. Army.*

The former professional tap dancer Tony Ruggerio *(left)* poses with Jack Kuhn, Len Lomell's heroic partner in disabling the big German howitzers which were poised to drive the D-Day invasion back into the sea. *Courtesy of the Descendants of WWII Rangers.*

Wielding his Browning automatic rifle from Normandy to the Hürtgen Forest, the slightly built and toothless Sergeant William "L-Rod" Petty became the "soul" of the 2nd Battalion's Fox Company. *Courtesy of Leon Bombardier.*

Handsome Herman "Bubby" Stein, L-Rod Petty's best friend and BAR running mate, established a reputation as the best climber in the 2nd Ranger Battalion. *Courtesy of the U.S. Army.*

Sergeants Five! From left to right, a gathering of some of the 2nd Ranger Battalion noncoms: Sigurd Sundby, Rex Clark, "L-Rod" Petty, Ed Secor, and Joseph Devoli. *Courtesy of the U.S. Army.*

Captured during the Rangers' assault on Hill 400, Fox Company's Captain Otto "Big Stoop" Masny escaped from a German P.O.W. camp and managed to journey nearly one thousand miles through enemy lines to freedom. *Courtesy of the U.S. Army.*

Col. Rudder tapped Major Max Schneider to lead the 5th Ranger Battalion into Europe following Schneider's exploits as a company commander under Bill Darby during the Mediterranean campaigns. *Courtesy of Dr. Thomas Hatfield/University of Texas.*

It was said that the 2nd Battalion's chief medical officer, Captain Walter E. "Doc" Block, "could cut a throat almost as well as he could sew one." *Courtesy of the U.S. Army.*

The former knife-fighting instructor Captain Harvey Cook proved invaluable as the 2nd Ranger Battalion's chief intelligence officer during the slog across Western Europe and into the Hürtgen Forest. *Courtesy of Dr. Thomas Hatfield/ University of Texas.*

The 2nd Ranger Battalion, led by Lt. Col. Rudder on the far right (with the smiling Lieutenant Bob Edlin nine rows behind him) marches toward the troop ship that will ferry them to Normandy Beach. Lieutenant Joe Rafferty, second from left in the first row, was among the Rangers who would never leave the beach alive. *Courtesy of the National Archives.*

Never an officer to lead from behind, "Big Jim" Rudder took command of the first wave of Rangers to hit the Normandy shores on D-Day. *Courtesy of the U.S. Army Military History Institute.*

Rangers who survived the landing on the beach and the scaling of Pointe du Hoc and D-Day take a break at the command post and aid station Col. Rudder established atop the cliff. *Courtesy of the U.S. Army Military History Institute.*

Rangers leading some of the scores of German prisoners captured atop Pointe du Hoc down the headland's escarpment. *Courtesy of the U.S. Army Military History Institute.*

Rangers marching down a typical mud trail in the Hürtgen Forest beneath some of the thousands of conifers destroyed by enemy "tree-burst" artillery shells. *Courtesy of U.S. Army Signal Corps.*

Captain James "Ike" Eikner *(far right)*, commander of the battalion's Headquarters Company, shares a bottle of "liberated" French wine with members of his staff (and "Ranger" the dog): left to right, Corporal Lou Lisko, Sergeant Stephen Liscinsky, and Sergeant Charles Parker. *Courtesy of the National Archives.*

"The Fool Lieutenant" Bob Edlin *(top left)* formed a scout team dubbed the "Fabulous Four"—"perhaps the most highly decorated patrol in the history of the United States Army"—whose exploits culminated in the capture of a Brest fortress housing 800 German soldiers. Standing next to Edlin is Sergeant Bill "Stoop" Dreher; kneeling before both are, at left, Sergeant Warren "Halftrack" Burmaster and Sergeant Bill "No-Neck" Courtney. *Courtesy of Dr. Thomas Hatfield/ University of Texas.*

The nineteen-year-old Dog Company rifleman Melvin "Bud" Potratz managed to scribble a note to his father moments before the battalion charged Hill 400: "Dear Dad: We're going on the line again. Gotta be big! I can see it in sergeant's eyes. He's scared." *Courtesy of the U.S. Army Signal Corps.*

Perhaps the stern-looking veteran Fox Company Sergeant Murrell Stinnette, at left, knew the fate that awaited him and his outfit atop Hill 400 as he posed with PFC Milt "Bunny" Moss in one of the last photographs taken of Stinnette. *Courtesy of Leon Bombardier.*

Born in what was then Czechoslovakia and hungry for revenge against the Nazis, the Dog Company Staff Sergeant Mike Sharik had only just transferred into the 2nd Ranger Battalion when the outfit was ordered to take Hill 400. *Courtesy of the U.S. Army.*

On loan to the Rangers from the U.S. Army's Fifth Armored Division for the assault on Hill 400, the fearless forward artillery spotter Lieutenant Howard Kettelhut was credited by "Duke" Slater as being the "best man we ever worked with." *Courtesy of Dr. Brett Kettelhut.*

Acknowledged as the Rangers' most stealthy pathfinder and scout, PFC Bill "Andy" Anderson died in "L-Rod" Petty's arms atop Hill 400; he was soon afterward joined in the battalion's makeshift morgue by his brother, Jack. *Courtesy of the U.S. Army.*

The German defenders in the Hürtgen Forest counted on the historically foul weather of the autumn of 1944 to slow the American advance across the dirt roads, trails, and firebreaks crisscrossing the woodland. *Courtesy of the U.S. Army Signal Corps.*

The splayed, lifeless bodies of both American and German soldiers were a disquieting sight across the breadth of the Hürtgen Forest floor; here a squad of Rangers passes the remains of a Wehrmacht machine gun nest. *Courtesy of the U.S. Army Signal Corps.*

The Hürtgen Forest was home to scores of hidden German pillboxes—here denuded of its camouflaging pine logs and conifer boughs and branches—that constituted but a small portion of the 390-mile-long Siegfried Line. It stretched from the Dutch border in the northwest to the High Rhine abutting Switzerland in the southeast. *Courtesy of the U.S. Army Signal Corps.*

The Ranger Battalion's "Doc" Block assigned an aid man to every patrol scouring the forest; they did not lack for work, nor did their Red Cross brassards prevent hidden enemy ambush sites from trying to kill them. *Courtesy of the U.S. Army Signal Corps.*

The forest hamlet of Bergstein—the jumping-off point for the assault on Hill 400 and home to the formerly quaint tourist lodge the Hurtgen Hotel—resembled nothing so much as a fetid pile of rubble by the time the Rangers arrived on the morning of December 7, 1944. *Courtesy of the U.S. Army Signal Corps.*

Hill 400 as seen from across the killing field the Rangers crossed as they charged the height. The German artillery-spotting tower is visible on the center right of the crest. *Courtesy of Bartek Kwasniewski.*

The mild-mannered Dog Company platoon sergeant Ed Secor almost single-handedly turned back one of the multiple German counterattacks atop Hill 400 on December 7. *Courtesy of the U.S. Army.*

In Czechoslovakia in June 1945, their mission accomplished, surviving 2nd Ranger Battalion soldiers are awarded medals by General Ernest Harmon. *Courtesy of the U.S. Army.*

James Earl Rudder in 1969, when he was president of Texas A&M University, and his World War II mentor, General Troy Middleton, who was president emeritus of Louisiana State University. *Courtesy of Dr. Thomas Hatfield/University of Texas.*

Among those attending the June 1984 ceremonies commemorating the fortieth anniversary of the Normandy invasion were *(left to right)* Amos Potts (U.S. Army Signal Corps photographer) and the Rangers Sid Salomon, Ted Lapres, Dick Merrill, Otto "Big Stoop" Masny, and Ralph Goranson. *Courtesy of Richard Merrill.*

of the enemy's 4711 aftershave from yards away.* And given the ubiquitous mud, Lieutenant Len Lomell advised his Dog Company platoon to wrap rags around the triggers and bolts of their M1s and to cover the muzzles with condoms to keep them clean. When the rags became too filthy and the condoms tore, waxed paper from ration boxes filled the bill.

True to his earlier vow, Lomell also somehow managed to convince the battalion's logistics officer, George Williams, to begin scrounging sacks of coffee beans from rear elements in Belgium. Crushing the beans with the flat of his trench knife and using jerricans of water and makeshift stoves assembled from abandoned oil tins, he constructed a coffee station in the corner of the bomb-blasted hotel basement that Dog and Charlie Companies had commandeered in Vossenack. When it came time to change watch shifts, Lomell ensured that hot joe and unrolled bedrolls awaited Rangers coming in from the cold.

What he could not requisition or pilfer, however, were fresh socks. To that end he assembled teams to gather buckets of snow to wash each man's filthy socks, which they would dry by the coffee-station fires or, in a pinch, by pressing them into their armpits. Lomell even took a foot-massaging course from a Britisher stationed in Vossenack as a forward observer. While men coming off the line settled into bedrolls, he personally removed their boots and rubbed circulation back into their feet. On particularly frigid nights he filled canteens with hot coffee and, braving snipers, prowled with his bounty from forward foxhole to foxhole. Recalled one Ranger, "Lomell thought he was our mother."

---

* The 4711, so popular with German foot soldiers, was the original eau de Cologne—*Echt Kölnisch Wasser*—produced in the eponymous city since the late eighteenth century. It was named after the address of the original *Parfumladen* at 4711 Glockengasse, Cologne's Clock Tower Square.

Meanwhile, less than a mile northwest of Vossenack, Able and Baker companies had settled into the basements of adjacent shell-pocked houses in Germeter. During their first night in the forest, as several of his Able Company Rangers were igniting a charcoal fire in a bathtub they'd hauled from an upper floor, Lieutenant Bob Edlin had an idea. He shared it with his CO, Bob Arman, who subsequently ordered all hands to grab entrenching tools and follow him outside. Arman's bemused Rangers then pretended to dig foxholes. When Baker Company's Sid Salomon noticed the activity from his command post next door, he followed suit. Both officers knew that they were being watched. When the Rangers finished their dummy digging, they celebrated by shooting and butchering a stray cow. As steaks sizzled over the bathtub "stove," another Ranger discovered a cache of potato wine.

The next morning the earth around the ersatz foxholes rose with the sun as the surrounding ridges echoed with artillery fire. The misplaced shelling continued for the next two hours until the Germans realized they had been duped. "The barrage woke everybody up," Edlin reported to Lt. Col. Rudder, "nothing much more."

The German cannoneers, however, had learned their lessons. The following day a second barrage collapsed the buildings housing Able and Baker Companies. None were killed, but seven of the thirty men in Edlin's basement alone were wounded—a mere portion of the sixteen casualties, including three fatalities, that the battalion would suffer from what became the daily and nightly bombardments. One of Bob Edlin's most terrifying nightmares manifested when, while screaming for a medic, he watched the loose tobacco from a shredded pack of Lucky Strikes disappearing into the cavity of a sucking chest wound suffered by one of his platoon sergeants.

Meanwhile, it was only natural for the old-timers to cast a wary if protective eye toward the eight officers and nearly fifty new enlisted men who had recently shipped into the battalion. Most were good soldiers—they would not have been accepted as Ranger volunteers otherwise. But they had not been blooded, had not seen the elephant. Some were soon gone, killed or wounded before their platoon mates could even learn their names. Others quickly picked up the cat-and-mouse nature of woodland combat. Squad and company commanders began to compare notes on which of the newbies racked up the most confirmed kills or brought in the most prisoners. Col. Rudder would want to know. The next Ranger job, however, called for experience.

27

The Return of the "Fabulous Four"

On November 16, the orders dropped from 8th Division Headquarters like a suicide note. Recon patrol. Schmidt. The belly of the beast.

Lt. Col. Rudder summoned the Fool Lieutenant.

Hiking from the other end of Germeter, it took Bob Edlin nearly thirty minutes to find his commander's new CP. With the headless German stinking up the forest master's basement, Rudder had left Ike Eikner's Headquarters Company there and moved into a tiny hunting cabin on the edge of the wood. There was barely room for the kerosene stove, a small wooden side table, a cot, and a couple of rickety chairs. Rudder nodded toward one. Edlin took a seat. The lieutenant colonel handed him a cup of hot coffee. Edlin lit a Lucky. The walls of the little hut were stained yellow with tobacco smoke and the floorboards still smelled of Wehrmacht hobnailed-boot leather.

It had only been forty-eight hours since Edlin had last seen Rudder, but he seemed to have aged ten years, "like a tired, worn-out old man." The purple sacks under his bloodshot eyes appeared to weigh down his entire face. His deep baritone, however, was as penetrating as ever. "In and out," he told Edlin. "Take just a couple of your guys." There was never a question of who.

Edlin returned to his musty cellar and gathered the usual suspects—Bill "No-Neck" Courtney, Bill "Stoop" Dreher, and Warren "Halftrack" Burmaster. He unfolded a topo map and laid out the mission. Division intelligence operatives needed to know the strength and disposition of the German forces at Schmidt, in particular the location of their artillery emplacements. They would travel light, just tommy guns and trench knives. Not even helmets, knit caps instead. They were not looking for a fight, only information. They left that night.

The temperature hovered near zero when the quartet disappeared into the dark. A new storm had coated the ground with eight or nine inches of fresh powder. For once they welcomed the snow. It would muffle their footsteps.

Fearing the minefields lacing the forest floor, they eschewed their usual diamond-shape formation, instead traveling single file down a firebreak, Edlin on point, Burmaster again the getaway man a hundred yards back. They walked low and slow and stuck to the edges of the trail, aware that they were crossing terrain riddled with enemy bunkers camouflaged to near invisibility behind thick meshes of pine-tree branches. Edlin stopped often, listening for snatches of German conversation. He wished he had the nose of Ralph Goranson's point man.

They waded the black and viscid Kall and scratched up the ridge that led to Schmidt. Picking up the blacktop road that led southeast, they followed it, eyes peeled for any lump in the snow that might indicate a buried *Tellermine*. Edlin signaled a halt on the outskirts of town. Something did not feel right. It was well after midnight, and light from kerosene lamps, even a few guttering candles, shone from windows. But not a single guard was posted. Edlin whispered to Burmaster to wait. He, Courtney, and Dreher moved forward. Halftrack knew the drill. He ducked behind a tree; if they needed him, he'd find them.

They had gone but a few steps when the tingling premonition again washed over Edlin. He stopped and ordered Dreher and Courtney back to Burmaster's position. They tried to argue. Edlin hissed through clenched teeth, "We're going to do this my way." The two retreated.

Edlin, sticking to the outer edges of the town, crawled up one alley and down another, hugging the base of buildings. Still no sign of a human being. He came to a corner structure, a barn of some sort that reeked of cow shit. He heard voices. First German. Then, a little softer, American. POWs? He could not make out what they were saying. He wished now he'd brought Courtney, with his high school German. Every nerve end screamed *fight*. Bum-rush the door and free those GIs. Deep down he knew better.

He lingered for a few moments, straining to make out a word in English. He could not. Finally, again keeping close to the shadowed foundations of shell-blasted houses, he slipped back to his patrol outside of town. Had it been daylight, the four Rangers would have had a clear view of Vossenack and Germeter below. They scrambled back down the ridge and reforded the Kall, still in single file, this time Burmaster on point, Edlin the rear guard.

The morning light was weak, the color of wet cement, as if the day was ending before it had even begun. It had been twelve hours since Edlin had received his recon orders, but Col. Rudder was still awake when he entered the CP. "Colonel," he said, "it isn't what I saw, but what I didn't see."

"What did you *not* see?"

"Germans," Edlin said. "It's like we could walk right through the town." Then Edlin told Rudder about the voices in the barn.

"You think it's a trap?" Rudder said.

Edlin nodded. "Like they were watching me the whole time." He paused. "Like Darby at Cisterna."

Rudder dismissed Lt. Edlin. He, Courtney, Dreher, and Burmaster made their way back to their basement digs in the blasted hotel basement. As he laid out his bedroll, Bob Edlin wondered what the intel guys would make of his strange report.

The last weeks of November were what passed for routine on the line in the Hürtgen—Ranger patrols avoiding minefields, snipers, and hidden bunkers. Plus, always, the shellings of Germeter and Vossenack, as regular as the Angelus. Sporadic at night to keep nerves frayed, more intense during the day when German spotters could sight targets. Evening after evening found the same sentence in the battalion diary—"Moderate to intense artillery and mortar fire fell in the Bn area throughout day."

To this point, the autumn of 1944 had produced weather of near record severity in the forest. It rained or snowed each day as the freezing temperatures—historically an anomaly along the German-Belgian border—came early and refused to leave. With thermometers hovering in the teens, leather on shoepacs cracked and soaking overcoats became so heavy with moisture and frozen mud that they were discarded. Some enterprising Rangers draped them over fenceposts in the hope they would draw fire. Hot meals forwarded from the rear were rare, and fresh clothing, particularly sorely needed socks, were mere rumors. To warm themselves, men would drape their soggy blankets over the embers of fires set during the day— never at night—and then throw the stinking coverlets over their shoulders like serapes. This provided at least a few moments of blessed relief from the cold.

Perhaps worst of all, there were no letters from home, no cookies crushed to crumbs, no local newspapers. Of course, only a fool
would chance a mail run into the Hürtgen. Perhaps taking their cue
from Gen. Hodges, senior officers visiting the front were nearly as
scarce as mail couriers. They were content to relay orders by radio
or phone lines in constant need of repair from bomb damage.

The Rangers, prowling with keyed-up nerves beneath the dark
umbrella of the fir branches, watched with a mixture of incredu-
lity and dismay as the 8th Division's battalion and rifle company
commanders, still pressing east through the forest, fell dead and
wounded with morose regularity. More than a few commanding
officers were relieved of duty by what one army historian diplomatically described as "the inconclusiveness of the advance."

It was soon apparent that the raw junior officers rushed in to
replace them were woefully unprepared to make tactical decisions
on the ground. Similarly, instead of sending cohesive squads or platoons with their own cadre of noncoms into the cold and rain to take
the places of fallen veterans, untested enlisted men were rushed forward willy-nilly into the maw. Predictably, for the most part these
poorly trained soldiers found front-line combat beyond their ken.
"Our missing men were mostly the replacements," a weary master
sergeant told the army historian Charles MacDonald. He added
that the shock of constant artillery bombardments caused many of
the new men to simply "scatter and run."

One visiting officer from the Ninth Army's Historical Section recorded a scathing memo from the forest's front lines. "The only thing
that higher headquarters contributed to the debacle was pressure,"
he wrote. "It had the effect of ordering men to die needlessly. Tactics and maneuver on battalion or regiment scale were conspicuous
by their absence. It never seemed to occur to anyone that the plan
might be wrong. The companies went into battle against the for-

midable Siegfried Line with hand grenades and rifle bullets against pillboxes."*

On November 19, the lethal tedium for the Rangers was momentarily broken when Charlie, Dog, Easy, and Fox Companies were ordered to send scouts to the rear to guide fresh GI reinforcements through the woods into Germeter and Vossenack. From there the new soldiers were bound for the front. Despite harassing salvos from enemy mortars and 88s, the mission went off without a hitch. Two days later, Sid Salomon's Baker Company was charged with moving east to protect the flank of an 8th Division regiment, the 121st, attempting to clear a paved ridgeline road connecting the tiny hamlet of Kleinhau to the village of Bergstein, north of Schmidt. Kleinhau? Bergstein? Did this mean they were bypassing Schmidt? Salomon did not ask. Above his pay grade.

Salomon's Baker Company moved out in single file at ten that night, each Ranger holding on to the belt of the man in front of him as they trudged through the Stygian darkness. A few hours later Salomon halted the men at the ridgeline that was to serve as their dispersal point. He kept his first platoon with him, hugging the fringe of the wooded heights, and sent the second platoon across a small clearing studded with a few scattered conifers. The first mine exploded within moments, killing Private First Class Paul Bryant.

It was as if the initial blast touched flame to the fuse of a string of murderous firecrackers. A second explosion blew off Sergeant John Zuravel's right foot; a third detonated beneath another PFC, Thomas Moore. By the time Sergeant Paul Donlin's leg disappeared in a rust-red mist of soil and snow, Salomon screamed a halt. No

---

* The same Ninth Army historian later calculated an odd fact unnoted at the time—some 50 percent of the GIs fighting in the Hürtgen Forest were from families of German-American descent. This meant that three-quarters of the combatants facing each other across the dark forest floor shared a Teutonic heritage.

man from the 2nd Platoon was to move again until dawn. Some Rangers froze like statues; others dropped to their knees.

As the 1st Platoon dug in along the periphery of the clearing to provide cover, the medic Willie Clark dashed into the minefield, heedless of the death underfoot. He raced between Zuravel, Moore, and Donlin, jabbing them with morphine syrettes and applying gauze bandages. There was nothing he could do for Bryant. Sid Salomon was exasperated; he couldn't afford to lose his only medic. Yet he couldn't fault Clark; he was doing what he was trained to do. Keeping one watchful eye on his roving aid man, Salomon dispatched a runner back to Col. Rudder. The message was brief. His company was cornered not far from the German front lines, and sitting ducks come first light.

28

"How Bad Is It?"

To Bob Edlin, it was déjà vu. The hut. The stove, the small table, the chairs, the cot. The hot cup of coffee. Only this time Able Company's Captain Bob Arman had joined Col. Rudder, who laid out Baker Company's predicament. Nodding toward Arman, Rudder explained that Arman's outfit was saddling up to relieve Sid Salomon's company. But, given the fluid front lines, that would take close to twenty-four hours. In the meanwhile, a volunteer patrol was needed to immediately access Baker's situation and evacuate the most severely wounded.

Rudder had come to view Edlin as a surrogate son of sorts, a Ranger whose feel for combat was only surpassed by—or perhaps due to—his love for his comrades. He looked at Edlin. Paused for a brief moment. Then spoke. "Bob, I'm not going to order you to go," he said. "But that's the situation."

A thousand crazy thoughts ricocheted through Edlin's mind. He thought of the fear he had felt both on the troop ship heading to Normandy and when Bill Courtney had first bounded into the Lochrist Battery: *I can't take any more of this. I'm tired and scared.*

This would be pure hell, and I can't stand to see any more of my platoon getting slaughtered.

He voiced none of these. He said he would go.

This time they chanced a jeep, even though it was daylight. Speed mattered. There were five Rangers—Edlin, Courtney, Dreher, Burmaster, and the medic Billy Geitz from Ike Eikner's Headquarters Company. Doc Block suggested they bring an aid man in case something had happened to Willie Clark. The squad was rounded out by a driver from the 8th Division who insisted his vehicle was not going anywhere without him. Snow was coming down heavily again, thick, dry flakes falling like a theater curtain. This was good. Maybe it would hide them. The closer they came to Baker Company's position, the louder the detonations of the German artillery and mortars and the long *braaats* of enemy machine guns echoing across the ridge.

It took less than an hour to reach the gunfight. The driver skidded the jeep to a halt, and the medic Geitz grabbed one stretcher. When the driver dismounted and slung a Thompson submachine gun over his shoulder, Edlin barked, "You stay here and watch the jeep."

The soldier stood his ground. "You think somebody's gonna steal it?" Edlin saw the logic. Geitz handed the driver a second stretcher.

The six men moved out, Edlin on point, Bill Dreher marking their path through the minefield with luminous engineering tape strung from tree stump to tree stump. The snow made it nearly impossible to see just a few feet ahead. They walked, bent low, toward the distinctive reports of M1 rifles and the "sickening sweet odor of cordite." A German flare lit up the area. Edlin was astounded. Trees hacked to kindling by artillery fire littered the forest floor like enormous spillikins, dead Germans and Americans splayed among them. One Ranger referred to the clearing as "the land of six-foot trees."

As Salomon had predicted, the sunrise had proven deadly. When the German gunners opened up with 88s and 150s, the 2nd Platoon's mortarmen had retaliated, firing blind. The Rangers trapped in the mined clearing had a choice—stand and die or scatter and maybe die. Most had somehow worked their way out of the minefield, but there were more men down now.

Suddenly Edlin felt frozen, unsure if he could take another step. A huge hand clapped his shoulder. "Drop back behind Courtney," Bill Dreher said, handing Edlin the roll of luminous tape. "I'll get point for a while." From behind him Edlin heard Courtney's voice. "Well, what the hell, Lieutenant, you volunteered, didn't you?"

From thereon they took turns out front, even the GI jeep driver. When they reached Baker Company's dug-in line, someone led Edlin to Sid Salomon's makeshift command post under a small log bridge beside a woodcutter's trail. The bridge had taken a near-direct hit from a German 88, wounding four of Salomon's staff but leaving the lieutenant unscathed.

Salomon and Edlin hugged. Edlin told Salomon that Able Company was not far behind. His patrol had marked a tape path through the minefield for Baker Company to follow out and to guide Able Company in. Meanwhile, he said, they had a jeep nearby to take out the most critically wounded. Salomon lifted his chin toward a nearby swale. Some Rangers, their bandages oozing blood, sat with their backs to tree trunks. Edlin spotted Willie Clark kneeling over a prone body. "Two at a time, let's carry them out," Edlin said.

Courtney and the jeep driver had already loaded an unconscious Ranger onto their canvas litter. Bill Geitz had rolled another onto the second stretcher and had picked up the front end. Geitz was a small, thin man, and he had no idea he was standing on a *Schümine* buried beneath the snow. When Edlin hefted the back end of the litter, he shifted the weight of the wounded Ranger toward Geitz. The detonation blew Geitz's left foot off and knocked Edlin backward. His head slammed hard into a tree. The last thing he remembered seeing was the wounded man's body soaring skyward amid snatches of torn canvas.

Bill Dreher threw Edlin over his shoulder like a rag doll and raced for the jeep. Bill Courtney and Warren Burmaster lifted Geitz on top of the Ranger already loaded on the first litter and followed. They laid all three men in the vehicle and told the driver to haul ass.

When Bob Edlin came to, he was still on the stretcher. He could make out a dim light. He couldn't feel his left hand, and assumed it was gone. He could only hear out of one ear but recognized Doc Block's voice. "Wash his eyes out with boric acid, it's just dirt and mud. Then get him on a truck to the field hospital."

Edlin's voice was little more than a croak. "How bad is it?"

"A little shrapnel in your hand and face. They'll fix you up in the rear. It's mostly shock and some mud."

With that someone jabbed a morphine syrette into Edlin's thigh. As two of Doc Block's assistants slid his stretcher into an ambulance truck, he asked about the others. Courtney and Dreher and Burmaster. The jeep driver. The medic Geitz. At that final name an aid man lifted his chin toward another body in the bed of the truck. Geitz, also full of morphine, was moaning softly.

Enemy artillery chased the ambulance west nearly to the edge of the forest. A morphine thought struck Bob Edlin: *It ought to be against the rules to shoot at you when you're leaving somewhere.*

The light was brighter here, wherever *here* was. Someone was running a washcloth over Edlin's face. His left hand now thumped with pain. He heard a voice, the words muffled, something about shipping him back to a hospital in Belgium. Edlin croaked as loud as he could: "Wait just a damn minute."

A doctor appeared. He wore the oak leaves of a major. He said he didn't have the time to treat minor wounds, there were too many serious casualties coming in. Nor did he have the inclination to argue with a lieutenant, even a Ranger lieutenant.

Edlin pled his case. A Ranger outfit was in a world of shit out there, and his own company was moving in to reinforce them. He had to be with them. The major stared, hard, at Edlin's left hand. "Lieutenant," he said, "if that hand gets infected, you'll lose it."

"I'd trade a hand for eighty men."

"I can't use anesthesia," the major said, "then you'd have to stay overnight."

Edlin nodded. There were suddenly two burly orderlies on either side of him. One threw his body across Edlin's legs, the other pressed down on his right arm. The major picked up a steel-bristled scrub brush and ran it several times across Edlin's left hand, debriding the wound. The pain was mind-numbing. Then the major produced a scalpel and a pair of tweezers. Edlin counted forty-eight pieces of shrapnel pinging into a pan of soapy water. He surprised himself by not passing out.

Finally, the major bandaged Edlin's hand. "You're on your own," he said.

Edlin asked the major if he had any kids. Two boys back home, he said. Edlin dug into his pocket with his good right hand and retrieved a crumpled wad of Reichsmarks he'd lifted off a dead German. "Send them this," he said. The major took the money. Edlin walked out of the tent.

Lieutenant Bob Edlin hitched a ride back to Germeter on an 8th Division water truck. When the usual mortar and 88 mm shells landed too close at Purple Heart Corner, he and the driver joked about abandoning the vehicle and hightailing it over the nearest ridgeline and out of the damn Hürtgen Forest. Neither had any idea that it was Thanksgiving night. They had missed out on the dense and chalky Hershey "D bars" that had been distributed for the holiday, as well as the dinner of slabs of turkey meat piled on stale corn bread sent up from the rear. After weeks of K rations and the by-now ubiquitous 10-in-1s—large food parcels intended to provide one meal for ten men—the Rangers had wolfed the sandwiches as well as the tins of cold mashed potatoes, stuffing, cranberry sauce, and even brussels sprouts. Edlin and the water truck driver might have counted themselves lucky. "We had our turkey today," reads Doc Block's entry in his journal for November 24. "Everyone got a stomach cramp and diarrhea, including myself."

It was dark when the water truck reached Germeter, and the cellar of the house that Edlin's Able Company platoon called home was deserted, the ashes from the bathtub charcoal fire gone cold. Bob Arman, Edlin realized, had already moved out to relieve Baker. He made his way to Col. Rudder's CP. It, too, was empty. He lit a crude lamp—an old canteen filled with kerosene, with a filthy sock for a wick—and slumped into one of the colonel's chairs. He thought of his men up on the line. Courtney and Dreher and Burmaster and the rest. Had he abandoned them? He wondered who was still standing from Sid Salomon's outfit. He was trying to summon the strength to head out when Doc Block entered the cabin. "Doc, if you give me something for the pain, I'll go back up there at daybreak."

"Boy, you ain't going anywhere. Get your butt in that bunk and stay there."

Okay, Edlin thought, *I'll just rest my eyes until sunrise.* He awoke twenty-four hours later. Col. Rudder was dozing on one of the chairs. As he listened to his commanding officer's soft snores, Edlin glanced at the table piled with paper. The most recent report from the front was dated November 26. The Rangers had entered the forest twelve days ago. It felt more like twelve months.

· · ·

Bob Edlin was not the only Ranger counting heads as Able Company limped back into Germeter at dusk on November 27. Enemy artillery had slacked off and Lt. Col. Rudder was also out, flanked by his XO, Ed Arnold, his intel officer, Harvey Cook, and the battalion's logistics officer, George Williams. Doc Block and a small squad of aid men hovered, eyes peeled for men who had not reported their wounds. They watched as Bob Arman led fifty-seven enlisted men and two officers into the village. An outside observer would have mistaken the company for no more than a platoon. All told, Baker and Able had taken fifty casualties across the previous four days of fighting.

Duke Slater welcomed Arman's outfit with hot food and coffee, warm blankets, and, finally, newly arrived dry socks. Most men ate in silence, collected their new supplies, and filed back to the wrecked basements that served as their living quarters. Some lit fires in makeshift stoves. The majority collapsed into deep sleep. By the time they awoke the next day, the elements of the 8th Infantry Division whose flank Sid Salomon and his Baker Company had been sent out to protect were finally driving forward on the little village of Kleinhau. It fell to the Americans the next afternoon, November 29.

Back in Germeter, the ensuing days felt like a rerun of the battalion's post-Normandy lull. Now officially attached to the 8th Infantry Division as a rapid-reaction force, the Rangers were pulled and stretched like taffy as the division's sundry regiments frantically summoned them for relief assignments, only for the missions to be just as abruptly canceled. With new faces filing in daily to fill in the dilapidated ranks of his rifle companies, Lt. Col. Rudder and his staff tried to keep the men combat ready.

Rudder recognized that prolonged exposure to a combination of bone-chilling cold and lethal living conditions led to emotional, mental, and physical fatigue even among his most battle-hardened veterans. The army system of deploying individual replacements into the battalion—as opposed to squads or platoons en masse—only contributed to the torpor by reminding the Rangers of friends they had lost. To offset any creeping malaise, Rudder revived dead-of-night tactical exercises, and though sporadic enemy artillery rounds still fell on the surrounding roads and firebreaks, daily speed marches were reinstituted. One of these training runs nearly turned disastrous when, on a rare clear day, a wayward flight of Messerschmitt fighter planes spotted the Americans bunched together on a road. But the Rangers scattered into the forest before the strafing began. No one was injured.

A few days into December, some twenty deuce-and-a-halfs rolled into Germeter. Lt. Col. Rudder, intuiting they were meant to move his battalion, radioed 8th Division headquarters. He was told to stand by for an imminent relocation. Rudder suspected his outfit was about to be attached to the incoming 83rd Division, which was relieving the 4th Division to his north. As it turned out, no follow-up orders ever arrived regarding the trucks, but Rudder managed to put the vehicles to use, instituting day-and-night practice alerts for motorized echelons. From the moment word was passed, each company was allotted thirty minutes to stow their combat gear in the vehicles and be ready to roll out. At first these scrambling dry runs, in particular lugging the heavy mortars and machine guns in the pitch dark, solidified what exhausted troopers groused as the "whiskey-tango-foxtrot" nature of war—"What the fuck?" Gradually, however, the Rangers became so squared away at packing and saddling up that Rudder reported to his superiors that his men were prepared to move toward any pending emergency within twenty minutes.

This was welcome news at 8th Division headquarters. The capture of the hamlets of Hürtgen and Kleinhau meant the Americans now controlled the hub of the best road network between the forest and the Roer River. It was, according to the War Department's official history, a "bridgehead" bypassing Schmidt and leading directly southeast to Bergstein, the sentinel that protected the commanding terrain of Hill 400. Just beyond that pernicious height lay the hydroelectric dams and, in the eyes of the First Army's Gen. Hodges, the pathway to the Rhine.

But the Germans could also read a map.

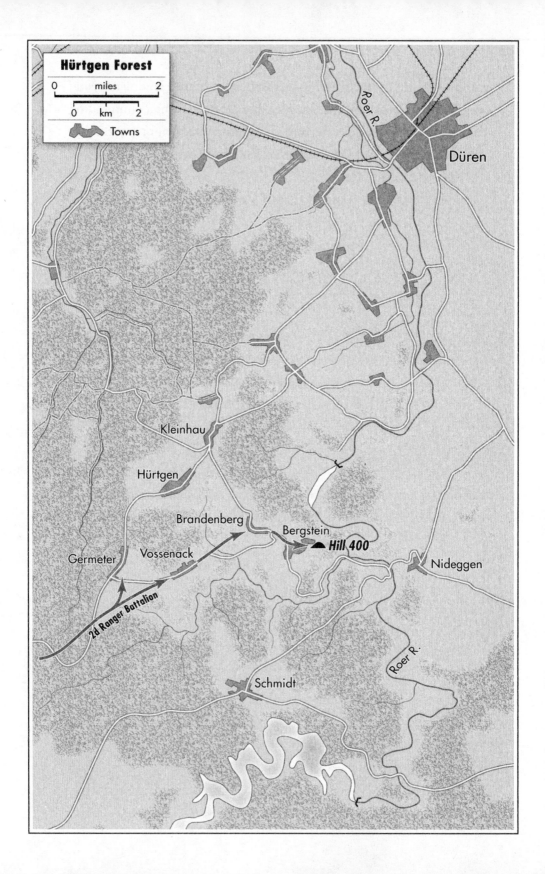

Hürtgen Forest

0   miles   2

0   km   2

Towns

Roer R.

Düren

Kleinhau

Hürtgen

Brandenberg

Bergstein

Hill 400

Germeter

Vossenack

Nideggen

2d Ranger Battalion

Schmidt

Roer R.

PART V

The Hill

Some people say D-Day, June 6, 1944, was their longest day. But for me, December 7, 1944—assaulting and climbing that steep and slippery hill in the Hürtgen Forest—was the longest, worst, and the most dangerous day of my life.

—LEONARD LOMELL

29

Bergstein

I t was soon clear to American commanders on the ground in the Hürtgen Forest that the so-called "bridgehead" to Bergstein and Hill 400 established by the capture of Kleinhau had altered a key combat metric. The GIs—specifically, elements of General William Weaver's 8th Infantry Division—could now avoid the troublesome town of Schmidt and approach the highest ground in the woodland from the north. This was so apparent that Gen. Weaver was already making plans for an assault down the highway with two battalions—the 10th Tank and the 47th Armored Infantry of the 5th Armored Division's Combat Command Reserve (CCR)—before the First Army's Gen. Hodges even delivered official orders to that effect.

As Hodges saw it, the only obstacle standing between Weaver's armored column and Bergstein was the tiny, German-controlled village of Brandenberg. Neither general officer was worried. Sherman tanks were finally getting into the Hürtgen game, taking advantage of the blacktop thoroughfare that ran south-by-southeast from Kleinhau to Brandenberg. The tanks, they felt, would make short work of any Germans occupying the latter. What the Americans failed to take into account was that running a convoy down that two-mile corridor was, as an army historian later phrased it, "like attacking down a fairway while the enemy controlled the rough on either side." This included the thick forest to the west, which separated the Kleinhau-Brandenberg highway from reinforcements fighting their way from Vossenack.

Like all previous American operations in the Hürtgen, the assault on Brandenberg initially faltered. First, elements of two 8th Division infantry regiments out of Vossenack were bogged down by strong resistance while attempting to clear the dense woods separating them from the armored column—the right rough, to extend the army historian's golf metaphor. Then, as the American convoy lurched south from Kleinhau shortly after sunrise on December 2, tank after tank moving in near single file—"canalized," in military argot—was disabled by *Tellermines* as they weaved through a steady rain of artillery fire directed from Hill 400.

The subsequent logjam created fat targets for German machine gunners and mortarmen secreted in bunkers to either side of the road. So ruinous was the three-pronged enemy defense—mines, artillery, and small-arms fire—that Weaver was forced to halt the convoy until sundown, when a nearby engineering company laying out culverts and drainage ditches was summoned to clear the mines under cover of darkness.

Working through the night, the engineers—still wearing their rubber hip boots—removed no less than 250 *Tellermines* from the highway, and the armored assault was again scheduled for dawn the next day, December 3. In what the Americans must have taken as an omen, for only the third morning in the last month the rising sun piercing the azure sky resembled a bright red dahlia, its blossoms ablaze. Gen. Weaver's ecstatic convoy commander called in air support. Soon the drone of P-47 Thunderbolts—the by-now dreaded *Jagdbombers, Jabos* to the Germans—was heard in the west. Within moments the aircraft appeared, their wings and fuselages painted in black and white stripes for easy recognition.

Combat air controllers, using VHF radio, directed the heavy fighters to their targets, and their 5-inch rockets and .50-caliber machine guns plowed a lethal path into Brandenberg. The armored vehicles on the ground followed fast in the furrows. Even when the point tanks reached the northern threshold of the village the convoy commander urged the fighter pilots to continue pummeling the hamlet. "Keep the buzz boys up!" he shouted to his radio operator. "We're at the critical stage."

"Six minutes later (at 09:26)," as the army's history of the operation records, American tanks were blasting Brandenberg's buildings to rubble as trailing CCR infantrymen leapt from half-tracks and boiled down into the town's basements to root out enemy holdouts. Shortly before noon an eerie hush fell over Brandenberg. The village, less than half a mile from Bergstein, had been secured.

Compared to previous assaults throughout the Hürtgen, the Americans initially rejoiced at the low casualty reports. Nonetheless, Gen. Weaver deemed his garrison's strength inadequate to continue pushing on to Bergstein. More disheartening, after the morning's brief sunny respite, the sky had again marbled, and reports of a blinding sleet storm riding the western winds toward the American air bases in Belgium forced the withdrawal of the P-47s. With no close air support available, the fight for Bergstein was going to be a ground-and-pound affair.

As Weaver's rifle companies disappeared into the ice-crusted woods east and southeast of the ridgeline leading to Bergstein to cover the convoy's flanks, the 10th Battalion's tanks, halftracks, and peeps—as armored units referred to their jeeps—halted in Brandenberg's town square. There they awaited reinforcement from Vossenack.

· · ·

The Rangers watched from the few rooftops still intact as the small task force of Shermans rolled down Vossenack's main street. Their mission: clear out the Rubble Pile on the eastern edge of the village. No one doubted that the tanks would make short work of the last fortified impediment on the road to Brandenberg. Incredibly, however, the Germans ensconced beneath the heaps of blasted brick and concrete held out for nearly twenty-four hours as salvo after salvo of 75 mm rounds reduced their position to dust. Finally, at sunrise on December 4, a white flag was hoisted through the cracks. By the next afternoon Gen. Weaver's convoy in Brandenberg, buttressed by the contingent of Shermans from Vossenack, was rolling into Bergstein and in view of Hill 400.

As one Ranger described it, the 2nd Battalion's frustrated special operators—not even called upon to help clear the Rubble Pile—felt rather like baseball fans hovering over a radio announcer's play-by-play as, on the morning of December 5, they followed the progress of the GIs moving on Bergstein. Although American planes had been grounded, the sky was still clear to the east, and a frisson of alarm roiled the Ranger ranks as word spread of a massive Luftwaffe attack, some sixty Messerschmitt Me 109s bombing and strafing Weaver's tankers and ground troops. But by midday it was reported that the bulk of Bergstein was in American hands, notwithstanding the small pockets of steadfast German resistance abetted by the feared Wehrmacht snipers.

Moreover, as casualty numbers trickled in from the 8th Division's forest-fighting units to the east and southeast, the realization dawned that the assault on Bergstein had been far more calamitous than originally thought. The Americans holding the town were down to sixteen working tanks and fewer than five hundred weary infantrymen. A decidedly weak occupying force. From Gen. Hodges down to the rawest Ranger, a perplexed thought prevailed—just how badly did the enemy want to hold that damn hill?

Of course, the Americans were unaware that even as GIs probed Bergstein's root cellars and hidden bunkers for enemy diehards, German army commanders along the Roer River were receiving urgent messages from General Walter Model. Despite Model's dreadnought pretensions, the monocled Prussian was widely regarded as one of the Wehrmacht's most adept minds when it came to both strategy and tactics. He well understood that the imposing heights of Hill 400 were the gateway to the Roer, which in turn opened a clear pathway across the Cologne plain, where his northernmost forces were already assembling in preparation for the Ardennes offensive. Model ordered Bergstein retaken and Hill 400 held at all costs, lest its capture jeopardize the execution of *Wacht am Rhein*—the forthcoming Battle of the Bulge.

In accordance with Model's instructions, his armored troop commander at the front, General der Panzertruppen Erich Brandenberger, redirected two battalions from one of his new *Volks-Grenadier* divisions, the 272nd, to the further defense of the area. It was a fraught decision. The 272nd was one of the twenty-nine infantry divisions that Gen. Model planned on folding into the assault force covertly assembling for the German counteroffensive. Model had in fact earmarked the ten-thousand-man unit to play a key role in the offensive through the Ardennes. Learning of Brandenberger's order, Model was unhappy. He could not afford to jeopardize the 272nd's existence.

Gen. Brandenberger, attempting to mollify his superior, assured Model that once the battalions from the 272nd had helped retake Bergstein and stabilized the state of affairs around Hill 400, the units would be returned to their parent division. Model nonetheless

fretted. For the 272nd stood out from the motley collection of un-
dertrained conscripts that constituted most *Volks-Grenadier* units.
Its troopers were fierce and, given the course of the war, such soldiers were becoming as extinct as the lion-killing Masai warriors
that the young Walter Model had read about as a cadet in *Kriegs-
schule*. Losing the unit in the Hürtgen would constitute one more
blow against the Reich's paling chances of survival.

Under the command of Lieutenant General Friedrich-August
Schack, the "new" 272nd had been reconstituted from Gen. Schack's
previous division of the same numerical designation. That unit had
lost more than half its strength during the summer's pitched battles
with British and Canadian forces on the Normandy coast around
Caen. In a quirk of fate, however, a sizable contingent of the "old"
division's hardened officers and NCOs had escaped from northern
France. They had subsequently overseen the integration of an inordinate proportion of *Kriegsmarine* sailors and Luftwaffe airmen
who had been transferred into the infantry. This combination of
veteran leadership and able-bodied war fighters had allowed the
272nd to "achieve a level of operational capability" more rapidly
than most, if not all, other *Volks-Grenadier* divisions.

  Prior to D-Day, the original three infantry regiments and one
artillery regiment of the 272nd had performed admirably in battles on the eastern front south of Moscow. That, as well as the
efficiency with which Gen. Schack had extricated so many of his
officers from France, led to his promotion to corps commander as
the unit was being reconfigured. He was replaced by the equally
capable Colonel Georg Kossmala. Despite the forty-eight-year-old
Kossmala's rough-hewn appearance—with his flattened nose, lop-
sided ears, and off-kilter chin he gave the impression of someone
who had been run over by a panzer and too-hastily reassembled—

the colonel was one of only 882 recipients of the Knight's Cross of the Iron Cross with Oak Leaves, awarded for his leadership and gallantry on the *Ostfront*.

By early December of 1944, American intelligence operatives were aware of the reinforcement of the area around Hill 400. Prisoner interrogations and radio intercepts had even provided them with the specific *Volks-Grenadier* battalions that had been diverted into the Hürtgen. Few Americans, however, took seriously the combat capability of what they referred to in shorthand as the reconstructed 272nd "VGD." Such was Gen. Hodges's overconfidence that these "old men and boys" would fold without a fight that they were specifically targeted with psychological warfare leaflets dropped over their lines by air and by shell. Alluding to the original 272nd's near annihilation at Caen, one of the propaganda messages read, "You know the fate that awaits you all. When we begin our major attack . . . the fate of the new 272nd VGD will be the same as the one experienced by the old. Surrender now!"

Yet the amalgamated officers and noncoms of the 272nd, having survived both the Russian front and Normandy, maintained a weary sense of detachment upon entering the Hürtgen. They assumed they had seen far worse.

They came in their heavy winter overcoats an hour before sunrise on December 6, their footsteps muffled by the carpet of freshly fallen snow. The *Volksgrenadiers* poured into Bergstein by the hundreds behind four tank-like assault guns and five Panzer tank destroyers, their approach obscured by the darkness.* The dazed Americans were taken aback by the automatic fire of the new *Sturmgewehr* 44

---

* Because of its angled armor and long barrel, the Panzer tank destroyer was often confused by the Allies with the Panzer tank, as was the case in the American after-action reports describing the German counterattack on Bergstein.

assault rifles the enemy infantrymen had been issued; GIs across the Western Front had grown accustomed to the sounds of the Wehrmacht's single-shot, bolt-action Mausers.*

As the Germans breached the American lines, close combat raged for two hours up and down Bergstein's streets and spilled into its shattered buildings. Streams of blood ran down staircases as vicious room-to-room fighting ensued. Select enemy soldiers stalked American tanks with recoilless, handheld *Panzerfausts*—light, single-shot, and disposable antitank weapons whose warheads, known as "armored fists," could shred the thin flank skin of a Sherman. American tank gunners, shaken by the *Panzerfaust* assault, strained to spot the enemy tank destroyers through the morning's thick haze. When they did manage to locate one, their 75 mm rounds bounced off the angled German armor like rubber balls.

Finally, the few American tank destroyers armed with 76 mm cannons bulled in and turned back the enemy's rolling thunder. What was left of the German foot soldiers—perhaps half of the two to three hundred *Volksgrenadiers* who had taken part in the assault—fell back with them.

The retreat, however, was merely the signal for the artillery spotters atop Hill 400 to direct what would become a daylong bombardment of Bergstein, interrupted only by two more *Volksgrenadiers* attempts to take the village. Although both failed, the American perimeter was contracting perilously, with the Germans even managing to establish a small salient on the southeastern edge of the hamlet. As darkness fell and the sleet storm from the west finally reached Bergstein, Gen. Weaver was forced to throw his engineering and reconnaissance platoons into the defense of the position. A regimental staff officer painted a grim picture of the enervated American troops:

---

* The *Sturmgewehr* 44, more colloquially known as the *Maschinepistole* 44, was the world's first modern assault rifle, and subsequently became a model for both the American M16 and the Russian AK-47.

"The men of this battalion are physically exhausted," he wrote. "The spirit and will to fight are there; the physical ability to continue is gone. . . . These men are shivering with cold and their hands are so numb that they have to help one another on with their equipment. I firmly believe that every man up there should be evacuated through medical channels."

Thus, with the enemy combing the western slope of Hill 400 and Bergstein open to further counterattacks from nearly all sides, a desperate Weaver reached out to Gen. Hodges. With only six Shermans and six tank destroyers still operable and entire companies from his armored infantry shredded, he reported that without more troops he was uncertain if he could hold his ground, much less seize Hill 400. He asked Hodges to release the 2nd Ranger Battalion to his command. Hodges complied. Weaver, relieved, gathered his staff. He told them that he would order the Rangers up Hill 400 just before first light the next morning. He added that he would leave it to Lt. Col. Rudder and his tactical officers to come up with a plan of attack.

30

Rudderless

Twelve hours before the 2nd Ranger Battalion was summoned to Bergstein—around the time that the leading elements of Colonel Georg Kossmala's *Volksgrenadiers* crept through the predawn darkness toward their surprise attack on the village—an odd radio message arrived in Ike Eikner's communications post in Germeter. Lt. Col. Rudder had been ordered to report to Gen. Hodges's First Army Headquarters, across the Belgian border at Spa. Rudder had immediately commandeered a jeep and a driver and departed.

When he had not returned by midafternoon, his subordinates began to fret. Eikner's increasingly agitated radio messages to Spa seeking Rudder's whereabouts went unanswered. Meanwhile, multiple reports from Bergstein indicated that far from pacifying the village, the American tankers and armored infantry were engaged in a series of debilitating firefights when not being inundated by incoming artillery. Rudder's senior staff correctly presumed that sooner rather than later the 2nd Battalion would be pulled into the fray.

It was long past sundown on December 6 when Rudder's jeep careered back down Germeter's main street at the same time that

Eikner relayed a radio directive from Gen. Weaver ordering the Rangers to depart for Bergstein. George Williams, unaware of Rudder's return, began distributing ammunition and food to company commanders—a one-day supply of K rations for each man—while Harvey Cook liaised with his 8th Division counterpart to obtain maps of Bergstein and Hill 400, overlays of friendly-force positions in and around the village, and passwords to be used for the next three days. When the two made their way to the 2nd Battalion's assembly point some two thousand yards south of Vossenack, awaiting them were Rudder, Duke Slater, and Ed Arnold.

With combat looming, Rudder did not have time to write out and distribute his usual tactical assault plan. Instead, glancing at the maps Cook had managed to gather, he merely told the officers that they were to divide into two task forces, one to establish a defensive perimeter around Bergstein and the other to take Hill 400. Then he dropped his bombshell—he had been transferred, effective immediately, to assume command of the 109th Infantry Regiment in Dutch Cota's 28th Division.

Rudder's officers were stunned. The transfer was technically a well-deserved promotion, from battalion commander to regimental commander. Still, given the circumstances, it made no sense. Cota's division was out of harm's way, still recuperating in Belgium from the beating it had taken at Schmidt. Meanwhile, the Ranger battalion's rifle companies were severely understrength—few replacements had arrived since it had entered the forest twenty-one days earlier—with several units operating at 50 percent capacity. How could Gen. Hodges deprive the undermanned outfit of their emotional and spiritual leader on the very eve of battle?

As four quizzical faces gazed at Rudder, he explained that he had tried to postpone the deployment, but Hodges had merely shrugged. The decision, Hodges said, was out of his hands. It had come down from General Troy Middleton, the army's VIII Corps commander. Hodges was not even certain if Gen. Cota was aware of the directive.

At the mention of Middleton's name, a grudging acceptance permeated the small circle of officers. Though Gen. Middleton was officially Gen. Hodges's subordinate, the bespectacled fifty-five-year-old was a legend throughout the United States Army. As a young 2nd lieutenant, he had skirmished against Pancho Villa on the Mexican border, and gone on to command a battalion at the Second Battle of the Marne during World War I. His crowning achievement was spearheading the forty-seven-day Meuse-Argonne offensive that brought an end to the Great War. In recognition of Middleton's rare combination of both strategic and tactical mastery, General John "Black Jack" Pershing had promoted him to colonel. This made Middleton, at twenty-nine, the youngest soldier to achieve the rank in Pershing's American Expeditionary Force.

Back in the United States following the 1918 armistice, Middleton had burnished his reputation while serving as an instructor at the army's Command and General Staff College at Fort Leavenworth—the school from which he had graduated with honors just ahead of his classmate George Patton. At one point during World War II, every general serving as a corps commander in the European Theater of Operations had studied under Middleton. It was at the college where Middleton and Dwight Eisenhower, then teacher and student, had bonded. That close relationship had only intensified as the United States declared war on the Axis powers. Middleton had also followed the exploits of Rudder's Rangers from Pointe du Hoc to Brest and was particularly impressed with the 2nd Battalion's near-bloodless capture of the Lochrist battery. As commander of VIII Corps, Middleton had been responsible for the Brest campaign, and as his star ascended, he was determined to take Rudder with him.

No one in that assembly area south of Vossenack doubted what was left unsaid that night: if Troy Middleton believed in someone, and wanted him promoted and transferred, those orders had come straight through Ike. Trying to reverse or even delay them was akin to cutting red tape sideways.

As his Ranger subordinates stood slack-jawed, Rudder imparted the only two pieces of good news he carried. George Williams had been promoted to major and would assume command of the battalion. And, in appreciation of Rudder's splendid service record, he had managed to negotiate one concession from Gen. Hodges—to be allowed to return to Germeter to bid farewell to his troops. He would even accompany them as far as Brandenberg, their jumping-off point to Bergstein.

That night a motley collection of quartermaster trucks, their blackout lights extinguished and traveling back roads, transported the 2nd Ranger Battalion on a roundabout ten-mile journey to the northern outskirts of Brandenberg. There, in a freezing rain, the men dismounted into mud up to their ankles amid scattered tree bursts and the rolling *ka-rump* of enemy artillery shells echoing from Bergstein, a half mile to the south. Because of the mortar threat, the men were told to assemble in small squads of a dozen or so. Harvey Cook ambled among these pods presenting the coming combat situation to each unit. During one of Cook's addresses a shell burst directly into an overhead conifer. The tree burst killed two Rangers and wounded nine. Cook was unhurt.

The nineteen-year-old Dog Company rifleman Melvin "Bud" Potratz managed to scribble a few words before the outfit jumped off. "Dear Dad: We're going on the line again. Gotta be big! I can see it in sergeant's eyes. He's scared." In fact, what Potratz mistook for fear was a burning desire for revenge on the part of the new staff sergeant Mike Sharik, who had just transferred into the outfit. Before his parents emigrated to the United States, Sharik had spent his early childhood in what was then eastern Czechoslovakia. He despised the Nazi boot on his country's throat. He felt his time for vengeance had arrived.

At five minutes past midnight on the seventh day of December 1944, Big Jim Rudder formally handed George Williams command of the 2nd Ranger Battalion. At the announcement, the former Ranger Robert Black describes Williams's fellow officers staring at the newly minted major "with a feeling of sympathy."

It was true, Black writes, that as a charter member of the 2nd Battalion, Williams had proven his professionalism both during stateside training and in the European theater, including his heroic salvage of most of the battalion's heavy equipment from the horrors of Omaha Beach. "But," Black also notes, "he had been primarily concerned with the logistical needs of the battalion, not in operations. He had not fought, planned, or controlled battles as a company commander. There was no time to become settled into his new assignment. The battalion was moving to contact, and no one could envision how serious this next fight would be."

Although Black could not know it, his last sentence in fact speaks to Col. Rudder's state of mind on that moonless night in Brandenberg. Duke Slater had long been considered Lt. Col. Rudder's heir apparent should Rudder be killed or incapacitated. And though Rudder considered Capt. Slater one of his fiercest fighters, if not the face of the battalion, he was also wary of Slater's aggressiveness. To Rudder's thinking, the Germans, with their western border broached, were already beaten. Despite the American blood that had soaked through the Hürtgen Forest floor, Rudder envisioned the coming weeks and months as a mopping-up operation. George Williams was a competent caretaker who would not take any lethal risks that might result in Rangers dying needlessly before Hitler—or at least his generals—surrendered.

Rudder, naturally, had no idea of the enemy's determination to hold Hill 400 while it prepared for its last-gasp counterattack into Belgium. In no small irony, it was General Troy Middleton, nearly alone among Eisenhower's war planners, who sensed that the Wehrmacht had one final large offensive in it. It was precisely why he had summoned a dependable officer like Rudder to Gen. Cota's command.

As the depleted Ranger battalion began its march on Bergstein, each man again gripping the cartridge belt of the trooper in front of him in order to negotiate the starless night, the throaty roar of a volley of German V-2 buzz bombs seemed to tear the leaden sky as they passed overhead on their journey to England. The noise, however, was small beans compared to the two pieces of news that had jolted the Ranger ranks like an electric current. The first—they were storming the murderous defenses of Hill 400 the next morning. This almost came as a relief; the outfit was built to attack, not to cower in filthy basements or hunker in freezing foxholes whose knee-deep sludge of rain, snow, and mud made their very existence so miserable. Even on those rare occasions when the enemy artillery had let up back in Vossenack and Germeter, a trained special operator could only stare at a poker hand or toss a pair of dice for so long before feeling the need to get back into action.

The second disclosure, however, thumped like a body blow—Big Jim Rudder had been transferred and was leaving. No one could understand why the "old man" was being pulled from the line at such a crucial juncture.

At the southern edge of Brandenberg, Lieutenant Colonel James Earl Rudder stood in the middle of the slick, icy track as the 396 officers and enlisted men of the 2nd Ranger Battalion approached. His helmet rode low, obscuring his broad forehead, and the collar of his overcoat was pulled high and tight against the rain and sleet. Most of the Rangers slogging south in parallel columns did not recognize him in the gloom until they came face-to-face with the only combat commander they had ever known. Rudder shook every man's hand as they passed. He thanked each for his service and repeated the mantra with which he had introduced himself seventeen months earlier at Camp Forrest. "Dig in fast and deep."

When the Fool Lieutenant Bob Edlin neared, Rudder grabbed his shoulder and half-jokingly admonished him, "Quit taking chances."

"No more chances," Edlin dutifully replied. This time he meant it. Or at least so he thought. He considered the lieutenant colonel's departure "probably the greatest loss that [the battalion] suffered during the war."

As Len Lomell shook Rudder's hand, he imagined he saw tears running down the colonel's cheeks, though it could have been the rain. For Lomell, Rudder's departure was a confusing "mix of love and loss."

Indeed, it was with "a heavy heart," as Rudder wrote to his wife, Chick, that he watched his Rangers trudge down that muddy road toward Bergstein. He waited until the last of the rear guard had disappeared before turning away. Then he was gone.

[31]

The Sugarloaf

The GIs in Bergstein were on edge, their nerves as taut as trip wires. After three counterattacks between the incessant shelling, no one doubted that the Germans would come again. The only question was when. Then the scuttlebutt wafted through the frigid village as if carried on a tropical breeze. The Rangers were on their way.

By this point in the war the U.S. armed forces comprised some twelve million men and women. The feelings of solace at the idea that a mere several hundred of these warfighters were rushing to the defense of the beleaguered soldiers from the 10th Tank Division and the 47th Armored Infantry Division seem either a jarring anachronism or a testament to the perceived notion of the special operators' fighting abilities. The official army historian Charles MacDonald opts for the latter. "Probably no news short of rotation to the United States," he observed, "could have cheered the men more than did word that the Rangers were coming."

In the meanwhile, Maj. Williams and his senior staff had worked out the assault plan. Upon reaching Bergstein, Bob Arman's Able Company, Sid Saloman's Baker Company, and Ralph Goranson's

Charlie Company would move through the village and establish defensive blocking positions against a flanking attack on the smaller ridgelines to the south and east. Eight tank destroyers had been attached to the three companies. Arman, Saloman, and Goranson would divvy them up depending on the terrain.

Simultaneously, Richard Merrill's Easy Company would clear any Germans from Bergstein's eastern rim before fanning out through the surrounding woodland to lay down suppressing fire for the Rangers assaulting Hill 400—Big Stoop Masny's Fox Company and the newly promoted Captain Morton McBride's Dog Company. Fox and Dog would attack at sunrise after a brief, predawn artillery barrage raked the heights in hopes of keeping the Germans bunkered up.

Perhaps more propitious than the addition of the tank destroyers was the arrival of the forward artillery observer Lieutenant Howard Kettelhut. Kettelhut, on loan to the Rangers from the 5th Armored Division, would be tasked with coordinating fire from eighteen separate American artillery batteries in support of the Hill 400 operation. Some of the hardier Rangers may have rolled their eyes at the blade-thin, sloe-eyed Nebraskan with the receding hairline and impossibly skinny nose. But the twenty-five-year-old Kettelhut's adroit handling of the big guns the ground pounders called the "King of Battle" would prove exactly what they needed in the coming hours.*

Lieutenant Richard Lewis of the 47th Armored Infantry was growing impatient. The cold rain had turned to a heavy sleet, and his small detachment, having taken a position at a crossroads north of Bergstein, were miserable. Lewis and his squad had been assigned

---

* If artillery was the regal patriarch, the infantry branch of the U.S. Army was dubbed the "Queen of Battle."

the task of guiding the Rangers into the village. But it was getting on toward 2 A.M., and the so-called commandos were already fifteen minutes late. Over the previous forty-eight hours, Lewis's rifle company had been reduced to thirty-seven effectives, and the "faint promise" of Ranger reinforcement was dimming by the moment. He wondered if the rumors about their imminent arrival were just that: rumors.

As the minutes ticked by, Lewis looked to his sergeant and let out a curse in frustration. His voice seemed to summon three wraiths from the darkness. Duke Slater, avoiding the ice-encrusted puddles that pockmarked the trail, whispered the password, and introduced himself and his two companions—Doc Block and the forward observer Howard Kettelhut. He asked Lt. Lewis which road to take. Lewis chucked his chin toward the lane leading into Bergstein.

Slater's voice was soft as church music. "Let's go, men," he said. With that, a half dozen Rangers from Slater's forward scout patrol stepped out from behind trees to either side of the astonished Richard Lewis. He heard their tommy guns click, locked and loaded. And then they vanished. "They moved out without saying a word," Lewis remembered. "Our morale went up in a hurry."

Reaching the northwestern fringes of Bergstein, Slater signaled for several Rangers to follow him through the village to get the lay of the land. Block and Kettelhut wanted to join the group. Slater forbade it; the town was taking intermittent artillery fire and he could not afford to lose either man. Slater's small patrol picked its way through the hulks of American tanks, halftracks, and jeeps littering the road, many still burning and throwing eerie shadows on the shattered homes and shops to either side.

Back in Vossenack, Slater had picked up rumors of American tank crews huddling helplessly under their disabled vehicles during the multiple German counterattacks, and even of shell-shocked CCR infantrymen refusing to leave basements and root cellars to fight. If they were true, he now saw why. The deeper his squad penetrated into Bergstein, the higher the piles of corpses seemed to rise. American medics and aid men had at least dragged the GI bodies, their flesh tinged blue, off the street. The Germans lay where they had fallen, not a few flattened into the cobblestones by the treads of heavy American armor. Several of the Rangers held rags to their noses to ward off the stench. The scarifying scene reminded one combat historian of "desolation such as one associated with the [American Civil War's] Battle of the Wilderness."

On the southeastern edge of the hamlet, about one hundred yards past the last cluster of buildings, Slater cautiously inspected a Roman Catholic church. Its stout walls, erected from heavy, uncut sandstone, had been blackened but not destroyed by artillery fire. Even its bell tower, constructed from the yellowish ashlar blocks quarried from the ruined schloss atop Hill 400, still stood. Beyond the church cemetery, he could hear Germans talking in their foxholes. Once Easy Company secured that salient, he decided, the Church of the Holy Moorish Martyrs would serve as his forward command post as well as Doc Block's aid station.

By the time Slater returned to the northwest edge of town at 2:30 A.M., Maj. Williams was waiting and Lt. Kettelhut was already on the radio coordinating fire support with the varied artillery units. Williams informed Slater that, as best as the intelligence boys could determine, they were facing three German infantry regiments backstopped by an armored outfit of indeterminate rolling stock. He added that the enemy's morale was reportedly extremely high.

As Able, Baker, and Charlie Companies calved from the main column at 3 A.M. and moved to occupy their defensive positions—without, the company commanders sardonically noted, the guides they had been promised from the 47th Armored Infantry—Dog Company's Morton McBride and Fox Company's Big Stoop Masny huddled with Harvey Cook. Given their unfamiliarity with the countryside, Cook suggested an immediate reconnaissance of Hill 400 was in order. The two company commanders agreed and called for volunteers. The ten-man squad would be led by Dog Company's Lieutenant Len Lomell and Fox Company's Lieutenant Kendall McClure.

McClure was new to the outfit, with scant combat experience. He later recalled that his flayed nerves were somewhat soothed when he was paired with Lomell, whose feats at Pointe du Hoc were already embedded in battalion lore. McClure was further heartened when his company's lead scout, Private First Class William "Andy" Anderson, stepped forward to join the patrol. It was said that Anderson, who had fought with Fox Company since D-Day, could see in the dark. His pathfinding reputation was only embossed when, on lone scouting missions through the woodland virtually devoid of wildlife, he usually somehow managed to return with enough venison to feed his entire platoon.

Before they moved out, Cook drew Lomell and McClure aside. If at all possible, he told them, he would dearly love to interrogate a German prisoner familiar with the hill's defenses. The Rangers nodded. Then Lomell lined up the patrol and had the men discard their musette bags and any loose equipment—canteens, spare ammo cartridges, gas masks—that might make a jangling noise and alert the enemy.

Hugging the foundations of Bergstein's shattered buildings, the recon team reached the church that Slater had eyeballed. From there they zigzagged through the church cemetery before clambering over a roadblock in the form of a thick tree felled across the street. Andy Anderson thought he heard someone whisper, "Halt." He ignored it. Though Harvey Cook had given Lomell and McClure a cursory glance at local topography maps, they had no idea where scattered American squads might be dug in. When they stumbled across a group of burrowing GIs from the 47th and asked directions to Hill 400, their queries were met with blank stares and shrugs.

Next, they descended into a sunken cart path leading east. Its cobblestones had been churned into a slippery morass by German vehicular and rolling armor traffic. Their movements grew more cautious as the forest thinned. At one point, Lomell turned and caught a glint of light from the pocket of one of the scouts' field jackets. The Ranger had left his flashlight on, and it was shining through the fabric. Lomell hissed at him to douse it. Less than fifteen seconds later, as they moved further up the road, a mortar shell detonated on the exact spot where Lomell had reprimanded the man.

After some two hundred yards they spotted the tree-covered hill rising in the distance. The objective had been code-named "Sugarloaf," after the stone peak looming over Rio de Janeiro's Guanabara Bay. Lomell had seen photographs of Sugarloaf Mountain. He thought Hill 400, studded with conifers, looked taller and steeper. More ominously, a swath of farmer's tract about the length of two football fields lay between the cart path and the hill, affording its defenders excellent fields of fire. There would be no surprising the Germans. Where were the damn trees when you needed them?

Lomell and McClure directed their scouts to fan out along the trail while they scrambled over its cantilevered embankment, perhaps four feet high, and belly-crawled across the ice-encrusted field. A low-lying fog covered their movements. With all five senses taut as a hound's, the two Rangers instantly recognized that the enemy was nearby from the strong aroma of cabbage, cheese, and wurst. They nearly jumped out of their skin at the muffled sound of voices conversing in German mere yards away. Lomell and McClure could not see them, and neither spoke the language. In any case the words were soon drowned out by the distinctive noise of a heavy machine gun being loaded.

Edging closer, they could just make out the contours of a log bunker built into the base of the hill. It was concealed beneath mounds of pine branches. Communicating in sign language, the Ranger officers decided to lie doggo in hopes of snatching one of the Germans on a piss break. Fifteen agonizing minutes passed before Lomell finally pointed to his wristwatch. It was time to go; dawn, and the pre-assault artillery barrage, were fast approaching. Harvey Cook would have no prisoner to interrogate. Lomell and McClure slithered away silently and collected their flanking troopers. Andy Anderson reported that he had reconnoitered the southeast slope of the rise. He'd heard no German voices.

As the returning recon patrol approached the outskirts of Bergstein, this time all the Rangers heard the word near the roadblock: "Halt." It was delivered in a German accent. They took off at a dead run. Bullets whistled through the branches around them as they hopped the felled tree and tore northwest.

One of the scouts, Fox Company's Private First Class Milton "Bunny" Moss, tripped and fell in the cemetery. Moss, who had only just joined the outfit, was disoriented, and not certain whether to move. He called softly for Anderson. A German burp gun opened up. Moss belly-crawled backward a few feet before he heard a familiar voice. "Over here, Moss; let's go." It was Anderson, squatting behind a headstone. The two crept away.

Back behind the jagged American lines, it was 6 A.M. when Lomell and McClure found Duke Slater studying topo maps. The two were so obviously shaken from the unexpected enemy encounter that Slater had to light the cigarettes he stuck into their mouths. Recovering his wits after several deep drags, Lomell described the location of the hidden bunker as best he could and reported that the terraced, sunken path was their best approach to the hill. Its embankment would provide some cover until they reached the open farmer's field that spread before the heights. As Lomell and McClure spoke, the sound of mortar shelling erupted to the southeast. The enemy fire was directed at Easy Company, already attempting to clear the Germans ensconced around the church and the roadblock.

32

"Let's Go Get the Bastards!"

By 6:40 A.M. on December 7, 1944—in other circumstances an anniversary date that would have resonated with most American servicemen—the Rangers of Easy Company had driven back the remaining *Volksgrenadiers* clinging to the eastern rim of Bergstein. Richard Merrill's outfit, taking no casualties, had captured seventeen prisoners before the enemy survivors fled back toward Hill 400. They had undoubtedly alerted the defenders on the crest that the Americans were coming.

Within moments incoming artillery fire picked up as the Rangers of Dog and Fox Companies, having stubbed their final smokes, passed through Easy Company's positions. Duke Slater was a man in constant motion, offering rough encouragement as he rushed up and down the snaking line of 130 troopers. If he harbored any ill feeling about being passed over for command of the battalion, he did not show it.

Slater and Howard Kettelhut peeled off from the column at the Roman Catholic church, stepping over the bodies of dead Germans sprawled across the front steps, and climbed to the top of the belfry. From beneath an enormous cast-bronze bell they had an unimpeded view of Hill 400.

Below them, in the church basement, Doc Block was already setting up a triage site. Block was without his chief assistant, Frank South. Two days earlier, before Col. Rudder had returned from his meeting with Gen. Hodges at Spa, Block had found South passed out in a puddle of his own watery shit at their aid station in Germeter. South was dehydrated and obviously suffering from some kind of gastrointestinal illness. With no idea that the Ranger battalion was about to be committed to combat, Block had ordered South to a field hospital straddling the western edge of the forest.* He had no time to worry about that decision now. His assistants were already carrying in litters loaded with Rangers felled by the latest enemy shelling.

Dog and Fox Companies had barely made the church graveyard before they were spotted. A red signal flare bursting overhead was followed by a barrage of machine gun and small-arms fire from the woods to their left. The Rangers, desperate for cover, dashed from tombstones to graves ripped open by shellfire. Fox's Lt. McClure, a self-described "lucky bugger," felt his pack absorb three separate slugs. They staggered him but failed to find flesh.

With their ranks already pared by a dozen or so shellfire casualties, by 7:15 the two Ranger rifle companies were spread out and in position along the sunken cart path and facing the mist-shrouded Hill 400. The veterans in the outfit did not fancy the idea of crossing that open field.

. . .

---

* Several weeks earlier South had refused evacuation after catching shell fragments in his arm; instead, he had sutured the wound himself. This time Doc Block insisted he leave the front line.

Orders arrived at Colonel Georg Kossmala's command post near the bank of the Roer at just after midnight on December 7. He was instructed to quick-march the remaining battalions of his 272nd Division toward what the Germans called *Burg-berg*, or Castle Mound, sweep up what was left of his two battered companies, which had taken part in the failed counterattacks the previous day, and fall on Bergstein at dawn. A regiment of Wehrmacht soldiers from Schmidt and a small unit of elite paratroopers—*Fallschirmjägers*—would be temporarily folded into his command to employ as he saw best. Eleven tank destroyers were also made available to augment the push. Kossmala's assignment was clear: the Americans must be driven out of the village before they could attack Castle Mound.

The extra armor and paratroops, Kossmala could use. But he was disappointed with the state of the regular-army *Landsers* sent from Schmidt. After having held the town over two straight weeks of heavy fighting, they were in sorry shape. He decided to hold them back in reserve. By 6 A.M. he had gathered his senior staff and begun formulating a plan of attack. He was stressing to his subordinates that they must avoid the mistakes of the previous day's assaults when word reached him. The Americans had stolen a march. Several companies of Rangers were already nearing the *Burg-berg*.

The American bombardment of the hill began at nearly the same time as the two Ranger companies fanned out along the road. With Howard Kettelhut relaying coordinates, the eighteen friendly artillery batteries unleashed a rolling barrage. The detonations began at the base of the rise and, with Kettelhut directing fire, marched up the slope by map quadrants. The cheers from the Ranger lines over the morale-boosting sibilance of this "outgoing mail" were silenced when German mortarmen began dropping shells several hundred yards to Dog and Fox Companies' rear. The assault force was caught in the middle, and every man recognized that it was only a matter of time before the enemy guns would reestablish their range projections and "walk their arty" straight up their butts.

With nowhere to go but forward, word was passed down the line to fix bayonets. Big Stoop Masny, on the left flank, dispatched runners to remind his Fox Company troopers that the moment the American artillery ceased, every man was to empty a full clip from his weapon into the base of the hill before charging en masse—a marching fire assault, in military terminology. Morton McBride on the right flank passed a similar message to his Dog Company charges. If the horizontal hail of bullets could keep the Germans buried in their hidden bunkers for even a few extra seconds, it might buy enough time to cross the icy clearing.

American shellfire was still erupting on Hill 400 when Fox Company's Lieutenant Thomas Rowland tapped the shoulder of the platoon sergeant, L-Rod Petty. Like Lt. McClure, Rowland was new to the outfit, a replacement only arrived in the last few weeks. The Germans in the bunkers at the base of the hill had yet to show their hand. Not knowing the enemy positions on the facing slope made Rowland uncomfortable. "Send out a scout," he told Petty.

The platoon sergeant looked at Rowland as if he had two heads. *And waste a man?* He shook his head, no.

Rowland repeated the order. Petty growled, "Fuck you, no way."

Angry and flustered, Rowland turned to the company staff sergeant, Bill McHugh. Before the officer could speak, McHugh shook his head. "No, sir." McHugh had stuck to L-Rod Petty's hip since the two had captured the enemy machine gun back atop Pointe du Hoc. He trusted the toothless BAR man's instincts a hell of a lot more than he did this newbie 2nd lieutenant.

Rowland finally found a Ranger to obey his command. Private First Class Gerald Bouchard humped over the road's embankment and made it two or three steps before a single bullet pierced his belly. An enraged Petty and McHugh grabbed Bouchard's heels and dragged the wounded private back to cover. Petty was still dosing Bouchard's gut shot with sulfa powder when, at precisely 7:30 A.M., the American barrage ceased. Behind the Ranger line, the German mortar detonations had crept to within thirty yards. Masny and McBride shouted near simultaneously, "Go!"

It was as if a tense and furious serpent had finally uncoiled to strike. The Rangers, firing at will, leapt from their defilade and surged across the open field. Bill McHugh, still seething over what he considered the new lieutenant's ineptitude, emptied the clip of his tommy gun. "Let's go get the bastards!" he hollered at the top of his lungs. He was answered by what Len Lomell described as a wild chorus of "Indian war whoops."

Enemy machine gunners and riflemen secreted on the slope finally opened up. Rangers dropped left and right. Not far from Lomell, Private First Class Kenneth Harsch had taken but a few steps when a mortar round "splattered" his head. Another trooper, new to the outfit, took one look at the raw meat that had once been Harsch's face and froze, dropping to the ground and curling up into a ball. Lomell did not begrudge him; combat, he had learned, turned men into mysterious animals.

Turning to wave his men on, Captain McBride took a slug in his right buttock. Bleeding and cursing—he considered it an insult to have been shot in the ass—he dropped to one knee and continued to urge his Dog Company Rangers forward. When the last man had passed him, he hobbled back toward Doc Block's aid station. He stopped often along the way to treat and mark the location of injured men. Among them was Fox Company's Bill McHugh. The bastards had got him before he could get them.

At the edge of the field where it met the path, McBride spotted the wounded Ranger Tony Ruggiero, the tap dancer from Massachusetts who had been with the outfit since Camp Forrest. A large piece of shrapnel had sliced through one of his legs. McBride remembered "Rugg" entertaining his platoon—and likely concealing his own anxiety—by dancing to the strums of a ukulele someone had smuggled aboard during the Channel crossing back on June 6. Ruggiero, who was all of five foot three, was lucky if he tipped the scales at 120 pounds. Despite McBride's own wound, he bent down and threw Ruggiero over his shoulder. Ruggiero puked all over his company commander's back.

It took less than two minutes for what was left of the assault force, little more than one hundred Rangers, to reach the base of the hill. The surrounding trees shook as scores of fragmentation grenades turned log bunkers into kindling. The Germans who had dug in on the slopes turned and ran for the top. The shrieking Rangers followed with no semblance of order, the frozen scree beneath their combat boots giving way as their adrenaline-infused momentum carried them up the forty-five-degree incline. The adjusted German mortar barrage nipped at their heels as they climbed. It was like scrabbling up a thirteen-hundred-foot child's playground slide while being shot at.

Watching the assault from the church bell tower, Howard Kettelhut called in a withering round of artillery. American shells—105 mms, 155 mms, 240 mms, 8-inch howitzers—raked the top of the hill. The ground shook from the force of the explosions. Kettelhut halted the barrage as the first wave of Rangers neared the crest. The fight on Hill 400 was now a chaotic brawl. Americans and Germans, many with no opportunity to reload, attacked each other with knives, entrenching tools, steel helmets, bare fists. "No quarter was asked," notes the army veteran and military historian Douglas Nash, "and none given."

By 8:35 A.M., sixty-five minutes after jump-off, Big Stoop Masny radioed George Williams at his command post in the only undamaged building on the west end of Bergstein. The Rangers, Masny reported, held the hill. They did not realize it, but theirs was now the deepest penetration into German territory by any American or British unit across the vast Allied front.

On the fight's far-left flank, Fox Company's Sergeant Herm Stein led his five-man squad in a semicircle around Hill 400. Stein was shaken. Midway across the field leading to the rise, he had seen a German rifleman rise from a foxhole, toss his gun, fall to his knees, and plead to be taken prisoner. A Ranger had shot him in the head. Before shipping overseas, Stein's father had told him, "I guess you'll gradually get used to [combat] as you go on."

No, Bubby thought now, the more you go on, the less you get used to it.

Nonetheless, he had a job to do. He and his team moved on and began climbing the northeastern slope of the hill. Midway to the top they were stopped cold by mortar fire. Two men went down, leaking blood from shrapnel wounds. Stein sent a scout, Sergeant Carl "Bomber" Bombardier, toward the crest while he and Milt Moss treated the wounded.

Bombardier was barely away when Len Lomell skittered down to Stein's position. Stein eyed Lomell's swollen left hand. It looked less like a hand than a red mitten, the pinkie finger nearly severed and dangling by tendons. Lomell had field-dressed the wound and bound his left arm to his body with the strap of his tommy gun. He saw Stein staring and lifted his weapon with his good right hand. The implication: he could still fire a gun. Milt Moss smiled and remembered what one of his staff sergeants had told him as they picked their way through Bergstein toward the hill. "Kid, stay away from officers. They just draw fire and may ask you to do something dumb that could just get you killed."

Moss was contemplating the advice when Lomell instructed him and Stein to link up with a contingent of Dog Company Rangers just a bit farther up the hill. Then he was gone. Stein and Moss moved out. They went the wrong way.

Stein knew something was amiss when he saw the Roer River below him. Too close. On the far side of the watercourse German Volkswagen command vehicles and the occasional Mercedes-Benz staff car were tearing up and down the road running parallel to the river. An Opel truck screeched to a halt beside what Stein took to be some sort of power station serving the dams and disgorged a squad of German riflemen, maybe ten men in all. They scrambled across a footbridge, heading in his direction. By this time in their wanderings Stein and Moss had picked up a Dog Company straggler, and the three Rangers burrowed into a crevice and let the Germans pass.

When the enemy squad disappeared, Stein and his fellow troopers followed their trail toward the top of the hill. They were some forty yards from the crest when Sgt. Bombardier miraculously reappeared. What was left of Fox Company, the Bomber told Stein, was spread along the hilltop's northeastern rim. Dog was to their left. Stein surveyed his downhill field of fire. "We dig in here," he said.

33

The Crest

Lieutenant Len Lomell fell to his knees, spent. Dead and dying Americans and Germans were strewn about him in grotesque positions. He focused. Through breaks in the banks of the blustering blue-gray clouds, he caught brief glimpses of Schmidt to the southwest and the winding Roer River directly east. Beyond the river he could see the hydroelectric dams as well as dozens of panzer tanks and German self-propelled 88s partially concealed behind farmhouses and barns. He shook his head in wonder. It had taken the Rangers just over an hour to capture a hill that three American divisions had attempted to roll up for months. All it had cost Lomell was the use of his left arm.

During the initial assault on the hilltop, Lomell had nearly run past an enemy troop shelter so adeptly camouflaged with pine boughs that at first he took it for a small ridgeline. When he'd realized what it was, he'd gathered a squad from Dog Company and surrounded it. The Rangers were pouring fire through the pillbox's rifle slits when a shell hit, sending shrapnel tearing through his left hand.

When a white flag attached to a tree branch emerged from the bunker's entrance, Lomell selected a brace of wounded yet ambulatory men to march the prisoners to the rear. He remembered Harvey Cook emphatically placing a premium on German captives during the previous evening's recon situation report, or sitrep. What good they would do the intel officer now, he was not certain. Still. As Lomell bandaged his wound he dolefully watched the little group of prisoners and their two guards disappear down the sunken path leading to Bergstein. The wounded Rangers had not wanted to leave, and he'd hated to lose the firepower. Perhaps Capt. Cook would find some good in it.

Now Lomell vaguely recalled seeing Morton McBride also limping back toward Bergstein. It took a moment for the thought to register. He was the highest-ranking Dog Company officer still standing. It was his outfit now. What was left of it. He had no idea how many of his Rangers had reached the crest.

Lomell's reverie was broken by the long *blaaaat* of a BAR followed by the familiar detonations of frag grenades. He turned to see Fox's Andy Anderson and L-Rod Petty exiting the door of a massive bunker complex just as a shell blast blew Anderson backward. Petty instinctively threw his arms around the scout to keep him from falling. With his left hand, Petty could feel the jagged chunk of shrapnel where Anderson's heart had been pierced. Petty, awash in his friend's blood, staggered and fell, cradling the dead scout. He was still hugging the corpse when Big Stoop Masny appeared out of the smoke like an apparition.

Petty gently lowered Anderson's body to the ground; he and Masny briefly conferred. The two then disappeared back into the bunker. The sound of more gunfire ensued before they reappeared leading a dozen prisoners. The Germans looked relieved to be marched back through the American lines.

Lomell got to his feet and headed toward Masny. He was startled to find the new Fox Company lieutenant, Ken McClure, walking by his side. Masny, a red worm of blood trickling from his ear, told Lomell that there were Fox Company Rangers, Herm Stein's BAR team among them, scattered across the eastern slope of the hill. Some, pumped by adrenaline, had slid down the hill and chased the Germans nearly to the Roer. These included the young Dog Company rifleman Bud Potratz and the newbie Sergeant Mike Sharik, in whose eyes Potratz thought he had detected fear.

Bring them all back up, Masny said. Lomell took off to find them.

Lt. McClure, meanwhile, had wandered over to the enemy bunker. It was the largest he had ever seen in his brief time on the line. The thick earthen banks covering its concrete roof and walls were pockmarked with shell holes. None had penetrated the blockhouse. McClure eased himself through the doorway as if there might be snakes inside. He saw what looked to be an old telephone switchboard. Sheets upon sheets of paper—maps, order forms, range-finding coordinates, pinup photos—formed a carpet beneath the bodies of the Germans dispatched first by Anderson and Petty, and then by Masny and Petty. Hemingway had been right: There was always much paper about the dead.

Then McClure noticed the wires, now cut. They had once led from the bunker to the top of a nearby fire tower, maybe forty feet high. It struck him that nearly every artillery shell that had sent an American soldier to his grave since September had been directed from that tower. It dominated the Roer River valley for miles in all directions. He was still examining the control room's field communications setup when Masny shouted at him to round up his platoon and dig in for the inevitable counterattack. Pockets of Germans still clung stubbornly to the north, east, and south slopes of Hill 400, with more in the ravines below. It was only a matter of time before they re-formed and came again.

• • •

Ken McClure looked left and right. Round up a platoon? From where? L-Rod Petty had vanished, and aside from the runner who had stuck with him during the charge up the hill, McClure could find only two men from Fox Company still in effective fighting shape. They would have to do.

McClure and his tiny cohort had barely begun to scrape fox-holes out of the frozen earth with their bayonets when a firestorm began to fall. The Germans, with an estimated two hundred artil-lery pieces of all calibers within range, were throwing everything they had at the hill with a lethal precision from the north, east, and south—mortars, 88s, 120s, even 75 mm tank shells. Rangers across the crest were blown to bits as McClure and his squad frantically dug. They cursed the immense tree roots that snaked through the near-impenetrable shale beneath the icy mud. Smoke as thick as volcano ash burned their eyes and nostrils.

During a lull in the shelling, Capt. Masny's runner stumbled into Lt. McClure's shallow hole. He motioned for the lieutenant and his runner to follow, and led them back to the captured enemy bunker. Masny and Lt. Rowland had organized it into a triage cen-ter. It was rapidly filling with wounded Rangers, and Big Stoop was angry. Men were bleeding out, dying unnecessarily up on this hill. Where the hell were the battalion stretcher bearers?

Masny told McClure and Rowland that he was heading back to Bergstein to fetch reinforcements. He'd march them back up this damn hill at gunpoint if necessary.

Not far away, L-Rod Petty had just deposited Andy Anderson's body onto the mounting "dead pile" in a separate room of the bun-ker. When he overheard Masny, he spoke up. He was certain, he said, that there were enemy soldiers, Germans they'd missed during the charge up the hill, still dug in on the western slope. He'd heard their voices. He begged Big Stoop to grab a couple of men to accompany him. Masny said no. He could not spare a trooper from the fight he knew was coming.

Otto Masny placed Lt. Rowland in command of Fox Company until he returned. Rowland was as new to combat as McClure, but he outranked him by time served. Big Stoop then instructed his radio operator to follow McClure back to his dugout near the hill's eastern rim. Keep Duke Slater and Howard Kettelhut informed of any enemy movements, he said. As Petty and the two young lieutenants watched their Fox Company commanding officer make his way back down the west slope of Hill 400, they had no idea that it would be nearly a year before they saw him again.

The enemy bombardment intensified within moments of Masny's departure. It was as if the entire hill wobbled like a colossal Jell-O mold. The big German guns were still firing proximity-fused shells, designed to burst above ground and rain down murderous storms of shrapnel. The bastards would not even provide shell craters to hide in. Rangers dived for cover beneath toppled trees and blasted rocks the size of doghouses. Amid the eerie tableau were a few who didn't make it yet remained slumped on their knees propped against their field shovels, their lifeless hands still clutching the digging implements.

As the sheets of artillery detonated above them, Ken McClure, his runner, and his new radioman slithered from their foxhole, making for a jutting ledge that overlooked the German positions in the ravine below. McClure could not do anything about the distant 88s and 120s. But if he could spot the small black plumes of smoke emanating from the closer enemy mortar tubes, he might be able to call in the coordinates to Slater and Kettelhut. He peered over the crest just as an explosion lifted him into the air.

McClure never lost consciousness, but he was momentarily

blinded. When his vision returned, he was still gripping the radio operator's telephone receiver in his hand. The line led to the destroyed fifty-pound communications pack fastened to the back of the dead radioman.* McClure rolled over. His runner had been stunned mute but, McClure thought, might be still alive. He grabbed the young private by the collar and began dragging him back toward the aid bunker.

By the time McClure reached the bunker entrance it took all his strength to heft his runner's body through the door. It was for naught. The boy was dead. McClure knelt over the corpse. He felt a hand on his shoulder. It was Tom Rowland, his fellow greenhorn lieutenant. Rowland asked if McClure had seen Len Lomell. McClure's world was upside down. He shook his head, no, and exited the bunker. Amid the awful confusion he thought he heard screaming. It was coming from the direction of the half-assed dugout where he had left the two Fox Company Rangers that formed his "platoon." He was running toward the sounds when a shell detonated several yards behind him.

McClure was "foggy" when he regained consciousness. He squinted at his watch; it was nearly nine-thirty. Still determined to find whoever and whatever was left of his tiny command, he rose to his knees. He took but a few steps before shrapnel from another explosion tore through his right leg. He was bandaging the wound as best he could when the Germans counterattacked.

---

* Although similar two-way field radios had been in use since the 1930s, the U.S. Army's backpack-mounted, battery-powered SCR portable radio transceiver, introduced during World War II, was the first radio to be nicknamed a "walkie-talkie."

34

Fallschirmjägers

L en Lomell knew what the green-and-mud-colored camouflage battle smocks signified. *Fallschirmjägers*. Luftwaffe
paratroopers. The elite of the elite. Over one hundred of
them. Their bayonets fixed and swarming like ants up the
southeast slope. Behind them, a bit farther east, another howling
German unit burst from what was left of the tree line. *Volksgrenadiers*.
The olive-green uniforms gave them away.

By this point in the war, not only was the Reich running out of
raw materials to fuel its war machine—iron ore, oil, copper, alumi-
num, nickel—but its mills were also bereft of wool. The consequent
reliance on synthetic fabrics meant that the sharp-pleated field grays
with their striking green lapels, in which Wehrmacht soldiers had
marched into Paris in 1940, had by now been replaced with a less
ornate version. Still, *Volksgrenadiers* or not, their weapons were
just as lethal. Lomell had seen the propaganda pamphlets dropped
over enemy lines. The horde now racing up Hill 400 did not look
like old men and boys to him.

Hours earlier, in the eerily quiet moments between taking the
hill and the beginning of the artillery barrages, Lomell managed

to gather ninety-one Rangers from Fox and Dog Companies. Platoon integrity had long been shattered, and Lomell recognized his force was too weakened to hold a continuous line across the hilltop. In anticipation of a counterattack, he'd assigned several two-man scout patrols to ease their way down the slopes facing the Roer River to determine where the enemy was reassembling. The intel had allowed him to mass his own defenses facing the direction from which the German paratroopers and *Volksgrenadiers* were now charging.

As they closed, the edgy Americans dug in as best they could to avoid the deadly sprays of lead from the barrels of *Sturmgewehr* 44s. They waited on Lomell's signal even as potato mashers seemed to darken the sky. And waited. Lomell remembered Robert Rogers's Thirteenth Rule of Rangering: *Reserve your fire till they are very near.* The two assaulting enemy groups had nearly converged when he hollered, "Now!"

A cascade of bullets tore into the Germans. They fell like dominoes.

L-Rod Petty had scratched out a shallow depression behind the thick trunk of a downed pine tree. His heart seemed to skip a beat when the Fox Company Private First Class Fred Dix suddenly fell in beside him. Petty's blood was boiling. Moments earlier he had carried the shredded body of Sergeant Jack Anderson into the aid bunker. Unlike his brother Bill, at least Jack Anderson was still breathing.*

Fred Dix, his right foot stitched by automatic rifle fire, had more bad news. His friend and fellow PFC Garness Colden was still out there in no-man's-land. Dix pointed to a spot some twenty yards downhill, where two small uplifts in the ground created a natural

---

* Since the deaths of the five Sullivan brothers two years earlier in the sinking of the battle cruiser USS *Juneau*, the army frowned upon—but did not strictly forbid—brothers serving in the same unit. Jack Anderson had only just joined the Ranger battalion on a temporary assignment and was due to transfer out in a few days.

crevice. Colden was in that narrow notch, Dix told Petty. Too hurt to move. Dix had tried to carry him. He couldn't.

Dix gimped away, and Petty shimmied out of his hole. Pressing his BAR lengthwise to his chest, he rolled in the direction of Colden's position.

Petty and "Garney" Colden shared a special bond. In the hold of the troopship carrying them from England to Normandy, Colden had pulled Petty aside and made him promise to write to his father— "his daddy," Colden had called him—if he was killed. Colden told Petty how his father had shaped his life, how much he loved him, and how he hadn't told him enough. A posthumous letter from his platoon sergeant saying just that would surely ease the pain of his son's death. The two Rangers had shaken on it, with Petty wondering what it must have been like to have had an affectionate dad.

Now, when Petty reached the slight furrow, he found the mortarman Murrell Stinnette, the former swabbie, already working on Colden. Sgt. Stinnette was pressing one hand on Colden's stomach to prevent his guts from squirming out. He was pouring sulfa onto the shrapnel wound with the other.

Stinnette's service shirt and half-opened field jacket were dripping with fresh blood. Petty assumed it was Colden's. Then Stinnette began bleeding from his mouth. Petty tore open Stinnette's jacket. The sergeant was leaking blood from multiple bullet wounds and growing paler by the second. Petty decided to get him to the medical bunker first and come back for Colden. Stinnette would not have it. He let Petty know it with a string of motherfucker-cocksucker oaths. The navy had taught Stinnette to curse well. Though Petty outranked Stinnette, he followed his orders like a yardbird.

Petty threw Colden over his shoulders and dashed madly through the shellfire. After handing the young enlisted man to a medic in the bunker, he asked after Jack Anderson. The aid man's look said it all. First Bill Anderson, now his brother Jack. Petty let out a primal scream—"There is no God!" Where the hell were Big Stoop Masny and the reinforcements? Where were Able and Baker and Charlie and Easy Companies? Didn't anybody know what was going on up here? Without Big Jim Rudder, the outfit had truly seemed to run SOL. Shit out of luck. Then he dashed back for Stinnette.

When Petty reached the crevice, Sgt. Stinnette was dead, bled out. He would only later learn that Garny Colden had joined the Anderson brothers and Murrell Stinnette on the 2nd Battalion's lengthening list of KIAs atop Hill 400.

The gunfight enveloping Len Lomell had devolved into a stalemate. The Germans who survived the initial broadside had taken cover behind the plethora of downed trees and were trying to pick off the dug-in Rangers. No more than twenty yards separated the combatants. A new sound had entered the fray, the *thlip-thlip-thlip* of burp guns. Lomell, who had nearly melted the barrel of his Thompson, eyed the battalion radio in his shallow hole. He thought about contacting Howard Kettelhut to call in artillery. No. As good as Kettelhut had proven, the enemy was too close. Friendly fire might kill them all.

Then, to his left, a shriek like Lomell had never heard before. He watched, astonished, as the Dog Company platoon sergeant Edwin Secor leaped from his foxhole and tossed aside his BAR, its stock mangled by an enemy bullet. Secor fell on two wounded Germans, seized their burp guns, and, still screaming at the top of his lungs, charged into the enemy flank firing the machine pistols from both hips.

Ed Secor was widely considered the most introverted, mild-mannered noncom in the outfit. Back at Tennessee's Camp Forrest—when Secor was still a private—few Rangers expected him to make Big Jim Rudder's final cut. One day outside of Brest, Secor and the brash, cigar-chomping technical sergeant Joe Stevens had briefly broken the Fabulous Four's single-day record for captured prisoners, bringing in just over a hundred. Afterward, Secor had retired to his tent without a word while Stevens larked about the battalion's bivouac like a conquering hero.

Now, apparently, Secor's pent-up emotions had slipped their brake as he barrelled into the German lines. In an instant one Ranger rose to follow him, and then another, and another, until a dozen men had caught up. By now Secor had emptied the burp guns and was firing his sidearm. Led by Secor, the Rangers slashed into the German flank and rolled it up in a frenzied feat of bloodletting. The fear in the panicked German paratroopers leached into the *Volksgrenadiers'* ranks. They began to fall back, at first by ones and twos, then by squads and platoons. Secor and his small band of warriors chased them nearly to the banks of the Roer.

Ken McClure had managed to fire off several bursts from his submachine gun at the approaching wave of attackers before his world went dark. When he came to, he was being carried toward the triage station by two Rangers he did not recognize. He grunted out a question, more like a series of slurred words. One of his litter bearers said that the Germans had been beaten back. McClure estimated that there were some two dozen wounded Rangers spread about the floor on top of the jumbled mass of papers he had noticed earlier. Someone jabbed a syrette of morphine into his leg just as the concrete blockhouse began to shake from multiple artillery hits. Amid the incessant shelling, McClure also thought he could hear the sound of scattered firefights. Then he lost consciousness.

It was just past noon on December 7 when Len Lomell entered the bunker to check on the wounded. Ken McClure, awake now but still groggy, tried to rise. He could not. Given the devastation atop the hill, McClure assumed that Lomell was now in command of the entire Ranger force. Lomell gave McClure a quick nod and headed for the doorway. McClure watched as Lomell conferred with a small circle of sergeants from Dog and Fox Companies, including Ed Secor, Mike Sharik, L-Rod Petty, and Herm Stein. The noncoms, their uniforms splotched with drying blood, all looked battered.

Lomell did not mince words. Captain Morton McBride had never even made the hilltop, and Big Stoop Masny was God-knows-where. Lieutenant Tom Rowland had been shot dead repulsing a German flanking probe, and—hitching his good right thumb over his shoulder—Lieutenant Ken McClure lay in a corner of the bunker with his right leg torn to hell, not far from where Lomell's fellow Dog Company platoon leader, Lieutenant George Kerchner, was nursing a shoulder wound.

Lomell was the last officer left standing on Hill 400. With disabled Rangers rasping out futile cries for medics across the crest, fear and frustration were slowly eroding the resolve of the combined thirty-two effectives remaining from the two companies. Lomell repeated the number. Thirty-two.

The United States Army was not a democracy, Lomell said, but in this case he was willing to make an exception. His eyes moistening with tears, he asked the sergeants for a vote on whether he should order a pullback to Bergstein. The Germans, he said, would treat the American wounded left in the aid bunker.

To a man, the noncoms voted no. They would hold the hill. One sergeant "prayed to God to be gentle with my parents when they learned of my death."

Down in Bergstein, they couldn't see the Panzers. But the German tanks, moving in from Schmidt, made their presence known. Able Company's Morris Prince, his clothes and equipment drenched and filthy, felt like "a duck in a shooting gallery." Prince wasn't even dug in, merely lying prone on his stomach behind a downed tree, "praying and sweating."

At one point Prince lifted his head and spotted a self-propelled *Sturmtiger* moving into a forward firing position. The odd-looking vehicle, likely rebuilt on the chassis of a damaged Tiger tank and equipped with a short barrel that fired a 380 mm rocket-propelled mortar, resembled a normal tank with its long nose lopped off. It would open fire and then withdraw to a concealed position among the trees before the American mortarmen, much less the artillery spotters, could even get a bead on it. It was as if there wasn't even an enemy to fire back at. Yet.

35

A Last Stand

L-Rod Petty did not know whether to laugh or weep. The platoon sergeant whom Lt. Col. Rudder had once tried to wash out of the 2nd Ranger Battalion because of his toothless smile was now in command of an entire rifle company. Or what was left of it, at any rate.

The surviving Fox and Dog Company Rangers were intertwined across the crest of Hill 400, and Petty was eyeballing the northeast slope when he spotted the Germans creeping up a draw through a tangle of felled conifers. A small patrol, maybe a dozen *Volksgrenadiers*. He signaled to the nearest man, a newbie to the outfit whose face he did not recognize. The trooper fell in behind Petty and the two began climbing to higher ground that overlooked the enemy approach.

They were still scrabbling up the small ridgeline when Petty caught the reflective glint of a sniper's scope out of the corner of his eye. Petty wheeled. He and the German fired simultaneously, Petty emptying the magazine of his BAR. The sniper slumped, dead. But not before the eight-millimeter slug from his Mauser *Karabiner* 98 passed through Petty's right shoulder and into the chest of the new man, killing him instantly.

Petty crumpled in sections. Hips first, then knees, finally ankles. He tried but could not lift his gun to reload. He leaned back against the hill as if he were holding it up. He watched three or four Rangers open fire on the Germans he had been trying to outflank. The enemy ran without putting up much of a fight. Within seconds Petty understood why. The shelling began again. Petty ran.

Milt Moss spotted L-Rod Petty zigzagging through the singing shards of shrapnel. He moved like he was drunk, stumbling over fallen tree limbs. Blood-flecked spittles of drool dripped from his chin. His right arm hung limp; he cradled his BAR in his left. Moss nudged Herm Stein, who lifted his head from behind a sandstone outcropping. Stein was taken aback. He'd never seen his friend like this. Stein jumped out from behind the rock formation, tackled Petty, and dragged him into his protected hole.

Petty, eyes glistening, mumbled almost incoherently, "Who's going to take care of my BAR? Who's going to take my BAR?"

"I'll take it, L-Rod," Herm Stein said, his voice gentle. "Don't you worry. I'll take good care of it."

Bunny Moss watched, astounded. He'd heard nothing but near-legendary stories about "Petty of the Pointe" since shipping into the battalion. Yet here the man was, apparently cracking up.

Since deploying overseas, Moss had carried a copy of the Ninety-first Psalm in his breast pocket. Now he absentmindedly fingered the creased and greasy piece of paper. *I will say of the LORD, He is my refuge and my fortress: my God; in Him will I trust.*

He watched as Petty handed Stein his precious gun and moved off toward the aid bunker.

. . .

The Germans came twice more that afternoon, both times in company strength. It was Howard Kettelhut who prevented a Custer-like massacre.

Len Lomell was in constant radio contact with Kettelhut. Each time the enemy assaulted, Lomell would relay their coordinates and watch in muted admiration as the forward observer directed a ring of shells around the remaining Rangers with the precision and timing of an orchestra conductor. Lomell made a mental note to put the GI up for a medal. If he lived to tell the story. By 4 P.M., Lomell was down to twenty-five effectives, including a few Rangers who had grabbed their weapons and limped or crawled from the aid station, preferring to die on the line. They joined the ever-shrinking perimeter encircling the bunker.

L-Rod Petty took it upon himself to find help. The bandage covering his shoulder wound was holding tight as he picked his way down the west slope of Hill 400. He paused often, listening for German voices. After the ear-breaking noise atop the rise, he found the sunken trail leading to Bergstein strangely quiet despite the sporadic mortar detonations. Without their spotters atop the hill to relay target coordinates, the Wehrmacht mortarmen were now dropping random shells in and around Bergstein, hoping to catch Americans coming or going.

When Petty reached the church command post, the first person he saw was a Ranger sergeant slumped against a wall dragging deep on a Lucky Strike. Petty snapped. He threw himself on the man, punching, kicking, cursing his cowardice. It took several medics to pull Petty away. As at the base of Pointe du Hoc, they made him swallow a pill. He was demanding to see Big Stoop Masny when he faded into unconsciousness.

· · ·

It was running toward dusk when it dawned on Herm Stein that, as Fox Company's highest-ranking noncom still standing, he had inherited the outfit from L-Rod Petty. Some inheritance. Ten able bodies, including himself. The rain had picked up. It would soon turn to sleet.

Working with Len Lomell, Stein had organized his negligible troop as best he could in one semicircle around the aid bunker. What was left of Lomell's Dog Company, fifteen Rangers, completed the belt. Stein took his line's center position and hunkered down in the shallow hole he had scratched out behind the sandstone rock. His rock, as he had taken to thinking of it. There were gaps in the Ranger defense large enough to drive a tank through, but at least the German artillery had fallen off. All day that had augured another infantry attack. Stein braced his men, waiting for the cock to crow. But for some reason they didn't come. Maybe it was Howard Kettelhut's pinpoint strikes. Maybe they were pulling back across the Roer. It did not matter. It was a moment of blessed peace.

Stein waited until it was completely dark before passing the word. "Get some sleep." He would take the first watch. Within moments the deep-throated rumble of Panzer tank engines idling on the other side of the river competed with the snoring to either side of his hole. Suddenly a pain in his gut jolted Stein. His bowels were about to crack open. He dared not chance leaving his position. One of his own men would likely shoot him. He dropped his pants, grabbed an empty K ration box, and did his business. He heaved the box down the hill.

The clatter woke the Ranger in the next dugout, who grabbed his M1 and began firing wildly in the direction of the noise. It took a few moments before Stein could stay the man's jumpy trigger finger.

When Fox Company had charged the hill that morning, the company's XO, Lieutenant Richard Wintz, had been left behind to act as a liaison to Duke Slater. Wintz had argued with Big Stoop Masny to join the assault, to no avail. As the hours ticked past with all hell obviously breaking loose up on that hill and no word from Masny, Wintz had hectored Slater to be allowed to lead a relief party. Finally, Slater received word from Maj. Williams to cobble together a squad from Easy Company's 1st and 2nd Platoons and find an officer to take them up the slope. Slater tapped Wintz. Howard Kettelhut insisted on joining him, arguing that he could more accurately call in artillery from the hill. Slater, aware that one of the first precepts of a combat officer's training was to "see the battlefield," reluctantly agreed.

It was just past 7 P.M. when Ken McClure bolted awake at the sound of the commotion. Peering down at him was a Ranger he had never met before. At first McClure wondered if he was hallucinating. He had read somewhere that soldiers in shock often saw things that weren't there. Then the man squatted and handed McClure two boxes of C rations, compliments of Easy Company. It was the first food McClure had seen since he'd left Germeter.

Besides the C rats, the tiny relief force had also hauled stretchers laden with cartons of ammunition, a radio to replace Fox Company's destroyed SCR, and bags of plasma. The most seriously wounded were quickly loaded onto the emptied litters to be carried back to Bergstein by a mixed squad of Doc Block's aid men and Charlie Company volunteers. Jeeps were waiting to transfer the injured to the rear; the dead would later be piled into trucks. Despite the gash in his leg, McClure did not qualify for evacuation. He would spend a restless night in the bunker.

When the new supplies were distributed and the litter bearers departed, Lieutenants Kettelhut and Wintz—carrying the new radio—humped the hilltop perimeter, such as it was, filling holes in the line with the ten Easy Company Rangers who had remained. Like Kettelhut, the twenty-seven-year-old Wintz was a native Nebraskan, and had been studying to be a mortician when the war broke out. He'd only just graduated from embalming school in St. Louis before enlisting, and naïvely thought he'd seen the worst of what the Angel of Death had to offer. But not even Pointe du Hoc could compare with the horrors he encountered atop Hill 400. The hilltop reeked of the rank odors of misery—of blood and sweat, of piss and shit and vomit.

German shellfire was falling hard again when Len Lomell appeared out of the darkness before Wintz and Kettelhut. Lomell had been hit again that afternoon, taking shrapnel in his left leg. He had also suffered a concussion, and was bleeding from his mouth and, unbeknownst to Wintz, from his anus. Lomell's leg wound was deep, but despite the urgings of his men, he had refused to shelter in the blockhouse. He gave Wintz his sitrep. He had to yell above the noise of the bursting shells. Wintz noticed that just raising his voice seemed to exhaust Lt. Lomell. When he was finished, Wintz and Kettelhut took a position outside the entrance to the bunker. Two hours later the stretcher bearers returned with more supplies and again began loading the wounded. Lt. Wintz made certain that Len Lomell was one of them.

It was nearing midnight when a *Volksgrenadier* runner reached the German command post beyond the east bank of the Roer. His report stunned the rear-echelon staff officers. The American Rangers, he said, still occupied *Burg-berg*. This despite Field Marshal Model's desperate offer—seven-day leaves and Iron Crosses, 1st Class, to any unit that could take back and hold the Castle Mound. The presiding officer in the CP, Brigadier General Walter Bruns, knew that Model would be furious at this latest news, and was loath to report the distressing state of affairs without eyes-on verification from a more trusted source than a *Volksgrenadier* messenger. The recon was ideally a job for Col. Kossmala, but he was out in the field, re-forming what remained of the 272nd *VGD* for yet another assault on Bergstein. Instead, Gen. Bruns dispatched a trio of veteran Wehrmacht officers across the river.

Evading sentries and dodging shellfire, American and their own, the enemy scout patrol managed to creep through the dark to the reverse, western slope of Hill 400. There they surprised two Ranger medics evacuating a soldier. They took the aid men prisoner and left the body. The Rangers had not noticed, but their human cargo had died en route.

Bergstein was a hellscape. The German batteries focusing on the small village had not bothered with proximity fuses, and as Bob Edlin shuffled and ducked through the shellfire it seemed to him as if every building in the village was aflame.

It was just past 3:30 A.M. on December 8, and Edlin and Able Company's 1st Platoon had been ordered to pull back into the village. Though the company had taken light casualties from artillery fire in its role as a blocking unit, Edlin knew they'd been lucky. Unlike Baker and Charlie, which had been forced to hack foxholes out of the frozen earth, Able had taken up position in a string of abandoned German trenches.

Now Edlin, eyeing the twenty-eight prisoners they were marching back into Bergstein, wondered if his platoon's redeployment was meant to bolster Duke Slater's stretched defensive line or whether his outfit was being put in motion to reinforce Dog and Fox Companies on Hill 400. The Fool Lieutenant prayed for the latter.

Edlin did not know exactly what was happening up on that hill, but he sensed it was bad. He and his fellow Able Company Rangers watched with sullen stares as jeeps transporting the few wounded men who had made it off the hill ran a gauntlet of artillery fire down Bergstein's main thoroughfare on their way back to the ambulance staging point in Brandenberg. But to Edlin, something was amiss.

For all the bomb blasts and small-arms fire emanating from the crest of Hill 400, there should be more wounded men being evacuated. His only guess was that they couldn't get them down. He could not understand why they had not taken him up on his plan.

Eighteen hours earlier, Edlin had listened intently from his outfit's position southeast of Bergstein as the screaming Rangers from Dog and Fox charged the heights. Then, after a brief hush, he'd heard the first enemy artillery bombardment followed by the counterattack. Edlin, like every veteran Ranger, had long since learned to differentiate the sounds of American M1s, tommy guns, and BARs from those of German automatic rifles and burp guns. Even explosions from potato mashers and frag grenades made distinct noises.

As the gunfire ebbed and flowed through the morning and afternoon, Edlin had requested permission from his company commander, Captain Bob Arman, to slip his platoon behind the hill and fall on the Germans from the rear. Arman liked the idea and had radioed the request to George Williams at his battalion command post. Maj. Williams had denied it, informing Arman that the 8th Division's Gen. Weaver had promised that reinforcements for the Rangers atop the hill were on their way. "Hold your positions," Weaver's radio message had emphasized.

Edlin was stunned when Arman relayed the reply. *Hold your positions? Until when? Until every man on that hill is dead?*

George Williams was waiting for no such thing. Shortly before he'd summoned Edlin's platoon back to the village to fill out Duke Slater's perimeter, a relief unit from the 121st Infantry had rolled into Bergstein to begin replacing the exhausted GIs from the 47th Armored Regiment. Williams managed to pry loose a heavy machine gun team from the new arrivals and sent them toward the hill. But they'd taken a wrong turn in the dark and walked into a German ambush. All fifteen GIs from the team were killed.

Now, as reports of German snipers creeping back into Bergstein reached him, Maj. Williams contacted Duke Slater. Williams worried that the infiltration signaled another all-out assault. Slater felt similarly and was worried enough about Bergstein being overrun that he had already sent word to his company commanders to order their men to throw away any Wehrmacht souvenirs they might have on them. A captured American discovered with German trophies was a dead American.

Slater also reported that the church had taken eighty-two direct artillery hits since he'd established his command post. But aside from two holes in the stout masonry roof, the structure—and the bell tower—were still standing. He reported two casualties and also commended the departed Howard Kettelhut to Williams. "Best man we ever worked with," he said.

Williams instructed Slater to collect all the working machine guns from the blackened hulks of the destroyed Shermans and halftracks strewn about the village and array them throughout the churchyard. If it came down to a last stand, the novice Ranger battalion commander felt, the grounds of the Church of the Holy Moorish Martyrs seemed an appropriate site.

36

Howls and Whistles

he sun had yet to rise on December 8 when the battered remnants of Colonel Georg Kossmala's *Volks-Grenadier* battalions stormed Bergstein. Binoculars raised, Kossmala watched from the nose of a small ridgeline as his soldiers were cut to pieces first by mortar shells and then by the machine gun emplacements that Duke Slater had spread throughout the churchyard. When his troops were pushed back in a shambles after barely twenty minutes, Kossmala and his officers hurriedly set about regrouping the assault lines for another charge. While Kossmala tried to convince his fractured infantry that the Americans were on their last legs, German artillerymen once again began methodically walking barrages up and down the village streets as well as across the crest of Hill 400.

They came at Bergstein a second time at 9 A.M., now supported by several of the tank-like self-propelled guns that Morris Prince had spotted the previous day. Behind the *Sturmtigers* were a string of armored cars spitting 20 mm shells from their long, thin cannons. Sid Salomon's Baker Company and Ralph Goranson's Charlie Company ran from their holes and massed behind the American antitank guns turning to meet the assault. The American antitank gunners made short work of the enemy's mobile guns, and the two Ranger outfits formed what can only be described as flying wedges to either side of the antitankers to sweep away the accompanying *Volksgrenadiers*.

One after-action report describes Bergstein as becoming "unbelievably quiet" following the second enemy attack. Even the German artillery gunners now made Hill 400 their priority. Mortar rounds still fell regularly on the village, but after the previous barrages from the big 88s and 120s, this felt like a respite.

On Hill 400, Herm Stein spotted an enemy squad break through a wide gap in the Ranger perimeter. Several of the Germans— paratroopers, Stein guessed—looked to be carrying flamethrowers. They were making for the entrance to the aid bunker.

Stein doffed his overcoat, hefted his BAR, and hand-signaled to Bomber Bombardier, now wielding L-Rod Petty's gun. As they rushed toward the bunker, Stein tapped Milt Moss's helmet. The three Rangers fell to their knees near the blockhouse entrance and put out a withering hail of bullets. What Germans they left standing turned back down the hill. Stein cursed the fact that they had managed to take their flamethrowers with them.

When Stein returned to his hole behind the sandstone rock, he found his overcoat shredded by shrapnel.

Not far from Herm Stein's position, it was Dick Wintz's turn to be amazed by Howard Kettelhut. The supply and evacuation teams had run telephone wires between the hilltop and Duke Slater's bell tower the previous night, but they had been blown to hell nearly as soon as they had been unspooled. Kettelhut was thus relying solely on the battalion radio, and Wintz would barely finish shouting coordinates to the forward observer before pinpoint American shell-fire ripped into the gathering enemy assailants.

Kettelhut was indeed a multifaceted maestro, taking time to scan Bergstein with his field glasses to range-find the positions of Koss-mala's *Volksgrenadiers* assaulting the village while simultaneously calling down a "curtain of fire" to support the Rangers ringing the aid bunker on the hill. The strikes on the crest were so precise that they detonated mere yards from the dug-in American positions. At one point, Kettelhut actually employed the big American guns as a broom, firing behind attacking Germans in order to sweep them into range of Ranger gunfire.

It was early afternoon on December 8 when the promised GI rein-forcements from Gen. Weaver's 8th Division rolled down Bergstein's main street. One of Weaver's battalion commanders conferred with Maj. Williams, and Williams radioed Duke Slater in the church belfry—the 8th was here to relieve the Rangers. As part of the handover, a division medical officer made his way to the church. Doc Block was busy ripping priests' vestments into bandages when Slater alerted him to be prepared to evacuate the wounded.

At 4:10 P.M., Block stepped outside to greet his relief. Block looked haggard. He had not slept since departing Germeter and missed Frank South more than he thought he would. South had developed into the best aid man on his team.

As Doc Block waited in the church nave for the new medic, he heard moans. Creeping out to investigate, he spotted a German soldier who had been wounded during the last counterattack. As he moved to assist the man, a shell powerful enough to dislodge the headstones in the churchyard detonated above him. Doc Block was dead before he hit the ground.

Harvey Cook was the first to reach the surgeon's body. With

Rudder gone and the Doc dead, it was as if the heart of the battalion had been sliced out. He lifted Block in his arms and carried him back into the church. Then he wept "for the only time in the entire war."

Cook somberly gathered Doc Block's things and found his journal. The last entry was dated December 3, five days earlier. "Still in the ~~Huret~~ Hürtgen woods," it read, "plenty artillery (enemy) shelling both day and night. Received a Christmas package from Alice and the kids yesterday—fur-lined gloves, wool scarf and wool socks. Sent some money to Duffy Floral Co. to buy Alice and [Block's youngest child] Jeffy flowers for their birthdays."*

Cook surely wondered if the flowers would arrive after the War Department's telegram. A bouquet from a ghost.

Not long after Harvey Cook carried Doc Block's mangled corpse into the church, scores of German signal whistles and guttural howls again rent the air around Bergstein. This final attack came from three directions, and a few of Col. Kossmala's *Volksgrenadiers* managed to claw their way as far as the church cemetery before they were churned to chum by machine gun and small-arms fire.

Simultaneously, as the sun set a similar scene was playing out atop Hill 400. In the interim between the morning and afternoon attacks, stretcher bearers from Charlie Company had managed to lug several .30-caliber machine guns to the crest before they departed with wounded Rangers. They were needed. Dog Company was down to twelve effectives, Herm Stein counted five Fox Company Rangers still able to fight, and even the Easy Company reinforcements had been whittled to the bone. But the attacking

---

* In an equally poignant passage in his journal dated November 2, Doc Block effused over the friendliness of the inhabitants of the Luxembourg town of Esch and vowed, "I will be back here again some day with my family."

Germans were not expecting the extra machine gun firepower and were mowed down in a murderous crossfire of machine gun, BAR, and tommy gun slugs.

Dick Wintz noticed that a machine gun position manned by the Dog Company sergeant Bill Roberson appeared to have been buttressed by a ring of sandbags. When Wintz crawled closer to inspect, he saw that what he took for sandbags were German bodies. The attackers who escaped the Ranger fire were torn to pieces by artillery directed by Kettelhut that fell so close to the aid bunker that shrapnel rattled off American helmets.

The Germans, beaten back again, went to ground in the ravine below Hill 400's eastern slope, and the Rangers could hear a roll call being taken. But something was off. The replies were ostentatiously loud, and to the Americans it sounded as if the same voices were answering to different names. They took it as a welcome sign—the enemy playing its last, desperate hand.

Milt Moss took advantage of the lull to make a gun run—collecting weapons from the dead. He had picked up a spare M1 rifle and several half-full bandoliers, a .45-caliber sidearm, and even a small satchel of fragmentation grenades when, crawling back to his foxhole, he spotted a German officer crouched behind a tree. The man, who had not spotted Moss, held a burp gun in one hand and was making signals to an unseen compatriot with the other. Within moments another German appeared, holding a white handkerchief tied to a pine branch. Moss hit the ground, sensing a ruse. He raised himself slightly, aimed his rifle, and hollered, *"Hände hoch; kommen Sie hier!"*

The words still hung in the air when slugs from a burp gun scattered the spare weapons Moss had spread before him. Bunny Moss shot the officer dead, wheeled, and killed the soldier holding the white flag. He stuffed the pistol and grenades into the folds of his field jacket and left the rifle. The burp gun's slugs had shattered its stock.

All told, the fifth and final firefight on Hill 400 lasted three hours. By the time the last of the attackers turned and fell back, the crest resembled an abattoir, with well over four hundred dead *Volksgrenadiers* and *Fallschirmjägers* littering the rise's nooks and crannies. For the assailants attempting to recapture the hill, in the words of the historian Douglas Nash, it was "truly the last gasp."

In fact, with so many of his men killed, wounded, and captured, Col. Kossmala's battalions had virtually ceased to exist. Yet he had no idea how close his men had come to retaking the heights. As the Germans licked their wounds, the Rangers took stock of their dwindling firepower. Milt Moss found Herm Stein to let him know that he had only two eight-round clips remaining for his M1. Stein patted his BAR and nodded. He, too, was down to his last couple of cartridges.

The night seemed colder and darker than usual, if that was possible. The driving sleet had turned to heavy snowfall by the time the last Germans limped away from Hill 400 toward the Roer. A thick white blanket soon obscured the contorted bodies splayed across the shell-racked heights. Ironically, it seemed to turn the killing fields into a serene and inviting scene from a prewar postcard.

The Rangers, their faces gaunt and expressionless, their bodies wrapped tight in overcoats and blankets "borrowed" from dead comrades, were too weary to notice.

37

Trudging Away

At 11:30 P.M. on December 8, after forty hours of continuous combat, the twenty-two effectives of Dog, Easy, and Fox Companies tensed at the sounds of boots tracking up the west slope of Hill 400. Swiveling in their holes, their hollow eyes narrowed over the sights of their near-empty weapons, they only relaxed when they recognized the insignias of the encroaching intruders. It was a company from the 8th Division's 1st Battalion. Their relief.

Medics and litter bearers swept through the aid bunker as Rangers who could still walk trudged for the last time down from the high outpost built on mud and wrath. A few Ranger sergeants—Herm Stein and Ed Secor among them—briefly remained behind to provide the newcomers with the lay of the fractured land.

The endless hours of incessant shelling and successive counterattacks in Bergstein and atop the small piece of real estate the Germans called *Burg-berg* had taken a mighty toll on the 2nd Ranger Battalion, whose fighting strength had been reduced by a third. Dog and Fox Companies had borne the brunt of the destruction. Out of the 133 troopers who had marched out of Bergstein toward the hill some forty-eight hours earlier, 4 were missing, 106 were wounded, and 23 would never see the sun rise again.

In the end, the U.S. Army's 8th Infantry Division had fared no better in the bloody forest than the 9th and 28th before it, suffering nearly fifty-two hundred casualties, including twelve hundred men pulled off the line for combat fatigue, trench foot, and other maladies caused by the severe elements.

These figures do not take into account the scores of thousands of casualties taken by the 4th, 78th, 83rd, 3rd Armored, and 5th Armored Divisions, which at some point also fought through the Hürtgen Forest. Meanwhile, in the three-month battle of attrition throughout the greater Hürtgen, German manpower and armor losses were close to an astounding thirty thousand casualties. The green hell of the Hürtgenwald ate men alive.

On the far side of the Roer River, Field Marshals Gerd von Rundstedt and Walter Model had mixed emotions. Not only had the fighting in and around the now-enemy-held Bergstein and the heights of *Burg-berg* pushed a salient into the German lines, but it had also severely impacted the counteroffensive force they planned to send into the Ardennes for Operation *Wacht am Rhein*—specifically the 272nd *Volks-Grenadier* Division, the remains of which Model had personally pulled out of the fight on December 8.

The Wehrmacht had been badly hurt by the Rangers' capture of Hill 400, which at the time constituted the Allies' deepest penetration into Germany. It caused the German general staff to narrow the approach of the upcoming assault through the Ardennes—with the loss of Hill 400, the enemy lost a large part of its ability to protect the northern flank of the German army with artillery fire when it made its last, desperate effort to turn the tide of the war. Moreover, the fall of the critical hill to a minuscule force of American Rangers had momentarily caused Wehrmacht morale to plummet even further.

It was, however, to be reanimated forty-eight hours later, when Adolf Hitler arrived at Rundstedt's field headquarters on the Western Front to personally take command of the offensive, which jumped off six days later.

Conversely, despite the Rangers' tenacity, Gen. Weaver's 8th Infantry Division was so decimated and exhausted that it was in no condition to press its advantage and push farther into Germany. Instead of advancing across the Roer, just one thousand yards away, Gen. Hodges ordered Weaver to begin the process of untangling his skewed front line by clearing and holding the ridges between Vossenack and Bergstein still occupied by scattered and undermanned German units.

Four days after relieving the Rangers on Hill 400, GIs from the 8th Division's 13th Infantry Regiment reported seeing "considerable" enemy troop train movements across the river in the town of Nideggen, four and a half miles away. Nideggen was, in fact, a major marshaling area for German soldiers preparing for Operation *Wacht am Rhein*.

Rather inconceivably, this discovery of Wehrmacht units massing for the Battle of the Bulge was not even mentioned in the 8th Division's daily intelligence summary.

At 6:15 A.M. on December 9, the remnants of the 2nd Ranger Battalion assembled on the northern edge of Bergstein. This time the deuce-and-a-half drivers had dared to venture all the way into the village. On the ride out of Germeter fifty-four hours earlier, the trucks carrying the Rangers had been loaded to overflowing. Now the vehicles were eerily empty except for the piles of duffel bags belonging to men who would never again need them.

Bob Edlin, daydreaming about the hot chow and coffee await-ing him in the rear, was walking toward the vehicle designated to carry the survivors from Able Company when Bob Arman stopped him. Lt. Arman told Edlin to report to Maj. Williams's battalion headquarters. The Fool Lieutenant's heart sank. *There's no way I can make another patrol right now,* he thought.

When Edlin reached the gutted building where Williams had set up his command post, he was greeted by the battalion's sergeant major, a gruff veteran named Manning Rubenstein who had re-placed Len Lomell when Lomell was promoted to lieutenant.

Rubenstein reached into a footlocker. Edlin could see piles of Purple Hearts. He felt a twinge in his left hand; the wound he'd taken outside of Germeter had never fully healed. And then he thought of the duffel bags piled into the deuce-and-a-halfs. The Pur-ple Hearts—General George Washington's profile on a heart-shaped purple shield bordered in gold—would soon be going out to griev-ing Ranger families across the United States.

He was about to remind Rubenstein that he'd already received his Purple Heart when the sergeant major dug out what he'd been searching for. He handed Edlin a citation and a box. Inside was the Distinguished Service Cross he'd been awarded for his actions at the Lochrist battery outside of Brest. The golden eagle on the medal, its wings spread athwart a cross, gleamed.

"Now get your ass out of here," Rubenstein said. "You're going back to the States. Thirty-day rest and recuperation leave."

It was Gen. Eisenhower's new policy, Rubenstein said, mandated for men with at least two decorations and six months of active com-bat service. Several wounded Rangers would be joining him for the voyage, Len Lomell among them, as would a dozen or so other Rangers who qualified for the month-long stateside leave. These in-cluded Bill "No-Neck" Courtney and Bill "Stoop" Dreher. The final member of the Fabulous Four, Warren "Halftrack" Burmaster, did not yet have the time served.

"What if I don't want to go?" Edlin said.

Rubenstein, stern, shook his head. "You're going. There's a jeep waiting for you up the road."

Edlin was torn. As much as he hated the thought of yet another patrol, he also abhorred the idea of leaving his Rangers to fight without him. Rubenstein must have read his thoughts. The sergeant major told him that the rest of the battalion was also slated for a month's R&R. Back in the Ardennes Forest. The Ardennes were safe, both men knew. They'd all been through the area. Cleaned and cleared, in military vernacular.

That eased Edlin's mind. No, the Fool Lieutenant thought, nothing bad is going to happen in the Ardennes.

Epilogue

On December 15, 1944, the 2nd Ranger Battalion's communications officer, Captain James "Ike" Eikner, was back in Eupen, Belgium. The Ardennes.

It was a week after the fight for Hill 400, and Eikner felt a strange mélange of relief, sadness, and ecstasy. "Civilization again," he said to his second-in-command, Lieutenant Tony Bazzocchi, as they checked into the small hotel that the U.S. Army had commandeered in the city center. Linen tablecloths. Feather beds, for god's sakes. Even espresso urns. "People living like human beings."

Eikner's only beef was that the rear-echelon troops had not been issued winter clothing. It was cold in Eupen, below freezing. He had no idea that the army's chief quartermaster had held back on shipping new cold-weather gear to the northern European front. The feeling at SHAEF was that the war was all but over in that sector. Given what he and the Rangers had just been through, Eikner figured he could live without woolen socks and long underwear.

Since being pulled from the line in the Hürtgen Forest, the two-hundred-odd surviving troopers of the 2nd Ranger Battalion—still attached to the 8th Infantry Division as a counterattack reserve—had eagerly shaved, showered, and donned clean uniforms before being billeted in towns like Eupen, Raeren, and Liège. Some of the veterans, like Len Lomell and three-quarters of the Fabulous Four—Bob Edlin, Bill Courtney, and Bill Dreher—were already making their way back to the States. Others had been granted travel passes to Paris for rest and recuperation. Wine. Women. Song was optional.

Major George Williams and his staff, meanwhile, were scouring the nearby replacement depots for volunteers to beef up the battalion's diminished ranks. Word from the various Allied fronts was once again positive, especially since Gen. Eisenhower's logistical supply lines to support combat operations along the Siegfried Line finally looked to be falling into place. Maybe "End the War in '44" had not been a pipe dream after all.

Not long after Eikner and Bazzocchi had settled into their hotel, a friend of Bazzocchi from V Corps asked if the two Rangers would be interested in joining the motor pool shuttling a USO troupe to and from the local theater where they were performing. The payoff was front-row seats to the show. Eikner and Bazzocchi jumped at the chance, and that night they found themselves driving two pretty blondes to the show. One of them was a perky comedienne. The other was the German-born international film star Marlene Dietrich, who had long since relocated to Hollywood. Eikner found Dietrich a pill. While the chatty comedienne laughed and flirted with the Rangers, the stony Dietrich, bundled in furs, refused to even look at them. When they reached the theater, she bolted from the jeep without a word of thanks.

Eikner was vaguely aware of the actress's Prussian roots and tried to sympathize with the thoughts that must have been running through her mind as she contemplated the destruction of her home country, just across the frontier. But he and Bazzocchi were so put off by Dietrich's haughtiness that they decided to skip the show. "Let her get back to the hotel any way she can," they agreed. The cute comedienne, they assumed, would have no problem hitching a ride.

The next morning in the hotel's basement restaurant, a waiter had just served the Rangers coffee when Dietrich strolled by. She lifted Eikner's cup off the table, uttered a curt, "Thank someone for ordering my coffee," and walked off. Before Eikner could say anything, he and Bazzocchi heard the whine of a shell and then an explosion in the distance. As they ran to the hotel entrance to investigate, their first thoughts were that an American tank gunner had overindulged on the potent Belgian beer and pointed his turret in the wrong direction before letting loose a round. But then another shell detonated. And another.

The two Rangers reached the street at the same moment that Eikner's jeep driver careened around the corner. Screeching the vehicle to a halt, he nearly ran over Eikner and Bazzocchi. Their orders, the driver said, were to pack immediately for reassembly. German divisions were pouring through the Ardennes.

The Battle of the Bulge had begun.

Chaos was too mild a description for what was occurring across Luxembourg and southeastern Belgium. It was not yet noon on December 16, and the First Army's 106th and 28th Infantry Divisions—including Lieutenant Colonel Jim Rudder's 109th Regiment—were close to being chewed to pieces by the nearly half-million advancing Germans. The assault included fifteen hundred tanks and tank destroyers, over twenty-five hundred artillery pieces, and close to one thousand Luftwaffe aircraft. The 2nd Ranger Battalion had been hurriedly trucked to the outskirts of the German village of Simmerath, near the German-Belgium border some twelve miles southeast of Aachen. When they arrived near midnight, the American troops in and around the area were taking heavy artillery.*

Maj. Williams established his headquarters in the basement of a ruined maternity hospital, the most prominent building in the town and therefore the most targeted by enemy artillerymen. Frank South, who had replaced Doc Block as chief medical officer, set up the outfit's aid station across the room. A switchboard was installed, telephone wires were unspooled, and Williams told his staff that, as far as he could learn, they seemed to be on the northern edge of the surprise German assault. They were miles, he figured, from the GIs bearing the brunt of the main thrust. But who knew? The sixty Rangers who had been issued passes to Paris had been recalled, but for now what was left of the battalion had been ordered to hold a line stretching across several snow-covered fields around Simmerath in an effort to shore up what would turn out to be the right flank of the enemy's bulging salient.

The manpower at Maj. Williams's disposal was still meager. Able, Baker, Charlie, and Easy Companies were platoon-sized at best, and the nineteen Dog Company Rangers who had survived Hill 400 had been designated as mortarmen. The remnants of Fox Company, with even fewer effectives, were converted into light machine gun teams. A few veterans noted that Charlie Company's Ralph Goranson was the only company commander still standing who had landed with the outfit on D-Day.

For the next nine days the Rangers, hunkered deep in their freezing, snow-encrusted foxholes, endured a steady barrage of rockets and shellfire. It was Herm Stein's idea to gather all the white sheets

---

* Such was the surprise with which the Allies were taken by the German counteroffensive that the U.S. Army's segregationist policy of keeping Black and white units separated was temporarily shelved in the name of the military necessity. Ironically, military necessity was the very justification which had kept Black and white American soldiers from integrating in the first place.

from the maternity hospital's linen closet and wear them like capes. The better, he figured, to blend in on the snowy ground. The Germans had again resorted to air-bursting proximity shells to drive the Americans from their open-topped dugouts. At least this time there were fewer trees to add lethal wood shards to the metal falling from the sky.

As returnees from Paris trickled in they were joined by fifty-three replacement troopers led by Lieutenant Ken McClure. McClure walked with a slight limp, but had convinced the rear-area doctors that he was hale enough to fight. A few of the new men were straight from basic training in the States without even having had the benefit of the individual infantry training; others had been culled from supply and signal units which had never seen combat. Some of the veterans never learned the names of their new platoon mates before their remains were shipped to the rear in shrouds, victims of what one veteran called "the mindless beast that was an incoming shell."

There were no all-out assaults by either side, though more than a few Rangers were thankful for the occasional German probes. The enemy patrols not only brought a merciful, if brief, hiatus to the continuous shelling, but provided warmth from movement otherwise impossible amid the cannonades. The temperatures continued to hover below freezing, and snow fell each day. "The warmest thing out there," noted Sid Salomon, "was the barrel of a BAR."

Then, on Christmas Eve, the clouds parted and the Rangers squinted in search of the Star of Bethlehem that had guided the Three Wise Men. Hours later, Christmas Day dawned cold and bright as the men whooped and hollered at the white contrails of counterattacking Allied fighter-bombers streaking the cornflower sky. Jerricans of hot coffee and turkey sandwiches were delivered from the rear sometime around midmorning. This time no one got sick.

Along with the food came word that the enemy offensive was

stalled short of Liège and the Meuse River. Although it would be another thirty days before all German forces withdrew back behind the Westwall, the Allies had effectively fought off Hitler's last-ditch *Wacht am Rhein*.

The remainder of the war in Europe proved somewhat anticlimactic for the 2nd Battalion, at least by Ranger standards. For the bulk of January, as the artillery barrages around Simmerath tapered, the Rangers held their positions while sending out nightly patrols. German prisoners taken invariably told the same story—their units were in retreat. In the meantime, replacement officers and enlisted men swelled the battalion to close to six hundred effectives. George Williams placed Duke Slater in charge of constructing firing ranges and rough-hewn classrooms to bring the newbies up to combat readiness. Speed marches took place each night.

In the last week of February, the outfit cleaved into two task forces and moved east, each unit attached to a separate cavalry reconnaissance group. Their combined mission: to secure a bridgehead over the Roer, the river that more than a few Rangers, dead and alive, had two months earlier glimpsed from atop Hill 400. By now the stubborn German enclave of Schmidt, deep in the Hürtgen, had finally fallen to GIs—the first Americans to enter the town since Bob Edlin's scouting mission back in mid-November of 1944. Over the first two days of March 1945, the Rangers of the 2nd Battalion waded through three feet of freezing water to the east bank of the Roer. The Germans had never blown their precious dams, which fell to American GIs from the 78th Infantry Division while the Rangers shielded their flanks. A captured Wehrmacht officer informed Maj. Williams that a mere few score *Landsers* remained in his unit still guarding the substations.

The following weeks found the Allies once again engaging in pursuit warfare, and a succession of German towns and villages between the Roer and the Rhine fell to the Rangers and their new mechanized cavalry partners—if, that is, "fell" is the proper verb. In each location with a bewildering name—Kreuzweingarten and Binzenbach; Kirchheim and Rissdorf—white sheets hung from flagstaffs once festooned with Nazi swastikas. In many cases the back alleys and garbage dumps were strewn with discarded Wehrmacht uniforms, and the American troopers could not help but notice men of fighting age wearing civilian coats, shirts, and pants that did not hide their hobnailed combat boots. Word was passed to check them for weapons and, if unarmed, leave them be for follow-up civil affairs units to handle.

In the defeated and starving nation, a Hershey chocolate bar or a pack of Lucky Strikes was worth its weight in gold, and Maj. Williams put Ike Eikner in charge of enforcing a no-fraternization policy. Any Ranger caught having sex with a German woman was to be busted a rank and have his pay docked sixty-five dollars.

Reminders of past travails, however, were never far. In the village of Vischel, just south of the city of Cologne, Able Company overran and surprised the rear guard of the retreating remnants of Colonel Georg Kossmala's 272nd Division. The once dauntless forest-fighting *Volksgrenadiers* were by now demoralized and unnerved. They formed a perfunctory skirmish line, but after eight Germans fell dead the rump of the unit surrendered. It was from Harvey Cook's interrogations that the Rangers learned of the capture of Big Stoop Masny and the two medics. Not long after, Sid Salomon summoned a mortar squad to chase off a platoon of Panzers accompanied by a unit of *Fallschirmjäger* paratroopers who, he suspected, had also fought on Hill 400. The tanks had inflicted five casualties on Baker Company while attempting to hold a railroad station overlooking an Ahr River bridge in the town of Altenahr.

Near the nondescript hamlet of Antweiler, a stray artillery shell found a column of Able Company Rangers, killing one and wounding five. Among the injured was Warren "Halftrack" Burmaster, thus drawing the final curtain on the adventures of the Fabulous Four. And on the outskirts of the quaint, wine-growing valley village of Mayschoss, Ranger scouts discovered a vast tunnel system protecting an underground power plant as well as the thirty-five hundred emaciated men and women from conquered countries who had been enslaved to keep it running.

By the last week of March, the 2nd Battalion had reached the juncture of the Ahr and Rhine Rivers, where, on the seventh day of the month, American infantrymen had stormed across an intact railroad bridge spanning the storied German watercourse. The Rangers followed on a pontoon bridge thrown up by army engineers. Three days later, forward elements from Dog Company made contact with units from Gen. Patton's 11th Armored Division thrusting into the Reich from farther south. The circle had been closed.

May 8, 1945, Victory in Europe Day, found the 2nd Ranger Battalion outside of the liberated city of Pilsen, several hundred miles across the eastern German border in what was then Czechoslovakia. The lilacs were in bloom. There they would remain for four months, providing protection for the new military government units and taking the occasional surrender of straggling German soldiers. They formed intramural softball teams and challenged outfits stationed nearby to basketball games and boxing matches. Not a few of the men closely followed the news from the Pacific Theater. Most assumed that this was their next deployment. When Japan surrendered, on August 15, a metaphorical sigh of relief pervaded their bivouac.

In recognition of their supreme service, General Omar Bradley decreed in early October that, unlike the majority of American infantry outfits, both the 2nd Ranger Battalion and the 5th Ranger Battalion—by this point attached to the 3rd Cavalry Reconnaissance Group and charged with securing the bridges over the Danube—

would be allowed to return to the States as intact units. George Williams's charges learned of the honor during the seventh-inning stretch of a softball game against a team of military police. Bob Edlin, who had returned to the battalion from his stateside leave, was on the mound.

On October 5, the 2nd Ranger Battalion once again boarded a string of French *quarante-et-huit* boxcars for the three-day journey to Reims, France. From Reims they were trucked to an assembly camp near the port of Le Havre. On October 16, they boarded the converted luxury liner USS *West Point* for the trip home.

Four days later, the 2nd Battalion debarked at Newport News, Virginia. At their final assembly at Camp Patrick Henry, no speeches were given, no parades were thrown. On October 23, the battalion's colors were furled without ceremony and each Ranger was issued a bus or train ticket. Sometimes their travel schedule permitted time to bid farewell to colleagues, sometimes it did not.

George Orwell is said to have remarked that we sleep soundly in our beds because rough men stand ready in the night to visit violence on those who would do us harm. Although the Rangers of the 2nd Battalion took different paths upon their return from the war, those veterans who stood ready in the night would always be connected by what Lincoln called "the mystic chords of memory."

For the survivors those memories included Omaha Beach, Pointe du Hoc, Fortress Brest, and, finally, the Last Hill in the Hürtgen Forest. Crucibles all.

Afterword

Writing about the Allied military struggles of late 1944 in the northwest section of the European Theater of Operations, it was left to Charles B. MacDonald, the rifle company commander who went on to become the deputy chief historian of the United States Army, to contextualize the too-often-overlooked combat that immediately preceded the Battle of the Bulge. "Some who have written of World War II in Europe have dismissed the period between 11 September and 16 December 1944 with a paragraph or two," MacDonald wrote in his seminal *The Siegfried Line Campaign*. "This has been their way of gaining space to tell of the [other] whirlwind advances."

MacDonald pointedly added that despite the Allies' overwhelming preponderance of air and sea power, the grisly combat of that autumn "belonged to the small units and individual soldiers."

As both a ground-pounding infantryman and a historian, MacDonald, who died in 1990, was a man of his era. He not only personally witnessed the carnage he chronicled along the Siegfried Line, but was later given access to the papers, public and private, of the American general officers who had overseen it. As a former junior officer, he may have been too tactful to suggest that those same generals, with the Nazis finally defeated, were relieved to have "dismissed the period" that the Germans called *die Hölle im Hürtgenwald*—"the hell in the Hürtgen Forest."

The American high command knew well, as did MacDonald, how much blood had been spilled in that woodland to accomplish so little. Over the three-month battle of attrition, the U.S. Army sent a total of 120,000 riflemen and tank crews into the dank forest. Thirty-three thousand of them became casualties.

Several historians have noted that the sacrifice in the Hürtgen was needless, and inadvertently stemmed from a general order issued by Dwight Eisenhower in mid-1944. In it, Eisenhower authorized his division commanders to anticipate their losses forty-eight hours in advance in order to accelerate the arrival of replacement troops. The Supreme Commander's strategic intentions—ensuring that Allied "pursuit" momentum would not be slowed to allow a desperate and retreating enemy time to regroup—certainly made sense on paper. But the general order's tactical consequences may have had the opposite effect of encouraging some staff officers who rarely visited the front to pour more and more manpower into the enigmatic campaign.

In any case, given their overall outstanding wartime leadership, neither Eisenhower, the future president of the United States, nor the U.S. Army's chief of staff, General George Marshall—whose surname personified the successful postwar plan to prevent the economic collapse of Europe and to contain the expansion of communism—suffered any repercussions to their reputations from the army's missteps in the bloodstained Hürtgen. Nor did any taint accrue to General Omar Bradley, whom the famed war correspondent Ernie Pyle dubbed "the GI's general." After the war, President Harry Truman tapped Bradley to head up the Veterans Administration before Bradley succeeded Marshall as the army's chief of staff. In 1949,

Truman appointed Bradley as the first chairman of the newly inaugurated Joint Chiefs of Staff; a year later he was promoted to the rank of General of the Army, the fifth—and last—soldier to achieve that rank.* In retirement, Bradley was, rightly, feted as a hero.

Even General Courtney Hodges escaped contemporaneous public opprobrium for his tepid Hürtgen Forest strategy.† Hodges's First Army rebounded from the Battle of the Bulge and went on to resume its penetration into the German heartland. This led Gen. Eisenhower to refer to Hodges as "the spearhead and the scintillating star" of the advance into the Reich. Eisenhower went so far as to urge the War Department's public relations department to steer newspapermen toward interviews with Hodges and, by intimation, away from the wildly popular and outspoken George Patton. And though General Norman "Dutch" Cota's disastrous divisional assault on the Wehrmacht's forest stronghold of Schmidt was the low point of Cota's otherwise illustrious military career, his postwar appointment as a director of the War Assets Administration, the precursor to today's General Services Administration, only served to enhance his formidable reputation.

The fate of the American commanders' German counterparts in the fight to defend the Hürtgen Forest was mixed. Contrary to his own bleak expectations, Field Marshal Gerd von Rundstedt lived to see Nazi Germany's unconditional surrender. Having been relieved of duty by Hitler after the Allies breached the Rhine River, Rundstedt was subsequently taken into custody by American forces on May 1, 1945, the day after the Führer's suicide in his Berlin bunker. As a field operations officer who claimed no political affiliation

---

* Bradley joined Marshall, Eisenhower, Douglas MacArthur, and Henry "Hap" Arnold in that pantheon.

† Judging from multiple foot soldiers' scathing journals, diaries, and even modern-day entries into World War II remembrances on blogs and websites, Hodges is still considered a bewildered butcher in certain quarters.

with the National Socialist regime, Rundstedt was spared an individual indictment for war crimes at the Nuremberg Trials. Impoverished and overcome with a disenchanted world-weariness that the Germans call *Weltschmerz*, he died of a heart attack at the age of seventy-seven in February 1953.

The end came more rapidly for the monocled Field Marshal Walter Model. After finding his 370,000-man Army Group B outnumbered and surrounded in the Ruhr Valley by two American armies in early April 1945, Model chose to honor his oath to Adolf Hitler and refused to formally surrender. Instead, he ordered the dissolution of his divisions and advised his soldiers to follow their consciences as to whether to lay down their arms individually or to fight on, guerrilla style. Close to 320,000 *Landsers* subsequently surrendered. In a dark coda, this decision earned Model the rabid vilification of Joseph Goebbels's desperate Nazi Propaganda Ministry. Labeled a traitor to the Reich by Goebbels and indicted for war crimes by the Soviet Union, Model shot himself in the head in a patch of Ruhr Valley woods on April 21. He was buried by his staff on the spot. Ten years later his son exhumed Model's remains from the field grave and reinterred them in a German military cemetery in the Hürtgen Forest.

On the opposite end of the spectrum lay the fate of the Wehrmacht officer Georg Kossmala. Not long after the 2nd Ranger Battalion overran the rear guard of what was left of his retreating 272nd *Volks-Grenadier* Division in early 1945, Kossmala, having been promoted to general, was killed while fighting the advancing Soviets in southern Poland's Silesia region.

As for the American senior officers with the most hands-on experience standing up the 2nd Ranger Battalion at Tennessee's Camp Forrest, General Ben Lear, having reached the army's mandatory retirement age of sixty-four in 1943, was administratively released from the service. Lear was then immediately recalled to active duty on a special exemption to serve on the Secretary of War's personnel board. In a trenchant touch, the Ranger-loving Lear replaced the commando-hating General Lesley McNair as commanding general of U.S. Army Ground Forces when McNair was killed by friendly artillery fire in France the following year.

Lear's successor at Camp Forrest, General Lloyd Fredendall—despite his discovery of a rough diamond in the then-Major James Earl Rudder to command the 2nd Ranger Battalion—could never erase the black mark left by his defeat at the hands of Erwin Rommel's Afrika Korps during the North African campaign's catastrophic Battle of the Kasserine Pass. Shipped home afterward, Fredendall spent the rest of his military career in stateside training assignments before his retirement in 1946.

The apparent lack of strategic purpose to the Battle of the Hürtgen Forest can in no way diminish the valor of the junior officers, noncoms, and enlisted men who fought and died there with such courage. No small part of that heroism accrued to the 2nd Ranger Battalion, which by 1945 had become one of the most highly decorated units in American military history, earning eighteen Distinguished Service Crosses, seventy-three Silver Stars, sixty-four Bronze Stars, two British Military Medals, and an astonishing 542 Purple Hearts. The outfit was also awarded a Presidential Unit Citation for its actions on D-Day. Inexplicably, a second submission for a Presidential Unit Citation, for the battalion's performance atop Hill 400 and in and around Bergstein during the first week of December 1944, was turned down.

The five-page narrative for the rejected Presidential Unit Citation, submitted by the XXII Corps commander General Ernest Harmon in August 1945, is as colorful and tightly woven as a Persian rug. Gen. Harmon chronicles in detail "the extraordinary gallantry and heroism [the 2nd Battalion] displayed . . . to seize and hold Hill

400." Harmon's proposed commendation concludes: "The fierce enemy artillery fire, the numerically superior enemy, the additional hardship of adverse weather, cold and hunger, failed to force these stubborn, fighting Rangers to withdraw. There was no panic, simply an indomitable will to hold this position."

It was never adequately explained why Gen. Harmon's petition was swept away in the postwar bureaucratic wash. The Rangers did not discover the apparent snub until several years later. After being informed of the slight, Captain Sid Salomon, then active in several Ranger alumni associations, drolly noted, "Further inquiry to re-open the matter was discouraged."

Following their understated demobilization at Virginia's Camp Patrick Henry in October 1945, the Rangers of the 2nd Battalion were left with only their battle scars and the memories of their comradery, their pride in their combat heritage, and, moving forward, the varied career opportunities open to civilian-soldiers of such special breed. Some participants of the European campaign, including the battalion's final commander, Major George Williams, seemed to vanish into the churn of postwar history. Others, such as the stalwart GI forward artillery observer Lieutenant Howard Kettelhut, picked up their prewar lives without seeming to miss a beat. After a brief stint living in Kansas City, Kettelhut, his wife, and his three young sons moved back home to Omaha, Nebraska, where he settled into employment as the director of purchasing for a trailer-truck manufacturer while winning numerous trophies for his trap- and skeet-shooting expertise. He apparently never lost his sharp eye. Kettelhut passed away in 1988, at the age of sixty-nine.

Still others found that combat had altered the course of their careers. The leg wound to Dog Company's professional tap dancer Antonio Ruggiero, for instance, never really healed, or never healed well enough for him to resume his show business vocation. Instead, upon returning home to Plymouth, Massachusetts, Ruggiero chose to dance up and down ladders as a fireman, retiring as a captain from the Plymouth Fire Department after a twenty-eight-year career. In 2009, the eighty-nine-year-old Ruggiero escorted President Barack Obama's first lady, Michelle Obama, across the tabletop of Pointe du Hoc during a ceremony commemorating the sixty-fifth anniversary of the Normandy landings. Ruggiero died seven years later. As for the officer who rescued the vomiting Ruggiero at the base of Hill 400 by throwing him over his shoulder and hauling him back to Doc Block's makeshift medical station in the Bergstein church basement, Captain Morton McBride returned to his hometown of Dickinson, North Dakota, and passed away in 1983 at the age of seventy-two.

Like Tony Ruggiero, Charlie Company's commanding officer, Captain Ralph Goranson, was another veteran who enjoyed a full and long postwar life, passing away in the northern suburbs of Chicago in 2012 at the age of ninety-three. After returning to the States, Goranson took a job with the nascent Zenith radio-manufacturing corporation, where he worked as an account executive for several decades while remaining active in his local American Legion post as well as his Lutheran parish church.

Many who knew Goranson saw the measure of the man captured by Tom Hanks's portrayal of Captain John Miller, commander of the fictional 2nd Ranger Battalion's Charlie Company, in Steven Spielberg's 1998 film *Saving Private Ryan*. Of particular relevance were the movie's grisly opening scenes on Omaha Beach. Although Spielberg took some artistic license regarding where Ralph Goranson's "real" Charlie Company actually landed on D-Day, it is quite apparent that Hanks's and the other actors' performances were infused with the spirit of Goranson's outfit as it crossed the bloody sands toward the outcropping of Pointe de la Percée.

Somewhat incredibly, the Dog Company sergeant Jack Kuhn made it to VE Day without suffering a serious wound. The noncom who amazed his fellow Camp Forrest recruits with his judo skills retired from the army with the rank of 1st sergeant only to re-enlist upon the outbreak of hostilities on the Korean peninsula five years later. Following the armistice agreement between North and South Korea, Kuhn returned to Altoona, Pennsylvania, and joined the city's police force. As he rose through the ranks, from detective sergeant to captain of the Criminal Investigation Division to deputy chief, Kuhn spoke little of his heroism atop Pointe du Hoc with Len Lomell in finding and disabling the German 155 mm howitzers and then spending that lonely night surrounded by enemy troops.

Upon Kuhn's appointment as Altoona's police chief in 1973, he did confide to associates how, during the 2nd Battalion's pursuit of the fleeing Germans after the Battle of the Bulge, he was a part of a Ranger squad that captured the massive if lightly defended Schaumberg Castle, outside the German town of Balduinstein. The *schloss* had been used as a *Kriegsmarine* book depository, and in its cellar Kuhn and the others discovered a vast collection of volumes detailing information about hundreds of American cities that the Nazis planned to conquer and administrate. The Altoona guide ran to an inch thick, and Kuhn liked to say that if he'd known he was one day to become the town's chief of police he would have held on to the book, as the Germans seemed to know more about his city than he did.

Kuhn retired from the Altoona Police Department in 1976 and, not one to take to a rocking chair or hammock, spent the next twenty-five years volunteering as a school bus driver. He died in December 2002, at the age of eighty-three. Kuhn, his commander Jim Rudder, and his running mate Len Lomell were the first three Rangers from the 2nd Battalion to be inducted into the U.S. Army Ranger Hall of Fame, in 1992.

Kuhn was not the only former Ranger to fight in the Korean War. Lieutenant Colonel Max Schneider and Captain Harold "The Duke" Slater both remained in the service following World War II, and both saw action in what was dubiously dubbed the United States' "police action" on that East Asian peninsula. Though their military careers never intersected after the Ranger campaigns of World War II, their psyches would deal with similar turmoil, albeit with very different outcomes.

After Schneider ceded his duties as commander of the 5th Ranger Battalion during the Brittany campaign in the summer of 1944, he returned to the States, graduated from the army's Command and General Staff College, and in 1946 was integrated back into the regular army with the rank of full colonel. Schneider went on to become part of General Douglas MacArthur's Inchon landing force and, following the Korean armistice, assumed duty posts in Japan and Germany. But Schneider's private demons were never far from the surface, and associates could not help but notice the palsy-like tremors that sometimes shook his body or the searing headaches for which he refused medication. In 1959, assigned to travel from the United States to a new posting in South Korea, Schneider instead disappeared for two weeks. He was discovered wandering the streets of San Francisco in a disoriented state. Instead of offering Schneider the psychological assistance he so obviously needed, the army charged him with being absent without leave. Weeks later, on March 25, 1959, Schneider took his own life at the age of forty-six.

Duke Slater, meanwhile, remained true to Col. Rudder's description of him as a soldier forever looking for a fight. He certainly found one in the Korean mountains. When hostilities broke out in June 1950, Slater, by now a colonel, was posted as an adviser to a Republic of Korea, or ROK, army regiment that in reality looked to him as their commander. During the year and a half that he "advised" his charges, he also incorporated into his command a battalion of deserters from the North Korean army that became known as one of the fiercest combat units in the war.

In May 1951, while fighting a rearguard action against the Red Army, Slater was captured by the Communist Chinese. Along with a bevy of American, ROK, English, Australian, and Turkish captives, he was marched to a prisoner-of-war camp near the Chinese border. Slater watched as those who could not keep pace through the rugged terrain were simply culled from the straggling line and bayoneted to death. When Slater was taken, he weighed 206 pounds. When he was released thirty months later, after surviving miserable conditions that included starvation rations and near-daily beatings, he weighed 110 pounds.

After his retirement from the army, Slater married and moved to Albuquerque, where he was an active volunteer in both the New Mexico Veterans Memorial Association and the local Salvation Army chapter. But the memories of his Korean incarceration never left him. He once told an interviewer that his wife, Inez, would wake him in the middle of the night because he was screaming and drenched in sweat. He added that after her death, he still awoke covered in perspiration, but did not know if he had been screaming because no one was around to tell him. Harold Slater died at ninety-two, in his adoptive city of Albuquerque, in 2011.

It is not recorded if Slater and his fellow Ranger Captain Otto "Big Stoop" Masny traded prisoner-of-war stories in the wee hours of the many Ranger reunions. As it turned out, L-Rod Petty's warning to Capt. Masny about scattered enemy forces still occupying the western slope of Hill 400 on the morning of December 7, 1944, proved prescient. Masny was indeed captured by German *Volksgrenadiers* as he descended the hill to collect reinforcements. He spent the next two weeks being questioned by SS officers who attempted to beat out of him any information he might have concerning the coming German counteroffensive through the Ardennes. Finally, with his inquisitors convinced that he knew nothing, Masny—minus his front teeth, which had been kicked out of his mouth during the "interrogations"—was shipped to Oflag 64, a prisoner-of-war camp for Allied officers in what is now the town of Szubin in northwestern Poland.

With the approach of the Soviet army in January 1945, Masny and the other captives were gathered for a projected forced march of nearly four hundred miles to another POW camp in the heart of Germany. In the haste and confusion of the retreat, Masny and several others managed to slip away and return to the abandoned Oflag 64. The Russians arrived soon after. Wary of relying on the tender mercies of America's Soviet allies—who were known to ransom any American prisoners of war they liberated—Masny and a few fellow Americans stole a Russian vehicle.

By various means and methods, over the next six weeks Masny trekked nearly one thousand miles to the Black Sea port of Odessa. There he secured a berth on an Australian supply ship bound for Port Said, Egypt, where he checked himself in to an American military hospital. Released from the service with full honors in late 1945, Otto Masny settled with his wife, Eileen, in Wisconsin, where he passed away in 1991 at the age of seventy-three.

The medic Frank South, whom Doc Block had sent to a rear-area hospital with a severe case of gastroenteritis just prior to the assault on Hill 400, was unaware that the 2nd Battalion had been thrown into combat atop the heights until wounded Rangers began to arrive at the ward where he was being treated. He immediately went AWOL, but by the time he caught up with his outfit outside of Bergstein, the fight was over. "I still feel guilty and somehow cheated that I was not part of that battle," he later wrote to Doc Block's son Jeff.

After mustering out of the army at war's end, South briefly

considered applying to medical school. In the end, however, academia beckoned, and he threw himself into the research atmosphere at the Berkeley campus of the University of California while earning a Ph.D. From there he embarked on a career teaching biophysics and physiology at the University of Delaware in his hometown of Newark, Delaware. Despite his near-lethal journey on the British landing craft that carried him to the cliffs of Pointe du Hoc, South developed a passion for sailing. Following his retirement, he and his wife, BernaDeane, were known to embark on ocean voyages from Maine to Key West. South died in March 2013, at the age of eighty-eight.

Campus life was not the cup of tea for South's best friend from the battalion, the medic Willie Clark. Perhaps influenced by the outfit's mop-up policing duties across the final few months of the war, Clark joined the Washington, D.C., police force following his discharge. There, as a detective sergeant, he served on the vice squad while also specializing in solving auto crimes. Like Howard Kettelhut, Clark was a far-too-young sixty-nine years old when he died, in February 1992. He was lowered to his final resting place in Arlington National Cemetery, not far from the future grave site of Sid Salomon, the Ranger with whom he had shared the perils of Omaha Beach.

Captain Sidney Salomon returned from Europe to New Jersey and the following year married his longtime sweetheart, Jocelyn Jungman. Together they raised four children. Upon Salomon's discharge from the Army Reserve in 1953, he was recruited by the corporation that was to become the American Can Company, where over a thirty-year career he rose to the position of regional sales manager. Salomon was also an active member of the WWII Ranger Battalions Association, serving as its national president from 1977 to 1979.

In 1982, following his retirement and the premature passing of his wife, Salomon joined a Philadelphia boat club and resumed his prewar rowing career. Known to his friends as the Iron Man, within two years of taking up his old passion Salomon was again competing in world-class competitions, winning over fifty gold medals, including eighteen United States Masters titles. Salomon continued to compete at regional, national, and international rowing regattas well into his eighties. He finally gave up rowing a month shy of his ninetieth birthday, several months prior to his passing in 2004.

When James "Ike" Eikner returned to Texas from overseas, his prewar supervisor at Southwestern Bell Telephone informed him that his old job as a telephone lineman was waiting for him. It was not long, however, before he was promoted to the position of senior engineer in the company's Special Services Department. It was from this office that in 1963 he was sent to the southwest-central Texas Hill Country to personally oversee the installation of secure telephone lines in the ranch and outlying buildings that became known as President Lyndon Baines Johnson's Texas White House.

Eikner eventually retired to Austin and devoted much of his later years to becoming the unofficial historian of the 2nd Ranger Battalion. In addition to his tape-recorded recollections and the personal papers he had accrued as the outfit's chief communications officer and commander of its Headquarters Company, he also collected a wide range of historical military materials and World War II memorabilia. This was the foundation of the James Wilmot Eikner Papers—which grew to 7.5 linear feet of documents housed at the Dolph Briscoe Center for American History at the University of Texas campus in Austin.

Eikner died on May Day, 2014, at the age of one hundred. In his eulogy, Eikner's son, Jim, remembered his father as a simple man: "He was a telephone installer and climbed poles and learned from the ground up." Similar sentiments could also be said to apply to Ike Eikner's stellar Ranger career.

Just as Eikner put his electronic communications skills to postwar use, Herm Stein did not allow his special Ranger talent for climbing to go to waste after his honorable discharge. Stein returned to New York and his bride, the former Lena Toirac, who had married him the week before he shipped out and with whom he would share the next sixty-eight years of his life. Stein initially found work with a construction company erecting Manhattan skyscrapers. Naturally, Stein was assigned to rivet the highest beams hundreds of feet off the ground. From there he tried his hand at truck driving, welding sheet metal, and even chicken farming, before discovering his true métier by starting a roofing company near his old haunts in the rapidly suburbanizing Westchester County, north of New York City. During these early, postwar perambulations, the Stein household doubled and then tripled with the birth of three daughters and a son.

In 1979, Stein relocated his roofing company to—of all places—Fort Pierce, Florida, where he was known to regale his new neighbors along the Indian River with tales of the excruciating swim and swat exercises that had tormented him decades earlier on the nearby beaches of Hutchinson Island. Stein continued to scamper across rooftops well into his eighties, and when it finally came time to pass the company reins to his son, Robby, Herm and Lena retired to Duluth, Georgia, where the nimble climber known as Bubby died in June 2012, at the age of ninety-one.

Whenever one of Stein's old war buddies passed, Stein would inevitably remark that he went to "Ranger Heaven"—a special place in the firmament, Stein believed, that was reserved for those who had worn the Ranger patch. With his own death imminent, Stein called his wife and children together to inform them that he was ready to finally again see his best friend and brother-in-arms, William "L-Rod" Petty, who had died twelve years earlier at the age of seventy-eight.

Following Petty's service discharge, he returned to the University of Georgia to finish obtaining his degree, and then opened a laundromat in nearby Dalton, Georgia. When that business failed to take off, Petty moved to New York City, where he earned a master's degree from New York University—the same school that Herm Stein had briefly attended, and played baseball for, before the war. Petty was once asked by a reporter the difference between the combat atop Pointe du Hoc and the fighting atop Hill 400. Petty replied that he "would personally take my three days at Pointe du Hoc as an annual holiday compared to my one day on that hill."

In the end, L-Rod finally found the parental peace that had eluded him as a child when he took over the operation of the Clear Pool Boys Camp in Putnam County, New York, which served New York City's disadvantaged youth. As one Ranger wrote of Petty's ultimate vocation, "For many mistreated children, he became the loving father that he and they had never known."

In contrast to the apprehension many Rangers felt after the Nazi surrender regarding an imminent deployment to the Pacific, Lieutenant Bob Edlin was eager for more combat. The army, he felt, and particularly patrolling for the army, had become his life. When he heard rumors that the 28th Infantry Division—which included Col. Rudder's regiment—might be Asia-bound to fight the Japanese, he even reached out to his old commander to inquire about transferring into his outfit. Rudder turned Edlin down, advising the "Fool Lieutenant" that he'd seen enough action, and suggesting strongly that Edlin return to the States and get on with his life. Rudder also promised to keep in touch. As it was, the atomic bombs dropped on Hiroshima and Nagasaki mooted Edlin's martial ambitions.

It is not recorded if Edlin tried to lasso his old "Fabulous Four" running mates Bill "Stoop" Dreher and Bill "No-Neck" Courtney into his scheme to hook up with Rudder's regiment. As it was, the quartet never rode again, as the shellfire wounds taken by Warren "Halftrack" Burmaster during the 2nd Battalion's pursuit warfare through Germany were serious enough to keep him hospital-bound for six months after he was shipped back to the States. Upon his recovery and release, Burmaster returned to Louisiana and joined the family business, operating a sawmill and several service stations, then driving an ice truck between his hometown of Belle Chasse and nearby Buras, Louisiana. Burmaster, who fathered a daughter and two sons with his wife, Alpha, died in 2015 at the age of ninety-two.

Burmaster's passing preceded by fifteen months the death of Bill Dreher, who upon his discharge enrolled in medical school and, after his graduation, served for thirty-two years as a staff psychiatrist for the Veterans Administration Medical Center in Gulfport, Mississippi, while also maintaining a private psychiatry practice. Three of the Fabulous Four outlived their compatriot Bill "No-Neck" Courtney, who died in La Grange, Illinois, in 1991, at the age of sixty-nine.

The Indiana homecoming of the Fabulous Four's leader, Bob Edlin, got off to a rocky start after he was discharged from the army with the rank of captain in March 1946. Edlin found working with his father at a furniture store mind-deadening, and his short stint as a commander in the Indiana National Guard was aborted when his superior officer refused to allow him to recruit Black soldiers. Even his brief career as a policeman turned sour when, ever headstrong, Edlin refused to engage in what he considered the overly political nature of the job.

Circumstances began to turn for Edlin when he married his girl-friend Dodie, with whom he would father a son and a daughter, and he found himself earning a decent wage as an insurance salesman. His life came full circle not long after when Jim Rudder, who would retire from the Army Reserve as a brigadier general, contacted him with the suggestion that Edlin and his young family relocate to Corpus Christi, Texas. From there, Edlin's unlikely career overseeing an import-export business and auction house took off. Given Edlin's fast-talking Ranger days, perhaps becoming an auctioneer was what he had been cut out for all along.

Meanwhile, twenty-five years after the events in the Hürtgen Forest, Edlin attended a Ranger reunion at which one of the invitees was a former officer who had fought through the forest with the 28th Infantry Division. The ex-GI explained to Edlin how he had been captured by a German patrol in early November 1944, and that he had been one of the American POWs whose voices Edlin had heard when he had snuck into Schmidt on the Fabulous Four's recon mission. He told Edlin that the Germans—as Edlin had suspected that night—were secretly watching the progress of his patrol, waiting in ambush in case the four Rangers were the point team for a larger force. For the first time in decades, Bob Edlin again thought of Cisterna and the trap set for Bill Darby's Rangers.

Perhaps appropriately, the "Fool Lieutenant" died on April Fool's Day, 2005. He was a month shy of his eighty-third birthday.

As with Bob Edlin, Lieutenant Len Lomell was also provided with a post-war epiphany when he discovered that you were never too old to learn something new about your own past—even if in Lomell's case, it was demonstrably false. Following Lomell's medical evacuation to the United States in December 1944, he was designated an ambulatory hospital patient. As such, the army found in Lomell's all-American looks and his heroic narratives the perfect stories to sell war bonds and, as Lomell once recalled with a sly smile, "to recruit WACs."

Following Lomell's discharge in 1945, he returned to his hometown of Toms River on the Jersey Shore and married the former Charlotte Ewart, with whom he raised three daughters. Upon his graduation from Rutgers Law School, Lomell set up a legal practice near the beach and, even after his retirement in the mid-1980s, remained one of his community's most active civic leaders as a bank and title insurance company director, a member and trustee of local education, hospital, and college boards, and president of the New Jersey Philharmonic Society.

Unlike Edlin, Lomell's revelatory moment arrived not at a Ranger reunion, but when he and several surviving Dog Company troopers returned to Hill 400 in 1989. When the now-elderly men clambered to the top of the rise they and their brethren had taken and held against multiple counterattacks forty-five years earlier, they were greeted by a welcoming committee of young German army officers. During the course of their conversation about the battle, one of the Germans translated an account of the engagement from a German textbook. The Americans were stunned speechless by the claim that the Wehrmacht soldiers defending what they called *Burg-berg* had been soundly outnumbered by the Rangers of the 2nd Battalion. Lomell broke the silence with a roaring laugh. "That's ridiculous," he told his interlocutors. "As a matter of fact, we were the ones outnumbered ten-to-one."

Lomell surmised that this was merely an attempt by a country that had lost two world wars to save a bit of face. But what really angered him for his entire life were the various misleading portrayals of the Rangers atop Pointe du Hoc produced by chroniclers from his own country. Particularly nettlesome was the account in Cornelius Ryan's bestselling book *The Longest Day* and the subsequent movie based on Ryan's narrative. In both, the Rangers who perished scaling the cliffs were depicted as having died in vain when the survivors reached the top only to find the German howitzers vanished. "They say, 'Wasn't it a shame, those boys climbed that cliff, there were no guns, the mission was in vain,'" Lomell told an interviewer in 1992. "That's not true," he continued, his voice rising. "The mission was to get those guns, wherever they are, as quickly as you can. And we did."

In 2001, in a modest statement submitted to a New Jersey congressman petitioning the Pentagon to consider awarding Lomell a belated Medal of Honor for his actions atop Hill 400, Lomell perhaps inadvertently penned his own epitaph. "Some people say D-Day, June 6, 1944, was their longest day," he wrote to Representative Chris Smith. "But for me, December 7, 1944—assaulting and climbing that steep and slippery hill in the Hürtgen Forest—was the longest, worst, and most dangerous day of my life."

Len Lomell died in his hometown of Toms River in 2011 at age ninety-one. Some thirty active-duty Rangers from the 75th Ranger Regiment stationed at Georgia's Fort Benning and the 2nd Ranger Battalion out of Fort Lewis in Washington State attended the funeral in honor of their forebear's valor.

The officer who recommended that Len Lomell receive a field promotion from battalion sergeant major to 2nd lieutenant needed a war chest to lug home the commendations he earned during World War II. When Lieutenant Colonel James Earl Rudder left the Rangers and assumed command of the 109th Infantry Regiment on December 8, 1944, his new unit was in near tatters, having sustained 1,367 casualties—44 percent of its effective manpower—over the previous five weeks of fighting in the Hürtgen Forest. Rudder had only just begun rebuilding and refitting the regiment when the German offensive now known as the Battle of the Bulge rolled through the Ardennes eight days later. Rudder's outfit, spread across a two-hundred-foot-high hilltop near the town of Ettelbruck in central Luxembourg, withstood repeated attacks for six days until, on December 22, American artillery broke the enemy's surge. Thereafter Rudder's 109th Regiment fell in with General George Patton's tank brigades and, as Rudder later recalled, "We stacked [dead Germans] in piles along the road from Ettelbruck." For his leadership, Rudder was promoted to colonel and awarded the Silver Star to go along with his Distinguished Service Cross, Bronze Star with Oak Leaf Cluster, Purple Heart, French Legion of Honor with Croix de Guerre, and Belgian Order of Leopold medal.

Anticipating the end of the war and his return to the States, Rudder wrote to his wife, Chick, "Our lives must be so complete that we can make up for that time that has been stolen from us." The couple, along with their five children, strove to do just that. Home in Texas within a year of V-J Day, Rudder was elected the mayor of the town of Brady, in the heart of the state, a post in which he served until 1952. Thereafter he declined to run for reelection and instead became a vice president of the Brady Aviation Corporation, a subsidiary of a tractor company expanding into manufacturing aircraft parts. Three years later, however, he was back in politics, drafted by the state's Democratic Party to run for the office of Texas land commissioner. Once elected, he was charged with reforming the notoriously corrupt and mismanaged Veterans Land Program. Such was Rudder's burgeoning reputation that, in 1958, he was named the vice president of his alma mater, Texas A&M; a year later he assumed the university's presidency.

Rudder's reformer's chops had been honed by his stint as land commissioner, and at Texas A&M he instituted a series of modernizations—allowing women to be admitted, integrating the campus, and making membership in the school's vaunted and cliquish Corps of Cadets optional. Those changes and more, while eliciting grumbles from traditionalist alumni, transformed the school from a small, all-male and all-white land-grant college into what is as of this writing the second-largest university in the United States. By 1967, Rudder was serving as president of the state's entire A&M university system when President Lyndon B. Johnson presented him with yet another honor, the Army Distinguished Service Medal, the service's highest peacetime award.

Rudder died in March 1970, two weeks shy of his sixtieth birthday. He was felled by a host of ailments, including a cerebral hemor-rhage and "circulatory collapse brought on by a kidney infection." He left a statewide legacy including numerous roads, buildings, and campus sites named in his honor, as well as the General James E. Rudder Medal to be awarded annually by the Association of the United States Army to the army reservist whose career in the Army Reserve best exemplified the traits of a citizen-soldier embodied by Big Jim.

At the conclusion of the memorial service held for Rudder at Texas A&M a few days after his death, the more than five thousand mourners—the former President Johnson and his wife Lady Bird Johnson among them—took notice of a dozen or so middle-aged men lingering off to the side. They were, of course, former Rang-ers, including Len Lomell, Ralph Goranson, and Bob Edlin. All had journeyed to College Station to bid their commander a final fare-well. A few months earlier, Rudder had written to his long-ago 2nd Battalion charges. In his letter he emphasized the wartime bond they had forged that, in his words, "an outsider cannot comprehend." It could only be understood, he continued, "by those of us who have had this privileged experience."

Rudder's Rangers snapped to attention when the caisson carry-ing his body pulled away, as the slow, sacred cadences of the univer-sity's traditional Silver Taps rendition of "Ave Maria" wafted above the procession.

Postscript

With the exhaustive fighting of World War II completed, the various branches of the United States Army naturally found themselves engrossed with the reconstruction of Japan and the occupation and defense of Europe from Soviet communism. Neither were jobs for special operators. Moreover, as the Ranger infantry battalions that had fought across Europe and the Pacific had been disbanded, reassembling them was low on anyone's priority list. In fact, by January 1950, the new combined-services Department of Defense, facing congressional budget cuts, found itself eliminating units across the services, delaying the purchase of new equipment, and even deferring maintenance on old gear.

Those and other proposed cutbacks vanished in June of that same year when the North Korean army swept south across the thirty-seventh parallel into South Korea. With that, the U.S. Army's chief of staff, General J. Lawton Collins, saw the need for some kind of commando-type units in Korea. He thus ordered the formation of a training center at Georgia's Fort Benning to stand up what he called "Airborne Ranger" companies. With memories of the accomplishments of the 82nd and 101st Airborne Divisions on D-Day still fresh, it seemed clear that highly trained American war fighters falling from the sky would be a more dramatic demonstration of United States firepower than mud-encrusted ground pounders. Several of these airborne outfits were in fact deployed to the Korean peninsula.

For myriad reasons, however, less than a year later even these companies were deactivated. The Ranger legacy hung by a thread via the continued existence of Gen. Lawton's Ranger Training Center at Fort Benning, which eventually grew into the Ranger Department of the infantry school, a course specializing in small-unit leadership. It took another twenty-three years before, in 1974, the then-army chief of staff General Creighton Abrams ordered the formation of two battalion-sized Ranger units. A decade later the service created the Ranger Regiment headquarters at Fort Benning and activated a third battalion.

Multiple rationales have been put forward regarding the decades-long interregnum. The general consensus among military historians is twofold. The first argument cites the lingering animosity among old-school regular-army officers toward what they still considered ill-disciplined commandos. This was evidenced by the disdain in certain army circles for the U.S. Navy SEAL teams blessed by President John F. Kennedy's formal recognition upon their creation in 1962.

The second, more subtle, reason flowed from the first. In short, throughout World War II it was apparent that senior army officers generally did not know how to deploy Ranger units, yet were loath to admit it. This theory was laid out succinctly by General Harold Nelson, who became the U.S. Army's chief of military history a generation after Charles MacDonald retired. "Regarding America's Special Operations in World War II, of which the Rangers are a component," Nelson wrote, "the Army's historical series on World War II treats the subject only in passing." This is attested to by the scant mention of Ranger activities in *First United States Army Report of Operations, 1 August 1944–22 February 1945,* and even in Mac-Donald's definitive *The Siegfried Line Campaign,* each an official accounting of the war published by the army's historical division.

Given the army's near-universal uncertainty about how to report the role of the Rangers in World War II, any contemporaneous public knowledge of the feats of the special operators was invariably lost in the publicity afforded to the larger fighting units to which they were attached. The 2nd Ranger Battalion in particular, Nelson noted, was such a numerically small component of the manpower being poured into the European theater that even when it was incorporated into a regular-army division "to put out the most raging fires," it was usually the parent unit that received the credit. By way of example, Nelson cites the four infantry divisions into which the 2nd Ranger Battalion was integrated during the Battle of the Hürtgen Forest alone. These dispersals led to the Rangers' story becoming obscured. This discrepancy was evident on Omaha Beach, during the Brittany campaign, and in the storming of Hill 400.

The exception, of course, was the derring-do of the Rangers atop Pointe du Hoc. But even then, it took President Ronald Reagan's 1984 speech on that once-shattered tableland on the fortieth anniversary of the Normandy invasion, specifically citing the Rangers' valor, to bring them into the public purview.* The historian Douglas Brinkley's well-received 2005 book, *The Boys of Pointe du Hoc,* put the final nail in the coffin of what Len Lomell and so many of his fellow Ranger veterans considered previous chroniclers' omissions and factual errors.

---

* It was at this ceremony that the sixty-three-year-old Herm Stein, a member of a contingent of World War II Ranger veterans who had traveled back to Normandy as guests of the French government, impetuously decided to once again scale the cliffs of Pointe du Hoc without assistance—rather astonishingly reaching the top ahead of a dozen active-duty American Green Berets who had been flown in to reenact the climb.

It can be argued that the Second World War was the first time since the Revolutionary War era that America's military leadership incorporated special operators into combat zones at a large scale. Further, any detailed study of the 2nd and 5th Ranger Battalions following the Normandy invasion only reinforces the notion that army commanders just did not always know how to deploy an elite, if unique, fighting force. That said, the Rangers' ability to accomplish any combat mission that the war called for undoubtedly shaped their military doctrine, in particular their special skills as a lightning attack force on the battlefield.

World War II was the crucible in which the Rangers birthed the future for special operations in the modern American army. It was the Ranger campaigns in the North African, Mediterranean, European, and Pacific Theaters that, for better or worse, foreshadowed the shape of future United States military operations from Vietnam to Afghanistan to Iraq. It is an interesting thought experiment to contemplate what the likes of Wild Bill Darby and Big Jim Rudder would make of that.

Acknowledgments

Researchers probing the extensive United States Army records of the Second World War confront such a daunting array of official histories, after-action reports, unit diaries and newsletters, and myriad autobiographies and biographies that they often compare themselves to mountaineers scaling soaring piles of paperwork. We were fortunate, as we had only one "last hill" to climb. That said, our deepest debts of gratitude must be directed to the men of World War II's 2nd Ranger Battalion whose contemporaneous and near-contemporaneous letters, journals, and personal reminiscences provided us with sturdy footholds during our ascent.

Moreover, we could not possibly have written this book without the assistance and courtesy of archivists, curators, librarians, historians, and others at multiple organizations and institutions devoted to America's participation in World War II. Those who often went above and beyond to provide us with essential information include David Williams at the Descendants of World War II Rangers; Thomas Hatfield, director emeritus at the Dolph Briscoe Center for American History on the University of Texas campus in Austin; Colonel (Ret.) Paul Zigo of the World War II Era Studies

Institute; Gary Dolan at the Ranger Hall of Fame; Jillian Acevedo, Jeff Hawks, and Colonel Mike Perry at the Army Heritage Center Foundation; Melissa Davis at the George C. Marshall Foundation; Mary Gasper, Justine Melone, and Duane Miller at the U.S. Army Heritage and Education Center; Tony Kiser of the National World War II Museum; Carrie Lund at the Pursuit of History; Alisa Whitley at the Army Corps of Engineers; Alan Millett at the Eisenhower Center; and the staff at the John Jermain Memorial Library.

We are especially grateful to Julie Belanger for her invaluable help in finding and supplying us with many of the images in this book, and to Lieutenant Colonel (Ret.) Tom Crowley, who was kind enough to share with us his hands-on military expertise.

Thanks also to Jeffrey Block, Karla Dadd, S. C. Gwynne, James Hornfischer, Phil Keith, Michael Levean, Megan Marks, Anne Gaines Rodriguez, and Janis Spidle, who were integral to our gathering and collating of facts.

Further, once again we cannot express enough appreciation for the insights and suggestions provided by our cadre of underground editors—Bobby Kelly, David Hughes, and Denise McDonald. In addition, the support of Jack Tassini, John Pierse, Ronnie D'Esposito, Sharon Borgatti, Bill Surdovel, and of course Bobby Crines, who knows how to read between the lines, proved most helpful.

Needless to say, despite the reporting paths of those who trod before us with the 2nd Ranger Battalion as well as all those mentioned above who helped to shape and sharpen this narrative, we take full responsibility for any and all errors that found their way into our text.

From the onset of this project through its completion we have benefited from the enthusiastic support of our editor, Marc Resnick. Others we are happy to thank at St. Martin's Press include Sally Richardson, Rebecca Lang, Lily Cronig, Tracey Guest, Danielle Prielipp, Rafal Gibek, Greg Villepique, Michelle McMillian, Rob Grom,

David Lindroth, and Andy Martin. Finally, and as always, we survive to write another day thanks to Nat Sobel and his merry band of elves at Sobel Weber Associates, particularly Adia Wright.

As with any lengthy research, reporting, and writing project, we depended on the ongoing support and encouragement of family. Allow us to single out the inestimable Leslie Reingold, Kathryn and James Vun Kannon, Brendan Clavin, Vivienne May Vun Kannon, Liam-Antoine DeBusschere-Drury, David Drury, and the Divine Ms. D.

Notes

Epigraph

xiii *"Rain and snow had turned the roads"*: Pogue, *Pogue's War: Diaries of a World War II Combat Historian*, p. 272.

Prologue

2 *"Everywhere the forest scowled"*: MacDonald, *The Siegfried Line Campaign*, p. 347.
2 *"Frost and cold making life so miserable"*: Prince, *Overseas and Then, Over the Top*, book 3, p. 1.
5 *"You might get hit"*: Block, 1944 Diary, Nov. 15, 1944.
5 *What an odd place for a church*: Edlin, *The Fool Lieutenant*, p. 206.
6 *"I wish you wouldn't go"*: Ibid., pp. 206, 207.
7 *one man down*: MacDonald, *The Siegfried Line Campaign*, p. 340.

PART I: THE RANGERS

9 *In general, when pushed upon by the enemy*: Robert Rogers's 13th Rule of Ranging, 1757.

1: Commandos

12 *"American officers"*: Hogan, *U.S. Army Special Operations in World War II*, p. 4.
13 *"big-unit"*: Ibid., p. 6.
14 *"arrow of penetration"*: Ibid., p. 7.
14 *"gentlemanly"*: Ibid., p. 6.
16 *"harvest of thought"*: Thoreau diary, August 7, 1854.
16 *"iron-mongering"*: Atkinson, *The Guns at Last Light*, p. 6.

2: Darby's Recruits

18 *"tough little boys"*: Hogan, *U.S. Army Special Operations in World War II*, p. 8.
18 *"predatory" face*: Atkinson, *The Guns at Last Light*, p. 196.
19 *"speed, vigor, and violence"*: Ibid., p. 197.
21 *even a circus lion tamer*: Hogan, *U.S. Army Special Operations in World War II*, p. 12.
22 *"death slides"*: O'Donnell, *Beyond Valor*, p. xv.
24 *"the raiding force also included"*: *New York Times*, Aug. 20, 1942.

3: Torch

25 *"to sever the Nazi jugular"*: Black, *Rangers in World War II*, p. 51.
30 *"that will top the instinctive and naturally dirty fight"*: Black, *The Battalion*, p. 10.

4: Heat and Dust

32 *"Rangerism is the doctrine"*: Ibid.
33 *"into clothing, bedding, weapons, food, and water"*: Ibid., p. 6.
34 *"the greatest battle implement ever devised"*: Pendergast, *Firearms*, p. 102.
39 *"We're heading for pay dirt"*: Black, *The Battalion*, p. 16.
39 *"the disposition of a constipated bull dog"*: Ibid., p. 17.

5: "Big Jim" Rudder

46 *"restore order"*: Ibid., p. 20.
46 *"volunteer out"*: Brinkley, *The Boys of Pointe du Hoc*, p. 39.
47 *"Dig in fast and deep"*: Black, *The Battalion*, p. 213.

6: A New Beginning

55 *"gruntland"*: Lomell, Eisenhower Center interview, Mar. 16, 1993, p. 2.
56 *"I'll promote you on the spot"*: Ibid.

7: Sea Change

59 *"gripe sessions"*: Hogan, *U.S. Army Special Operations in World War II*, p. 40.
61 *"the soul of Fox Company"*: Black, *The Battalion*, p. 4.
62 *"The dead were buried"*: Ibid., p. 23.
63 *"the boondocks"*: Stein, Atlanta History Center interview, p. 2.
63 *"training and waiting"*: Jones, *Veritas* magazine, vol. 5, no. 1.
65 *"Not for every soldier"*: Clark et al., *The Narrative History of Headquarters Company*, p. 25.

8: Swim and Swat

68 *"undesirables"*: Black, *The Battalion*, p. 34.
69 *"drew nearly all the blood"*: Clark et al., *The Narrative History of Headquarters Company*, p. 29.
69 *"over-stuffed waffles"*: Ibid.

70 *"general exhilaration of spirit"*: Black, *The Battalion*, p. 32.
74 *"always anticipate"*: Frank South, letter to Jeff Block.
75 *"Doc Block could cut a throat"*: Black, *The Battalion*, p. 36.
75 *"final readiness"*: Hatfield, *Rudder: From Leader to Legend*, p. 78.
77 *"You will have to pardon"*: Ibid., p. 80.

9: The Cliffs

82 *"One Yank and they're down"*: Black, *The Battalion*, pp. 52–53.
86 *"suicide squad"*: Quistorff, "The U.S. Army's 2nd Ranger Battalion: Beyond D-Day," p. 9.
86 *Even these Rangers don't care*: Edlin, *The Fool Lieutenant*, p. 65.
87 *"You look like a Ranger"*: Ibid.

PART II: THE BEACH

89 *"We knew where France was"*: Ibid., p. 79.

10: "The Most Dangerous Mission of D-Day"

92 *"hysteria"*: Taylor and Reister, *Medical Statistics in World War II*, p. 43.
96 *was the most dangerous mission of D-Day*: Hogan, *U.S. Army Special Operations in World War II*, p. 41.
96 *"trying to scare me"*: Bradley, *A Soldier's Story*, p. 269.
96 *"Destruction of the [155 mm] battery"*: Hogan, *U.S. Army Special Operations in World War II*, p. 41.

11: Gin Blossoms

101 *"episodes"*: O'Donnell, *Dog Company*, pp. 38–39.
101 *"a neurasthenic condition"*: Ibid.
103 *"still the storm"*: The Bible, Psalm 107.
103 *"In effect"*: Williamson, *Field Marshal Erwin Rommel's Defense of Normandy During World War II*, History.net.

12: Charon's Craft

112 *"talking American"*: Astor, *June 6, 1944: The Voices of D-Day*, p. 248.
113 *"Guys, look on this as a big football game"*: Ibid., p. 205.
114 *"a turkey shoot"*: Black, *The Battalion*, p. 122.
114 ACHTUNG! MINEN!: Hodefield, "I Climbed the Cliffs with the Rangers," *Saturday Evening Post*, Aug. 19, 1944.

13: Charnel Ground

118 *"Get off the beach"*: Black, *The Battalion*, p. 90.
119 *"a small, fat old Irishman"*: McClarey, *The American Catholic*, June 6, 2009.
119 *"When you land"*: Ibid.
123 *"Cover me"*: Edlin, *The Fool Lieutenant*, p. 93.

14: Thermite

124 *It was equivalent to the bomb:* Ambrose, *D-Day: June 6, 1944,* p. 406.
125 *"Okay":* Lomell, Eisenhower Center interview, Mar. 16, 1993, p. 9.
125 *Digging our own graves:* Ibid., p. 10.
126 *"like rabbits":* Ibid.
127 *"How bad":* Frederick and Masci, *World War II* magazine, July 2001.
127 *"Save the bullet":* Ibid.
128 *"You're just a goddamn pessimist":* Ryan, *The Longest Day,* p. 93.
129 *"Hell, L-Rod":* Black, *The Battalion,* p. 130.
130 *"Let's take a chance":* Lomell, Eisenhower Center interview, Mar. 16, 1993, p. 14.
132 *"in case one of them":* Ibid., p. 23.
132 *"to maintain and defend":* Lisko, *The Guns of Pointe du Hoc,* p. 2.

15: "No Reinforcements Available"

134 *"Located Pointe du Hoc":* Black, *The Battalion,* p. 135.
135 *"a new kind of warfare":* Hodefield, *Saturday Evening Post,* Aug. 19, 1944.
136 *"Heinie prisoners":* Block, 1944 Diary, June 8, 1944.
138 *"There are no snipers":* Black, *The Battalion,* p. 129.
141 *"Orders are to hold":* Astor, *June 6, 1944: The Voices of D-Day,* p. 329.

16: "All Rangers Down!"

146 *"All Rangers down":* Stein, Eisenhower Center interview, Dec. 21, 2005.
147 *"George," he'd hollered:* O'Donnell, *Dog Company,* p. 104.
148 *"Thirteen":* Ibid., p. 121.
149 *"not despair or terror":* Owen, *The War Poems,* 1944.

17: Graves Registration

152 *"Hold fire":* O'Donnell, *Dog Company,* p. 124.

PART III: THE FORTRESS

18: Hurry Up and Wait

160 *"booze patrol":* B Company Combat History, June 1944.
163 *"The cow was not supported":* Black, *The Battalion,* p. 156.
163 *"a black line on a war map":* Atkinson, *The Guns at Last Light,* p. 409.
164 *"repo depot":* Eikner, Eisenhower Center interview, Apr. 3, 1986.
169 *"Being a separate battalion":* Salomon, *2nd U.S. Ranger Infantry Battalion,* p. 42.
169 *"Having accomplished the task":* Hogan, *U.S. Army Special Operations in World War II,* p. 43.

19: The "Fabulous Four"

171 *"just pulling some of the ligaments together":* Edlin, *The Fool Lieutenant,* p. 112.
173 *"Lt. Edlin returned":* Hatfield, *Rudder: From Leader to Legend,* p. 171.

173 *"old timers"*: Edlin, *The Fool Lieutenant*, p. 124.

174 *"two mismatched tinhorns"*: *Overland Monthly*, Jan. 1916.

174 *"The only casualties"*: Block, 1944 Diary, July 19, 1944.

174 *"Fabulous Four"*: Black, *The Battalion*, p. 161.

175 *"magic number"*: Ibid.

176 *"It's simple mathematics"*: Edlin, *The Fool Lieutenant*, p. 135.

20: Brittany

179 *"fire brigade"*: Jones, *Veritas* magazine, Nov. 1, 2009.

179 *"there aren't more than ten thousand"*: Atkinson, *The Guns at Last Light*, p. 151.

180 *"to the last man"*: Ibid., p. 152.

181 *"I was pretty upset"*: Edlin, *The Fool Lieutenant*, p. 136.

183 *"I believe I can hit [him]"*: Ibid., p. 148.

185 *"the political part of warfare"*: Ibid., p. 137.

185 *"They wanted to fire a few rounds"*: Ibid.

21: *Festung* Brest

186 *"Stay in your hole"*: Black, *The Battalion*, p.169.

187 *"Hell, no"*: Stein, Eisenhower Center interview, Dec. 21, 2005.

189 *"the muzzle blast alone"*: Jones, *Veritas* magazine, Nov. 1, 2009.

189 *"Bullets were whizzing by"*: Hatfield, *Rudder: From Leader to Legend*, p. 83.

22: The "Fool Lieutenant"

194 *"I'm just a little down"*: Edlin, *The Fool Lieutenant*, p. 25.

195 *"I think I see a way through"*: Ibid., p. 160.

197 *"Hände hoch"*: Ibid., p. 161.

199 *"What do you want"*: Edlin, *The Fool Lieutenant*, pp. 163–65.

23: Credentials

202 *"'Fool Lieutenant' Breaches Bastion"*: Gannett, *New York Herald Tribune*, Sep. 9, 1944.

202 *"Where's his pistol"*: Edlin, *The Fool Lieutenant*, p. 170.

203 *"What would you have done"*: Ibid., p. 171.

205 *"romance overcame language"*: Black, *The Battalion*, p. 185.

205 *"I have been recommended"*: Edlin, *The Fool Lieutenant*, p. 175.

207 *"These are my credentials"*: Black, *The Battalion*, p. 186.

PART IV: THE FOREST

209 *Thinking of the Hürtgen now*: Hemingway, *Across the River and into the Trees*, p. 138.

24: "End the War in '44"

211 *"Pursuit warfare"*: MacDonald, *The Siegfried Line Campaign*, p. 4.

212 *"to rapidly starve Germany"*: Ibid., p. 6.

213 *"It looks like the war"*: Edlin, *The Fool Lieutenant*, p. 114.

214 *"pea soup mud"*: MacDonald, *The Siegfried Line Campaign*, p. 618.

214 *"A soldier's mind"*: Ibid.

214 *"One of the severest"*: Prince, *Overseas and Then, Over the Top*, book 3, p. 1.

216 *"Yeah. How come"*: Edlin, *The Fool Lieutenant*, p. 194.

217 *"soldier's soldier"*: MacDonald, *The Siegfried Line Campaign*, p. 20.

217 *"hold ground against"*: Hatfield, *Rudder: From Leader to Legend*, p. 208.

217 *"to act as moving targets"*: Pogue, *Pogue's War: Diaries of a WWII Combat Historian*, p. 351.

217 *"He was flabbergasted"*: Hatfield, *Rudder: From Leader to Legend*, p. 208.

218 *1914*: Edlin, *The Fool Lieutenant*, p. 200.

218 *"Is all of me still there"*: Atkinson, *The Guns at Last Light*, p. 321.

219 *"thrashing through the underbrush"*: MacDonald, *The Siegfried Line Campaign*, p. 371.

220 *"upside-down ice cream cone"*: Black, *The Battalion*, p. 208.

220 *"We had respect"*: *Die Welt* newspaper, June 23, 2001.

25: The Green Hell

225 *"until annihilation"*: Atkinson, *The Guns at Last Light*, p. 251.

225 *"The fight in the west"*: Ibid.

226 *"bow and arrow infantry"*: Ibid., p. 391.

227 *"out of sheer terror"*: Ibid.

227 *"in combat in wooded areas"*: First United States Army, *Report of Operations, 1 August 1944–22 February 1945*, p. 80.

228 *"God gave him a face"*: Atkinson, *The Guns at Last Light*, p. 310.

228 *"temperamental"*: Bradley, *A Soldier's Story*, p. 422.

229 *"Smash ahead"*: Atkinson, *The Guns at Last Light*, p. 311.

229 *"[Hodges] was pretty slow"*: MacDonald, *The Siegfried Line*, p. 619.

229 *"Surely [Hodges's] approach"*: Ibid.

230 *"At a moment when"*: Atkinson, *The Guns at Last Light*, p. 246.

230 *"calm and dependable"*: MacDonald, *The Siegfried Line Campaign*, p. 20.

232 *"for reasons of prestige"*: Ibid., p. 38.

26: The Queen's Gambit

234 *Purple Heart Corner*: Edlin, *The Fool Lieutenant*, p. 207.

235 *"Don't worry if you don't"*: Hatfield, *Rudder: From Leader to Legend*, p. 198.

235 *"the last big assault"*: MacDonald, *The Siegfried Line Campaign*, p. 409.

237 *"stumbling off the stage"*: Ibid., p. 411.

237 *"knee deep in bloody bodies"*: Lomell, *Letter to Ranger Hall of Fame*, Sep. 1997.

237 *"crimson tirade"*: Atkinson, *The Guns at Last Light*, p. 321.

238 *"Roll on"*: Ibid.

238 *"Attempts by American artillery"*: MacDonald, *The Siegfried Line Campaign*, pp. 442–43.

239 *"In trench warfare"*: Orwell, *Homage to Catalonia*, p. 16.

240 *"Without a map"*: MacDonald, *The Siegfried Line Campaign*, p. 336.

241 *"Lomell thought"*: Black, *The Battalion*, p. 197.

242 *"The barrage"*: Edlin, *The Fool Lieutenant*, p. 208.

27: The Return of the "Fabulous Four"

244 *"like a tired, worn-out old man"*: Hatfield, *Rudder: From Leader to Legend*, p. 214.
245 *"In and out"*: Edlin, *The Fool Lieutenant*, p. 210.
246 *"We're going to do this"*: Ibid., p. 211.
247 *"Like they were watching me"*: Ibid, p. 215.
247 *"Moderate to intense"*: Hatfield, *Rudder: From Leader to Legend*, p. 213.
248 *"the inconclusiveness of the advance"*: MacDonald, *The Siegfried Line Campaign*, p. 444.
248 *"Our missing men"*: Ibid., p. 455.
248 *"The only thing that higher headquarters"*: Herr, *The Worst of the Worst*, p. 3.

28: "How Bad Is It?"

251 *"Bob, I'm not going to"*: Edlin, *The Fool Lieutenant*, p. 219.
251 *I can't take any more of this*: Ibid.
252 *"You think somebody's gonna steal it"*: Ibid., p. 219.
252 *"sickening sweet odor"*: Black, *The Battalion*, p. 202.
252 *"the land of six-foot trees"*: O'Donnell, *Dog Company*, p. 167.
253 *"Drop back behind"*: Edlin, *The Fool Lieutenant*, p. 220.
253 *"Two at a time"*: Ibid.
254 *"Wash his eyes out"*; *"How bad is it"*; *"A little shrapnel"*: Ibid., p. 221.
254 *It ought to be against the rules*; *"Wait just a damn minute"*: Ibid.
255 *"Lieutenant, if that hand"*; *"I'd trade"*; *"I can't use anesthesia"*; *"You're on your own"*; *"Send them this"*: Ibid., p. 222.
256 *"We had our turkey today"*: Block, 1944 Diary, Nov. 24, 1944.
256 *"Doc, if you give me"*; *"Boy, you ain't going"*: Edlin, *The Fool Lieutenant*, p. 223.
259 *"bridgehead"*: MacDonald, *The Siegfried Line Campaign*, p. 451.

PART V: THE HILL

261 *Some people say D-Day:* Lomell speech, Eisenhower Center, May 8, 1995.

29: Bergstein

264 *"like attacking down a fairway"*: MacDonald, *The Siegfried Line Campaign,* p. 451.
265 *"canalized"*: Roquemore, *The Operations of the 2nd Ranger Battalion at Hürtgen Forest*, p. 25.
265 *"We're at the critical"*; *"Six minutes later"*: MacDonald, *The Siegfried Line Campaign*, p. 453.
268 *"achieve a level of operational capability"*: Nash, *Victory Was Beyond Their Grasp*, p. 41.
269 *"old men and boys"*: Ibid., p. 80.
269 *"You know the fate"*: Ibid., p. 81.
270 *"armored fists"*: Ibid., p. 18.
271 *"The men of this battalion"*: MacDonald, *The Siegfried Line Campaign*, pp. 456–57.

30: Rudderless

275 *"Dear Dad"*: Potratz, "Remembering the Blood Spilled on Hill 400," *Milwaukee Journal*, Oct. 30, 1994.

276 *"with a feeling of sympathy"*: Black, *The Battalion,* p. 211.
278 *"Dig in fast and deep"*: Ibid., p. 213.
278 *"No more chances"*: Ibid., p. 229.
278 *"mix of love and loss"*: Ibid., p. 213.
278 *"a heavy heart"*: Hatfield, *Rudder: From Leader to Legend,* p. 216.

31: The Sugarloaf

279 *"Probably no news"*: MacDonald, *The Siegfried Line Campaign,* p. 461.
281 *"faint promise"*: Pogue, *Pogue's War: Diaries of a WWII Combat Historian,* p. 285.
281 *"Let's go, men"*: MacDonald, *The Siegfried Line Campaign,* p. 462.
281 *"Our morale went up"*: Pogue, *Pogue's War: Diaries of a WWII Combat Historian,*
        p. 285.
282 *"desolation such as one"*: Ibid., p. 271.
285 *"Over here"*: Milt Moss, letter to Sid Salomon, circa 1989, p. 2.

32: "Let's Go Get the Bastards!"

288 *"lucky bugger"*: Kendall McClure, letter to Paul Zigo, Jan. 15, 2007.
289 *"outgoing mail"*: Milt Moss, letter to Sid Salomon, circa 1989, p. 2.
290 *"Send out a scout"; "Fuck you"; "No, sir"*: Black, *The Battalion,* p. 218.
291 *"Go!"*: Ibid., p. 219.
291 *"Indian war whoops"; "splattered"*: Kenneth Harsch, letter to Paul Zigo, Jan. 9, 2007.
292 *"No quarter was asked"*: Nash, *Victory Was Beyond Their Grasp,* p. 100.
293 *"I guess you'll gradually"*: Herm Stein, interview with Atlanta History Center, Dec.
        21, 2005, p. 26.
293 *"Kid, stay away from"*: Milt Moss, letter to Sid Salomon, circa 1989, p. 8.
294 *"We dig in here"*: Ibid.

33: The Crest

300 *"foggy"*: Kendall McClure, letter to Paul Zigo, Jan. 15, 2007.

34: Fallschirmjägers

302 *Reserve your fire till they are very near; "Now"*: Leonard Lomell, letter to Ranger Hall
        of Fame, 2001.
303 *"his daddy"*: O'Donnell, *Dog Company,* pp. 54–55.
304 *"There is no God"*: Black, *The Battalion,* p. 225.
306 *"prayed to God"*: O'Donnell, *Beyond Valor,* p. 285.
306 *"a duck in a shooting gallery"; "praying and sweating"*: Prince, *Overseas and Then,
        Over the Top,* book 3, pp. 14–15.

35: A Last Stand

309 *"Who's going to take"; "I'll take it"*: Black, *The Battalion,* p. 225.
311 *His rock*: Leonard Lomell, letter to Ranger Hall of Fame, 2001.
311 *"Get some sleep"*: Black, *The Battalion,* p. 227.
315 *"Hold your positions"*: Ibid., p. 226.

315 *Hold your positions:* Edlin, *The Fool Lieutenant,* pp. 234–35.
316 *"Best man":* MacDonald, *The Siegfried Line Campaign,* p. 462.

36: Howls and Whistles

318 *"unbelievably quiet":* Roquemore, *The Operations of the 2nd Ranger Battalion at Hürtgen Forest,* p. 21.
319 *"curtain of fire":* Ibid., p. 22.
320 *"for the only time":* Hatfield, *Rudder: From Leader to Legend,* p. 216.
318 *"Still in the":* Block, 1944 Diary, Dec. 3, 1944.
320 *"I will be back":* Ibid., Nov 2, 1944.
321 *"Hände hoch; kommen Sie hier":* Black, *The Battalion,* p. 231.
322 *"truly the last gasp":* Nash, *Victory Was Beyond Their Grasp,* p. 101.

37: Trudging Away

326 *There's no way:* Edlin, *The Fool Lieutenant,* p. 236.

Epilogue

329 *"Civilization again":* James Eikner, Eisenhower Center interview, April 1986.
331 *"Let her get back":* Ibid.
331 *"Thank someone":* Ibid.
333 *"the mindless beast":* Black, *The Battalion,* p. 237.
333 *"The warmest thing out there":* Salomon, *2nd U.S. Ranger Infantry Battalion,* p. 17.

Afterword

339 *"This has been their way":* MacDonald, *The Siegfried Line Campaign,* p. xi.
341 *"the spearhead":* Morelock, *Generals of the Bulge,* p. 299.
343 *"the extraordinary gallantry":* Harmon, Recommendation for Presidential Unit Citation (Oak Leaf Cluster), Aug. 16, 1945.
344 *"Further inquiry":* Salomon, *2nd U.S. Ranger Infantry Battalion,* p. 72.
349 *"I still feel guilty":* Frank South, letter to Jeff Block, Mar. 29, 1993.
353 *"would personally take my three days":* O'Donnell, *Beyond Valor,* p. 217.
353 *"For many mistreated children":* Black, *The Battalion,* p. 285.
355 *"to recruit WACs":* Lomell, Eisenhower Center interview, Mar. 16, 1993, p. 3.
356 *"That's ridiculous":* Len Lomell, letter to Representative Chris Smith, Apr. 1, 2001.
356 *"They say":* Lomell, Eisenhower Center interview, Mar. 16, 1993, p. 3.
357 *"We stacked":* Hatfield, *Rudder: From Leader to Legend,* p. 237.
358 *"Our lives":* Ibid., p. 257.
359 *"circulatory collapse":* Ibid., p. 389.
359 *"an outsider cannot comprehend":* Ibid., p. 391.

Postscript

362 *"Regarding America's Special Operations":* Hogan, *U.S. Army Special Operations in World War II,* p. iii.
363 *"to put out the most raging fires":* Ibid.

Selected Bibliography

Books

Altieri, James. *The Spearheaders: A Personal History of Darby's Raiders*. New York: Bobbs-Merrill, 1960.

Ambrose, Stephen. *D-Day: June 6, 1944, The Climactic Battle of World War II*. New York: Simon and Schuster, 1994.

Astor, Gerald. *The Bloody Forest*. Novato, CA: Presidio, 2000.

———. *June 6, 1944: The Voices of D-Day*. New York: Dell, 2002.

Atkinson, Rick. *An Army at Dawn*. New York: Henry Holt, 2002.

———. *The Guns at Last Light: The War in Western Europe, 1944–1945*. New York: Henry Holt, 2013.

Baer, Alfred E., Jr. *D-for-Dog: The Story of a Ranger Company*. Memphis, 1946.

Bahmanyer, Mir. *Shadow Warriors: A History of the U.S. Army Rangers*. Oxford, UK: Osprey Publishing, 2006.

Baldwin, Hanson W. *Battles Lost & Won*. New York: Konecky & Konecky, 1966.

Balkoski, Joseph. *From Beachhead to Brittany: The 29th Infantry Division at Brest, August–September 1944*. Mechanicsburg, PA: Stackpole Books, 2008.

Black, Robert W. *The Battalion: The Dramatic Story of the 2nd Ranger Battalion in World War II*. Mechanicsburg, PA: Stackpole Books, 2006.

———. *Rangers in World War II*. New York: Ballantine, 1992.

Boesch, Paul. *Road to Huertgen: Forest in Hell*. Houston: Gulf Publishing Co., 1962.

Bradley, Omar. *A Soldier's Story*. New York: Henry Holt, 1951.

Brinkley, Douglas. *The Boys of Pointe du Hoc*. New York: William Morrow, 2005.

Brokaw, Tom. *The Greatest Generation*. New York: Random House, 1998.

Clark, George M., Gerhard Stalling, William Weber, and Ronald Paradis. *2nd Ranger Bn, The Narrative History of Headquarters Company, April 1943–May 1945*. Privately printed in Czechoslovakia, 1945.

Currey, Cecil B. *Follow Me and Die: The Destruction of an American Division in World War II*. Reston, VA: Military Heritage, 1988.

D'Este, Carlo. *Patton: A Genius for War*. New York: HarperCollins, 1995.

Dickson, Paul. *The Rise of the G.I. Army*. New York: Atlantic Monthly Press, 2020.

Doubler, Michael D. *Closing with the Enemy: How GIs Fought the War in Europe, 1944–1945*. Lawrence: University Press of Kansas, 1994.

Dupuy, Trevor N. *Hitler's Last Gamble: The Battle of the Bulge*. New York: HarperCollins, 1994.

Edlin, Robert, as told to Marcia Moen and Margo Heinen. *The Fool Lieutenant: A Personal Account of D-Day and World War II*. Elk River, MN: Meadowlark Publishing, 2000.

Eikner, James W., ed. *2nd Ranger Battalion: The Narrative History of Headquarters Company, April 1943–May 1945*. Houston: Privately published, 1946.

Ewing, Joseph H. *29 Let's Go! A History of the 29th Infantry Division in World War II*. Washington, D.C.: Infantry Journal Press, 1948.

First United States Army. *Report of Operations: 1 August 1944–22 February 1945*. Vol. 2.

Glatthaar, Joseph T. *The American Military: A Concise History*. New York: Oxford University Press, 2018.

Hatfield, Thomas M. *Rudder: From Leader to Legend*. College Station: Texas A&M University Press, 2011.

Heinl, Robert Debs, Jr. *Dictionary of Military and Naval Quotations*. Annapolis, MD: United States Naval Institute, 1966.

Hemingway, Ernest. *Across the River and Into the Trees*. New York: Simon and Schuster, 1950.

Historical and Pictorial Review of the 28th Infantry Division in World War II. Atlanta: Albert Love Enterprises, 1945.

Hogan, David W., Jr. *U.S. Army Special Operations in World War II*. Washington, D.C.: Center of Military History, Department of the Army, 1992.

Jeffers, H. Paul. *Onward We Charge: The Heroic Story of Darby's Rangers in World War II*. New York: NAL, 2007.

Kennard, John V. O. *D-Day Journal: The Untold Story of a U.S. Ranger on Omaha Beach*. Virginia Beach: Koehler Books, 2018.

King, Michael J. *Rangers: Selected Combat Operations in World War II*. Fort Leavenworth, KS: U.S. Army Command and General Staff College, 2017.

Ladd, James. *Commandos and Rangers of World War II*. New York: St. Martin's Press, 1978.

Lane, Ronald. *Rudder's Rangers: The True Story of the 2nd Rangers Battalion D-Day Combat Action*. Manassas, VA: Ranger Associates, 1979.

MacDonald, Charles B. *The Battle of the Huertgen Forest*. Philadelphia: University of Pennsylvania Press, 2003.

———. *The Last Offensive: United States Army in World War II*. Washington, D.C.: Office of the Chief of Military History, 1973.

———. *The Siegfried Line Campaign: United States Army in World War II*. Atlanta: Whitman, 2012.

Marine Corps Command and Staff College. *Herringbone Cloak: GI Dagger Marines of the OSS*. Damascus, MD: Penny Hill Press, 2015.

McDonald, Joanna M. *The Liberation of Pointe du Hoc: The 2nd Rangers at Normandy, June 6–8. 1944*. Redondo Beach, CA: Rank and File, 2000.

Miller, Edward G. *A Dark and Bloody Ground: The Huertgen Forest and the Roer River Dams, 1944–45*. College Station: Texas A&M University Press, 1995.

Miller, Robert A. *Division Commander: A Biography of Major General Norman D. Cota*. Spartanburg, SC: Reprint Company, 1989.

———. *Reflections of Courage on D-Day and the Days That Followed: A Personal Account of Ranger "Ace" Parker.* Elk River, MN: DeForest Press, 1999.

Monnartz, Rainer. *Hürtgenwald 1944/1945: Militärgeschichtlicher Tourenplaner.* Aachen, Germany: Heilos Verlags und Buchvertriebsgesellschaft, 2006.

Morelock, Jerry D. *Generals of the Bulge.* Mechanicsburg, PA: Stackpole Books, 2015.

Nash, Douglas E. *Victory Was Beyond Their Grasp: With the 272nd Volks-Grenadier Division from the Hürtgen Forest to the Heart of the Reich.* Bedford, PA: Aberjona Press, 2008.

O'Donnell, Patrick K. *Beyond Valor: World War II's Ranger and Airborne Veterans Reveal the Heart of Combat.* New York: Touchstone, 2001.

———. *Dog Company: The Boys of Pointe du Hoc.* New York: Da Capo, 2012.

Orwell, George. *Homage to Catalonia.* 1938; reprint, Morningside Heights, NY: Bibliotech, 2018.

Owen, Wilfred. *War Poems.* London: Chatto and Windus, 1944.

Pogue, Forrest C. *Pogue's War: Diaries of a WWII Combat Historian.* Lexington: University Press of Kentucky, 2001.

Prince, Morris. *Overseas and Then, Over the Top.* Washington, D.C.: BiblioGov Project, Library Command and General Staff College, 1972.

Rogers, Robert. *Journals of Major Robert Rogers.* New York: Corinth Books, 1961.

Ryan, Cornelius. *The Longest Day: June 6, 1944.* New York: Simon and Schuster, 1959.

Salomon, Sidney A. *2nd U.S. Ranger Infantry Battalion: Germeter-Vossenack-Hürtgen-Bergstein-Hill 400 Germany, 14 Nov.–10 Dec. 1944.* Doylestown, PA: Birchwood Books, 1991.

———. *Second U.S. Ranger Infantry Battalion 14 Nov.–10 Dec. 1944.* Doylestown, PA: self-published, 1991.

Sizer, Mona D. *The Glory Guys: The Story of the U.S. Army Rangers.* Taylor Trade Publishing, 2009.

Steinbeck, John. *Once There Was a War.* New York: Penguin Classics, 2007.

Stimson, Henry L. *On Active Service in Peace and War.* New York: Harper, 1948.

Taylor, Richard R., Frank A. Reister, and John Lada. *Medical Statistics in World War II.* Washington, D.C.: Office of the Surgeon General, Department of the Army, 1975.

Taylor, Thomas. *Rangers Lead the Way.* Nashville: Turner Publishing, 1996.

Thoreau, Henry David. *The Journal of Henry David Thoreau: 1837–1861.* New York: NYRB, 2009.

Whiting, Charles. *The Battle of Hurtgen Forest.* New York: Orion Books, 1989.

Zaloga, Steven J. *Rangers Lead the Way: Pointe du Hoc, D-Day 1944.* Oxford, UK: Osprey Publishing, 2009.

Magazines, Newspapers, and Internet Sites

Astor, Gerald. *"The Deadly Forest."* World War II Magazine, Nov. 2004.

Farley, Robert. "Why So Many Historians Look Down on Ulysses S. Grant." 19FortyFive.com, Sep. 17, 2021.

Finlayson, Kenneth, and Robert W. Jones, Jr. "Rangers in World War II: Part I—The Formation and the Early Days." *Veritas* 2, no. 3 (2006), 64–69.

———. "Rangers in World War II: Part II—Sicily and Italy," *Veritas* 3, no. 1 (2006), 49–58.

Frederick, Michael H., and Joseph F. Masci. "D-Day: Interview with Two U.S. 2nd Ranger Battalion Members Who Describe the Attack at Pointe-du-Hoc." *World War II Magazine,* Jul. 2001.

Gannett, Lewis. "Americans Win Strongest Fort Guarding Brest." *New York Herald Tribune,* Sept. 9, 1944.

Herr, Ernie. "The Worst of the Worst: The Battle for the Hürtgen Forest." ww2live.com, Sept. 25, 2016.

Hodenfield, G. K. "I Climbed the Cliffs with the Rangers," *Saturday Evening Post,* Aug. 19, 1944.

Jones, Robert W., Jr. "Beyond the Beach: The 2nd Rangers Fight Through Europe." *Veritas* 5, no. 1 (2009).

Lomell, Leonard G. "The Guns of Pointe du Hoc." *World War II Chronicles,* Spring 2004.

Lisko, Louis. "The Guns of Pointe du Hoc."

Margry, Karel. "The Battle of the Hürtgen Forest." *After the Battle* 71, 1991.

Marino, James. "Taking Hill 400: Army Rangers vs. Fallschirmjägers." Warfare History Network, May 2017.

McClarey, Donald R. "Father Ranger." *The American Catholic,* June 6, 2009.

McMaken, Linda. "Andrew Jackson Higgins: The Man Who Won the War for Us." *Elks Magazine,* June 2020.

New York Times, Aug. 20, 1942.

Potratz, M. G. "Remembering the Blood Spilled on Hill 400." *Milwaukee Journal,* Oct. 30, 1994.

Williamson, Murray. "Field Marshal Erwin Rommel's Defense of Normandy During World War II." History.net, June 2006.

Archives

James Eikner Papers at the Dolph Briscoe Center for American History, University of Texas at Austin.

The Robert W. Black Collection and the Lou Lisko Collection at the U.S. Army Heritage and Education Center, Carlisle, PA.

Eyewitness Accounts

Block, Walter. 1944 Diary.

"Interview with James Eikner." Eisenhower Center, New Orleans, Apr. 3, 1986.

"Interview with Ralph Goranson." Eisenhower Center, New Orleans: July 3, 2000.

"Interview with Len Lomell." Eisenhower Center, New Orleans: Mar. 16, 1993.

Lisko, Lou: National Historian of the Ranger Bn. of World War II.

Lomell, Leonard G., Kendall B. McClure, Sigurd Sundby, Kenneth R. Harsch. Compiled by Paul Zigo, Founder and President, World War II Era Studies Institute.

Stein, Herman. Eisenhower Center interview, Dec. 21, 2005.

Speeches

Lomell, Leonard G. Address to the Eisenhower Center, University of New Orleans. May 8, 1995.

Letters

Kenneth Harsch to Paul Zigo, Jan. 19, 2007.

Leonard Lomell to Ranger Hall of Fame, Sept. 1997.

Leonard Lomell to Representative Chris Smith, Aug. 30, 2000.

Kendall McClure to Paul Zigo, Jan. 15, 2007.

Milt Moss to Sidney Salomon, undated.
Representative Chris Smith to Major General Galen Jackson, June 8, 2007.
Frank South to Jeffrey Block, Mar. and Apr. 1993.
Frank South to Gerald Astor, Mar. 8, 1997.
Sigurd Sundby to Joseph Monti, June 10, 2007.

Citation

Recommendation for Presidential Unit Citation (Oak Leaf Cluster), Aug. 16, 1945, Major General E. N. Harmon.

Dissertations

Roquemore, Frank U. "The Operations of the 2nd Ranger Battalion at Huertgen Forest, 6–8 December 1944: Personal Experiences of a Platoon Leader." World War II Collection, Donovan Research Library, Fort Benning, GA.
Quistorff, Alissa. "The U.S. Army's 2nd Ranger Battalion: Beyond D-Day." Florida State University, 2005.

Index